the alps

approach

resource book

accelerated learning in primary schools

**A practical approach to using brain-based
methods in the primary classroom**

**ALISTAIR SMITH
NICOLA & CALL**

First Published by
Network Educational Press Ltd
PO Box 635
Stafford
ST16 1BF
www.networkpress.co.uk

Published in the USA by
Crown House Publishing Ltd
PO Box 2223, Williston, VT 05495-2223, USA
www.CHPUS.com

First published 2001
Reprinted 2003

© Alistair Smith and Nicola Call 2001

ISBN 1 85539 078 7
Library of Congress Control Number: 2003104611

Managing Editor: Janice Baiton
Editorial Work: Janice Baiton
Design: Neil Hawkins - Network Educational Press Ltd
Illustrations: Pam Pierce & Oliver Caviglioli

Printed in Great Britain by MPG Books Ltd., Bodmin, Cornwall

Contents

Foreword   5

Preface   6

How to use this book   7

Acknowledgements   8

Introduction: Extending the horizons of possibility

Memory map and preview of Introduction   9

❶ A visit to the ALPS   11

❷ The ALPS model explained   27

❸ The children who journey with you   33

❹ Nine 'brain-based' principles   43

❺ Five dispositions for lifelong learning – five Rs   47

❻ Take a map on your journey   53

Review of Introduction   63

Part One: Establishing base camp

Memory map and preview of Part One   65

❶ Preparing for a learning journey   67

❷ Exceeding expectations   81

❸ The motivational loop   87

❹ Twenty positive strategies   95

Review of Part One   99

Part Two: Into the foothills of learning

Memory map and preview of Part Two   101

❶ Goals and targets that work   103

❷ Positive classroom talk   109

❸ Providing educative feedback   115

❹ Brain breaks   131

❺ Music in the classroom   143

Review of Part Two   149

Part Three: The learning journey

Memory map and preview of Part Three   151

❶ Using beginnings and endings   153

❷ VAKplus   159

❸ Structuring time on task   167

❹ Demonstrating understanding   171

❺ Using review for recall   177

❻ Success in standardized tests   181

Review of Part Three   189

Part Four: Appendices

❶ Where to begin with the ALPS method™   193

❷ Your engagement chart   196

❸ The 'how good am I at learning?' questionnaire   197

❹ The self-esteem questionnaire   206

❺ The emotional intelligence questionnaire   208

❻ The homework questionnaire   215

❼ Contact list   218

❽ Key vocabulary and definitions for pupils   219

❾ The ten best of everything (almost)   220

Index of resources   222

Foreword

ALPS stands for 'Accelerated Learning in Primary Schools'. It is a structured approach to organizing learning based on well-proven methods. *The ALPS Approach Resource Book* derives from the models described in the books *Accelerated Learning in the Classroom* (Network Educational Press, 1995) and *Accelerated Learning in Practice* (Network Educational Press, 1998) by Alistair Smith, and *The ALPS Approach* by Alistair Smith and Nicola Call (Network Educational Press, 1999). *The ALPS Approach Resource Book* complements the work on accelerated learning that has gone before. Permission is given (see page 2) for materials to be copied and used to help accelerate the learning of children within the purchasing institution.

Preface

The metaphor of the journey occurs across cultures and throughout history. The concept of the journey has always played its part in shaping thinking. The journey has expressed itself in cultural artefacts and proved fascinating for philosophers, theologians, anthropologists and explorers of time and space. Our original book, *The ALPS Approach*, was structured around the metaphor of the journey. We identified travellers (the pupils) and guides (the teachers), a destination (towards the development of the 3Rs), and a means of journeying (using the strategies and techniques described in *The ALPS Approach*). The book and the subsequent training programmes related to it proved a surprising success and so we have assembled in this book a more detailed set of tools to extend the journey. Within these pages you will find a great deal of material to enliven your teaching and to continue on your way to enhancing the life chances of those with whom you work. Should we visit you in the midst of your journey, we would expect to see this book a little dog-eared, with the pages marked and perhaps stained through constant use and we would also hope that some pages had felt the heat of the photocopier. Use the tools, apply the principles, share the ideas. We know they work. Many of you have told us how successful you have been with them.

You make a difference! A teacher spends her life sending messages of hope into the future. The true worth of those messages of hope may never become apparent to you, but a principled positivity is part of what you are and part of what you hope the children you influence will become.

In our original text we described the new three 'Rs' as resilience, responsibility and resourcefulness. We feel that we were at once premature and parsimonious with our allocation of desirable learning dispositions! We would wish to add a further two and so make a case for 5 Rs! Our new list consists of resilience, responsibility, resourcefulness, reasoning and reflectivity–reflexivity. We feel that the disposition to reason in a considered and methodical way is not only desirable but can also be nurtured and instructed. To be reflective leads, over time, towards becoming more reflexive, so there is a relationship between these two. As an individual reflects on a learning experience, they construct sense and participate in their own making of meaning. The more this happens, the more automatic the likelihood of it continuing to happen until it becomes a more automatic or reflexive response.

By pursuing the five Rs in her teaching, we feel a teacher moves towards the provision of a balanced and lifelong learning inheritance for her pupils. The ALPS approach provides a clear structure for the organization of learning. If you visit an ALPS classroom, we hope you will be impressed by the high level of professionalism and the self-awareness of the classroom teacher you observe there. When a teacher uses the ALPS approach she:

* has an interest in, and some understanding of, current theories of learning and brain development;
* creates the right environment for learning – what we call 'base camp';
* is aware of how physical needs affect learning and has strategies to intervene;
* builds self-esteem in the learner so that he is willing and able to take the risk of learning;
* sets clear and ambitious targets for and with the learners – these are the signposts for the journey;
* plans lessons effectively;
* optimizes *rather than maximizes* the use of time;
* teaches relaxation techniques and uses structured breaks to enhance learning;
* uses and teaches memory mapping techniques;
* uses VAKplus to present lessons in visual, auditory and kinesthetic ways with quality questions;
* uses RAP – recognition, affirmation and praise – to shape feedback to and motivate learners;
* is aware of the different models of intelligence as she plans and delivers lessons;
* uses motion and e-motion to consolidate learning;
* teaches children to be metacognitive – to understand *how* they learn;
* provides tools for improving memory and recall;
* uses review purposefully.

How to use this book

For the sake of simplicity, throughout this book we generally refer to the teacher as 'she' and to pupils as both 'he' and 'she'.

This book is complementary to *The ALPS Approach* by Alistair Smith and Nicola Call (Network Educational Press, 1999). ALPS stands for Accelerated Learning in Primary Schools. Our organizing metaphor is that education is a lifelong journey. The journey into the ALPS is one that each individual child makes in his own way but with a guide to direct and to challenge and sometimes to comfort. The teacher is the guide.

This resource book is intended to support the teacher who wishes to use Accelerated Learning in her classroom. This book can be used independently of *The ALPS Approach*, although we do recommend that a copy is available for reference. Ideally, teachers should have access to copies of both books. Some schools may choose to keep copies of *The ALPS Approach* in a central location, while teachers use this handbook as a practical reference and resource in their classrooms.

There is no right or wrong way to begin the journey into the ALPS. Dip into this book as you please and use ideas that appeal to you. Adapt them to fit in with your school routines and requirements. Pages 193–5 give some ideas about how other schools began work on the ALPS method™. Refer back to *The ALPS Approach* to read more at any stage, or use our resources lists at the back of both books to do your own research. Some schools choose to implement certain aspects of ALPS as whole school policy, while in other schools teachers work as individuals to trial our ideas. Do whatever works for you in your situation.

Acknowledgements

The ALPS Approach Resource Book is the result of a further genuine collaboration between Alistair Smith in London, Great Britain and Nicola Call in California, USA.

Alistair

Alistair acknowledges the contribution of his colleagues Nicky Anastasiou, Ian Harris, Oliver Caviglioli and Sarah Mook. Horsenden School in Ealing provided and trialled many of the ideas and provided fresh inspiration. The Bo'ness Cluster in central Scotland wrote a resource pack of their own, based on accelerated learning methods and were good enough to give me a copy. Alweena Zairi and Headfield Junior School provided research data on movement, hydration and learning. Many, many thanks to all those primary teachers who have given me ideas, taken me into their classrooms and shared their energy. Thanks for children's drawings to Laura Davis and her class at Birdlip School, Cheltenham.

Nicola

Thank you to those teachers who shared with me their experience of working with the ALPS method™ in their classrooms. In particular, thank you to Vicky Desmond and Siobhan Burrows for their continued support and feedback. My husband Josef encouraged me to keep writing while expecting our baby. Two weeks after I completed this book, Alysia Sophie was born. I watch in awe as she grows and learns, and I am humbled by the experience. May she live and learn in a world of positive experiences, and may all her dreams be realized.

A special thanks to Liz Knox for supplying some of the design ideas used in this book.

Introduction

Extending the horizons of possibility

In the Introduction you will:

* read three case studies from schools with success in using these methods;
* be reminded of the Accelerated Learning Cycle and how it works;
* find a brilliant method for helping children be more understanding of what helps them learn;
* rediscover the nine principles for what we are calling 'brain-based' learning and how the resources in this book can be used to apply them;
* be given some ideas about how to promote five dispositions for lifelong learning – Resilience, Responsibility, Resourcefulness, Reasoning, Reflectivity–reflexivity – in your classroom;
* learn about memory mapping and how to make a 'life map'.

Key vocabulary for Introduction:

Accelerated Learning Cycle	Dispositions for lifelong	Positive and supportive
Brain-based learning	learning	learning environments
Chardonnay	Magic spelling	School ethos
	Memory mapping	Switching on the learning lights

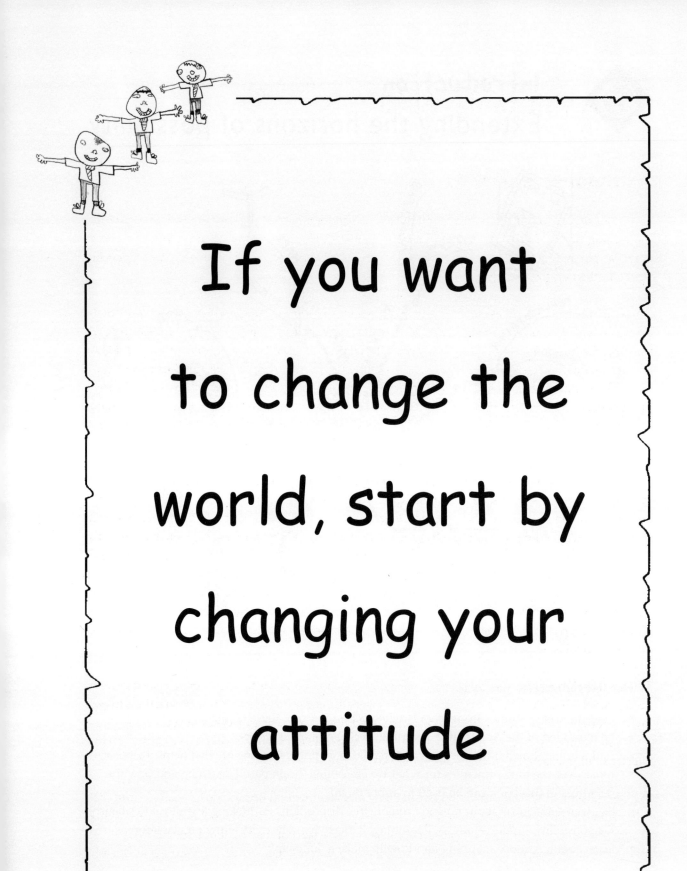

If you want to change the world, start by changing your attitude

A visit to the ALPS

A school in consolidation

If you can successfully negotiate yourself off one of London's busiest through roads. If you can find the turning north. If you can manoeuvre your way through narrow streets, and if you can find a parking spot amidst the builder's rubble. Then you may have arrived at Horsenden. A very special school in the London Borough of Ealing.

Horsenden School is in Greenford. It is surrounded by a mix of housing and is tucked away down a narrow lane. If you were to stand on the roof you might catch a glimpse of a green field. Do not stand on the Junior School building however – it collapsed in 1996. There is no playground to speak of. Management meetings are held in a shed. Otherwise, for the moment, the school is hemmed in by a construction site, shops and housing. It is a primary school with 760 pupils including a 100-place nursery. It is oversubscribed. In all there are 82 staff, including administrative, care and support staff at the school. What makes it special? – a *consistent* and *coherent* concern for learning.

If you were to ask the headteacher, Liz Walton, what characterizes the school, she would say that it was 'about maximizing what everyone can achieve and congratulating children and adults for what they do achieve'. Many, maybe most, headteachers might say something similar. After all, schools do exist in an age of 'vision and mission'. What impressed Alistair about this headteacher was a steeliness that belied the small frame and the gentle manner, and the impression given that 'yes, this is what the school is about'. Throughout the school the emphasis is on identifying how children and adults learn and structuring all the experiences to take account of this. You can walk any corridor and you will not hear a raised voice. Children are on task for 99 per cent of the time they are learning. You will not see any child sitting outside a classroom or queuing outside the headteacher's office for a reprimand. The atmosphere is calm, positive and purposeful. Which leaves us with the question: so what?

The 'so what?' question is a good one: it is a good question for a learner, it is a good question for a professional educator. The 'so what?' question suggests a curiosity about finding connections to our own experience. How does what happens at Horsenden connect to me? What lessons if any can I derive from this? What benefits will my school get from thinking about theirs? Their story contains many useful pointers for enhancing the provision in similar schools.

The school staff handbook is a weighty tome. When Alistair takes it on staff development courses it is looked at with some reverence and awe. It contains the distilled wisdom behind years of steady improvement at the school. The headteacher's letter at the start of the handbook states, 'everything that exists at the school is there because, ultimately, it ensures the best learning outcomes for the children'.

Ask the headteacher, the deputy headteacher, the Key Stage managers, the year group co-ordinators or any teacher what characterizes the ethos of the school and the response is remarkably consistent.

'Teachers affect eternity – no one knows where their influence ends.'

11

Seven features get talked about. The features are talked about in different ways and with differing emphases but they remain there nevertheless. They are:

* All children and all adults know and appreciate how they learn.
* A clear commitment from the top.
* All successes are celebrated.
* A focus on achievement.
* Delegation and empowerment is everywhere – roles are made explicit.
* All new and temporary staff participate in an induction programme.
* All procedures and systems are clearly communicated and summarized in the handbook.

This is the sort of list that you can read in any school improvement handbook and if you have read one in the last ten years, and there have been many, you would have seen all these features with the possible exception of the first feature. Horsenden makes the distinction that it is important for all children and all staff to be aware of the variety of ways in which we learn and the variety of possible ways in which to structure learning. If you went to a Year 1 class, you would see learning occurring through visual, auditory and kinesthetic channels. You would see children passing around squishy vowels – large foam letters that, when squeezed, make the appropriate vowel sounds. In the Year 6 lesson on *Midsummer Night's Dream* you would see visual overviews, discussion in pairs and in small groups, brain breaks and movement between tables. The commitment to structure for variety runs throughout the school. A prerequisite for this is a positive and supportive learning environment where children and adults can 'take the risk of learning'.

For the past five years the school has worked on securing a positive and supportive learning environment starting with 'quality behaviour'. Some of Horsenden's steps to 'quality behaviour' are as follows:

* Building on an existing and strong personal social and health education culture.
* Establishing a training programme led by an external consultant – paid for by Standards Fund monies – for all staff, including school meals assistants and governors.
* Coming back to the professional development via staff updates, weekly and daily briefings and through peer observation against a VAK monitoring form.
* A common induction programme for all staff incorporating accelerated learning, learning styles, what makes effective learning.
* Clear codes of behaviour devised by and with the children.
* Building in comprehensive schemes for quality lunchtimes, quality playtimes and quality behaviour in class with a consistent approach across each.
* Relentless attention to positive reinforcement.
* Encouraging reflective practice. Especially successful has been the headteacher logbook, which is written daily, and the newly qualified teacher six-weekly focus.
* Good home–school links incorporating carefully monitored letters, a quality newsletter that contains information, dates for the diary, what's happening in class, games to play with your child and other useful tips.

'First he wrought, and afterward he taught.'
(Geoffrey Chaucer, recipe for teacher training)

- Attention to detail. A good example is the 'To Do list'. At the end of each day, a 'To Do list' for next morning is placed not only on the classroom whiteboard but also on the classroom door. This allows parents collecting their children to see what is happening next morning and encourages them into the school.

- Workshops for parents across a range of issues – impact maths, confident parents–confident children, VAK, friendships – and including positive behaviour.

Target setting is an important part of the learning approach at Horsenden. The situation had been that there was an assessment record folder comprising an A4 sheet and the staff were used to recording and analysing the data held there. However, children 'were not let in on the secret' and parents and others were only shown the record at the end of the year. What was wanted was a mechanism to maintain the focus on quality teaching and learning, involve the children in the process and 'switch on, and keep on, their learning lights'.

Horsenden Code of Conduct at KS1

General
Say kind things
Don't pull a funny or a nasty face
Talk quietly

Around the school
Walk quietly and sensibly
Only use your hands and feet to play games
Play with new children and take time with them

Trips
Listen to the grown ups and do what they say
Sit down quietly and put your seat belt on in the coach
Stay with the adult in your group

Quality Lunchtimes
Let others join in your games
Be polite to everyone
No punching, pushing, pinching or kicking!

So what happened was an attempt to bring the targets to life so that:

- children use them daily;
- they are visible in the classroom;
- they are available as criteria for marking;
- we celebrate when they are met.

A number of things can go wrong in target setting and the school was aware of these. There can be a focus on quantity and presentation rather than learning. Children can be made to suffer in a game where overemphasis of comparisons with others is the norm. Children who are not sufficiently involved in setting the targets do not develop positive learning dispositions towards their achievement. Without being fully involved, children can fail to see their purpose. The feedback from the targets can be too readily used for social engineering or managerial purposes rather than learning.

'If you are travelling with a child, put on your own mask first'
(In-flight instructions, recipe for teacher training)

Literacy session – Thursday 30.09.99   **Lesson Plan** – 10.25 – 11.25

Observation for VAK by EAD

Children in three mixed ability groups – A, B, C

Time	Literacy session	Resources	VAK
10.20	**Class enter** aims of lesson on each table (coloured paper) and on the OHP. Classical music playing.	OHP – aims & 8 colour p/c.	
10.25 10 min 5 min	**Whole class – shared reading and writing.** 'Rhyming Doggerel' by Michael Rosen. (OHP and 4xA3 copies around room on walls) Teacher to read through once – Identify the rhythm of the poem and clap it. What gives it/or helps the rhyme? – The rhyme. Identify the words that rhyme – write on board in <u>coloured chalk</u>. What makes the words rhyme – how they are spelt or how they <u>sound</u>? Recap – Spelling families from yesterday, ain, ane, eign. Use the letters on the board to make new rhyming words.	OHP – poem. 6 x A3 (2x for V.F & C.S) Coloured chalk Enlarged – Alphabet letters / spelling family words.	
10.40 10 min 5 min	**Whole class phonics, spellings, vocabulary and grammar.** Rhyming activity – Using doggerel sheets (yellow paper) and A3 activity sheets. Work in pairs – using coloured pens. Spelling family activity – Working as a table group – use the spelling families and alphabet letters to make new rhyming words.	OHP poem. Poem p/c x 16 (yellow paper) Activity sheet 16 x A3 Alphabet activity envelops.	
10.55	**STOP** – Brain gym. Spelling word of the day / figure of eight exercise. Ear rolling.		
11.00 20 min	**Guided / independent tasks.** Independent – Groups C & A. Using the p/c sheet to help them write their own rhyming doggerel & spelling family words if useful. Individual work. Guided – Group B – Shape poems. Look at examples and read through the instructions as a group. Teacher gives 3 example shapes (already drawn) – spider, cat & an abstract star. Divide group into 3 – each has to write either an interesting sentence/s about that object or a repeating work pattern that describes the object. Once they've decided, fill the shape with their 'poem' – using coloured pens. (Music played quietly while working)	Doggerel sheet x 22 Reasons for writing textbooks x 4 Shape poem examples x 10 A2 Shape templates x 3 Pack of coloured pens	
11.20	**Plenary** Group B – Each of the three mini groups to report back to whole class and show their shape poems.	Shape poems	

There were factors enabling the school's target-setting approach to take place. There was an agreed aim for children to take more control of their own learning. This was supported by an investment in training that allowed staff to build in the established assessment system. Staff had become used to seeing, handling and analysing data and were becoming more familiar with using targets for planning and for focused teaching. This meant that the system became consistent even when the staff using it changed.

Now in every lesson the learning objectives are shared at the beginning, during and at the end of the lesson. There is time for reflection on these objectives and on individual targets. Assessment breakdowns are used to identify one positive target per child. Four or maybe five general targets are used for the class as a whole. Children use homework planners to set themselves and record their own weekly targets. The target cards are out in every lesson. Marking always refers to the targets.

Imaginative ways of recording and displaying target cards helps. For example:

See pages 216–7 for more on target cards

* Laminate the targets.
* Have standardized laminates and individualize with the child's name.
* Have class, group and individual targets.
* Put a numeracy target and a literacy target on each side of the card.
* Suspend them on thread above the desks.
* Write them as postcards to yourself.
* Write targets as circus- or concert-type posters announcing when the target will be met and by whom.
* Celebrate noisily and with movement when someone hits their target.
* Have a target-setters wall and display them there.
* Build up the target cards on the wall to see if collectively you can reach certain target heights or marks by the end of the week, term or year.

Structuring for variety in learning at Horsenden can be boiled down to three letters: VAK. Throughout the school, VAK provides the baseline or structuring variety in lessons. The school has invested in developing an understanding of adult learning styles, accelerated learning methods and strategies for children of high ability. National testing scores have improved year on year and with detailed analysis teachers found that certain groups of children who were performing poorly at national and local level were doing very well at Horsenden. After observing lessons, the headteacher noticed, 'the improvements in what was happening with teachers using accelerated learning techniques compared to observations carried out before we had started to consciously think about learning'. External inspections validated the improvements. Classroom observations for the last two years have taken place using a VAK proforma (see page 14) that played a part in cementing the adoption of VAK as a whole school approach. The teaching of spelling is a good example of how VAK is put to work.

'In the practice of tolerance, one's enemy is the best teacher.' (Dalai Lama)

15

After data analysis identified improvement in children's spelling as a need, a whole school strategy was introduced in 1996. The strategy was launched through a series of professional development activities that considered the stages involved in spelling, the visual and perceptual skills and the links with motor skills including handwriting. A new approach was launched that contained progression from KS1 to KS2. It was introduced to parents via the newsletter and through after-school sessions and a children's sharing assembly. KS1 scores are now well above national averages.

The school found that spelling lists did not work, nor did drilling whole class. A multi-sensory approach was the key. There are weekly targets, which are individualized, and VAK spelling is a daily routine for KS1. The VAK method described opposite is taught to the children and they work with the methods they find suits them best. High frequency words are printed on laminated card that is colour coded and then manipulated via an easily seen velcro board. The most charming part of this is when the children are memorizing the look of the word and take an imaginary photograph – 30 or more tiny and wholly imaginary cameras clicking at once!

Horsenden's Magic Spelling strategy

- Have the word properly spelled on a card
- Think of a good feeling and make it stronger
- Close your eyes
- Open your eyes and look at the correct spelling
- Move the card with the correct spelling up and to the left and see it there
- Remove the card and see if you can still see the word
- Write down what you are seeing
- Look at the word and give yourself a tick for every letter you get right
- When you have done it u r a mgc spllr

At KS2 spelling strategies that owe their origin to Neuro Linguistic Programming (NLP) have been widely adopted and given the label 'Magic Spelling'. Magic Spelling is multi-sensory and involves first getting the child to feel good about the experience, then manipulating the word by seeing it, hearing it and its component parts and then physically rehearsing its organization in some way. To complement magic spelling we have active punctuation. When punctuation is read or used the child mimics the punctuation using fingers. This helps get it into the muscle memory and so it resists forgetting.

Recruiting and retaining staff are issues for many UK schools. Horsenden has gone some way to overcoming the problem. It does what it can within its own remit. There is high morale among staff, brought about in part by 'keeping true to our direction whatever the local or national circumstances'. There are positive and secure relationships with parents and carers, achieved by paying attention to detail and being sensitive to parenting issues and some adult insecurities about schooling. They provide ongoing and imaginative staff development for existing staff and carefully considered induction programmes for both NQTs and supply teachers. Finally, established response protocols itemized in the staff handbook – which every individual working in or with the school receives – makes potential disruption easier to manage.

Attendance has been a school priority recently. If you make something important, give it attention, it changes as a result. This simple psychological methodology can work. This is how the headteacher describes what they have done.

'Who dares to teach must never cease to learn.' (John Cotton Dana)

Horsenden Primary
Reception Literacy through VAK

- **Brain Gym-**   Lazy 8's/ 88's
Rub –a-dubs
Cross crawl

- **VAK spelling-**   1. Hold up word, repeat word 3x
2.Say letter names, sound out if appropriate.
3.Discuss word, are there words within words, is there an ee monster, what happens if....
4.Write the word with your magic pen.
5. Take a photo of the word.
6. See the word in your head (close eyes if you want), spell the word. (loud, soft, rap it, sing it)

Funny words- keep a collection of favourite/ unusual words e.g. into because it is made of two words; look because of the double oo etc)

Magnetic Letters- word building, missing letters, jumbled Letters, name games.

- **Big book front covers are displayed on wall with high frequency words learnt in that book displayed as a visual reminder and tool for independent learning**

- **The Singing Alphabet-**
  - o   VISUAL- hold up the picture with the letter and sentence.
  - o   AUDITORY- sing the phonics song
  - o   KINESTHETIC- do the action to go with the words and song.

- **Letter/ Number recognition and writing**
  - o   VISUAL- turning letters into characters, what do they remind us of.
  - o   KINESTHETIC- write letters with magic finger or hands, write the letter on a partners back, guess what it is. Play dough letters, trace letters in sand etc. The letter/number feely bag game
  - o   AUDITORY- describe the letter shape e.g. Down-up-flick, tongue twisters, jingles

'The man who can make hard things easy is the educator.' (Ralph Waldo Emerson)

- **Phonics**- Kim's game, odd one out, letter of the week table, the sound button machine.

- **Big books**

  o VISUAL- use of story props to support the story
  o KINESTHETIC- role play the story
  o AUDITORY- use musical instruments to denote main characters or events; really dramatise the stories; make deliberate mistakes; children model teacher

- **Alphabetical order/ word order**
  o VISUAL- use of ABC washing line
  o KINESTHETIC- get up and do it using ABC cards, jumbled sentences
  o AUDITORY- clap it, shout it, whisper it...

VAK GROUP ACTIVITIES

- Sorting objects by sound and recording (V A K)
- Alphabet soundtracks (V A K)
- High frequency word BINGO (V A)
- Letter of the week in language books using objects, jingles, dictionaries (VAK)
- Phonic art activities (V A K) eg. Letter r paint rainbows, make 3d rockets
- Literacy through PE (K) e.g. making letter shapes in groups of threes
- Bringing books to life (VAK) e.g. Goldilocks and Three Bears- role play story, make porridge, write recipes, sing songs to sequence the story, set up situations for creative writing (leave out porridge for goldilocks, find out bears have eaten it, read letter from bear, write back, draw a map of where they live etc....
- Draw story maps
- Make unusually shaped books.

'Study to be what you wish to seem.' (John Bate)

The actions taken to establish a climate conducive to learning have been numerous, planned and all are trackable. For example, the actions taken to improve attendance. Our attendance figures were improving year on year. Children were frequently checking if they had, or would be receiving the end of term or end of year certificates. They told staff they wanted the certificates to keep or to put on their bedroom walls. We had managed to create a strong desire within the school for this to happen. At staff meetings and at meetings with colleagues from outside the school such as the educational social worker, we discussed how we would best achieve our attendance goals. Success was measured family by family, not by school percentages. Many individual success stories were noted; mothers with low self-esteem were helped to be in control. Simple expedients such as a colleague going to talk to them outside the school gates were gently put into place. The children of these mothers then began to attend school more regularly. We tracked assiduously. An administrator has responsibility for distributing class registers. She feeds the registers through an Optical Mark Reader (OMR). She then provides all data to teachers, parents, governors, the LEA and notes reasons for absence. She prepares the paperwork for meetings with the regular Educational Social Welfare (ESW) meetings. Joint decisions are then taken as to appropriate actions for children with irregular attendance. I then meet with parents/carer. We specifically target certain children on their improved attendance. End of term assemblies occur to congratulate and present certificates to those with 100 per cent attendance and for those with the highest improvements. Super gold awards are presented at a public occasion to children with 100 per cent attendance for the whole year. Although, at the end of the day, all costs can be identified, it was the ways in which we were working which were important and which we agreed made the difference.

The staff at Horsenden talk of learning as a shared journey. The headteacher says,

from the moment we set off on our effective learning journey all the staff in the school knew it was improving what was happening in the classroom. All staff are firmly committed to our lifelong learning focus. I can honestly say that there have not been any barriers or obstacles. Office staff know their role, instructors, nursery nurses, teachers, caretakers, cleaners, welfare assistants, classroom assistants, governors, PTFA, lunchtime assistants and classroom helpers know theirs. Managers at all levels know their role in the process – children theirs. As we have seven newly qualified staff in the school who started in September, this may blow us off course temporarily but we will get back there. Our target is to ensure that we all become lifelong learners; we will all have control of our learning and know how we learn.

A school in transition

A different set of circumstances prevail at Eastover County Primary School, in Bridgwater, Somerset. Until very recently, Steve John was headteacher there and he told us what had prompted change at his school.

'Facts are like fish, eventually they go off.' (Oscar Wilde)

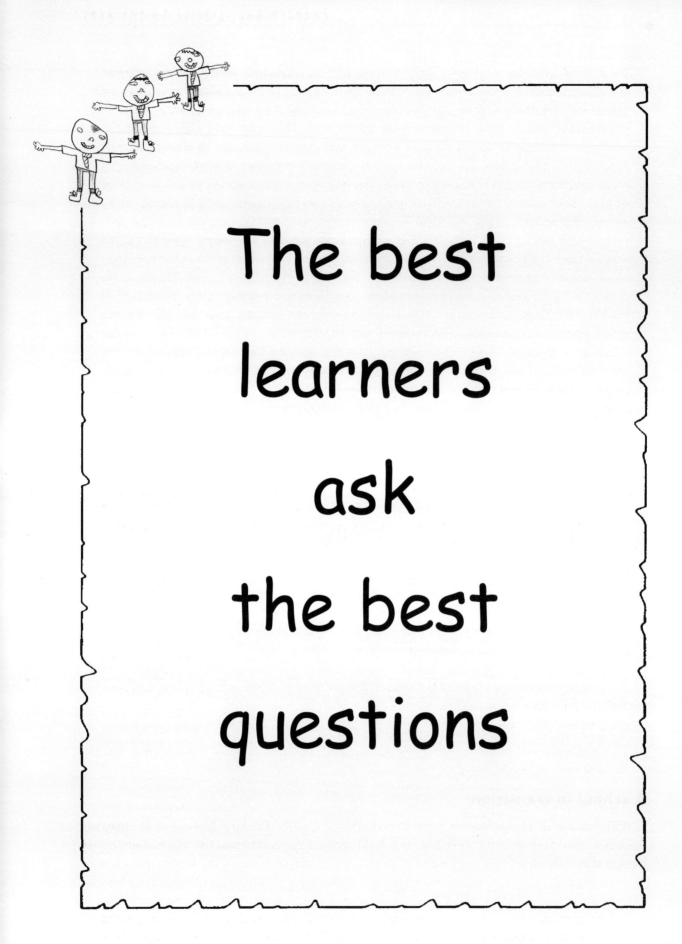

The best learners ask the best questions

Despite being in the rural county of Somerset, Bridgwater is a town with the kinds of problems that one would expect to find in the inner city: high unemployment, poverty, a high crime rate, one of the highest incidences of child abuse in the country and a serious drug problem.

Eastover, a school of 420 children, lies in the very centre of the town with no playing field and bounded on three sides by roads and on the fourth a railway siding where nuclear waste from Hinckley Point power station is stored prior to being sent to Sellafield for treatment.

When I took over as headteacher in 1995, a number of key issues became apparent:

◆ The low self-esteem felt by many Bridgwater people was reflected in the children at the school.

◆ SATs results were low.

◆ The expert and highly professional staff were ready to commit themselves fully to the many changes and initiatives coming into school as long as they had real impact on teaching and learning in the school.

◆ WE ALL WANTED OUR CHILDREN TO BECOME LEARNERS AND NOT SIMPLY 'KNOWERS'.

These key points offered huge challenges – our problem was how to do something about them.

Often the most significant things in our lives come about through chance and coincidence – enter stage right Accelerated Learning. Following a successful OFSTED report in 1997 and knowing how 'flat' staff can feel after the experience, I was keen to give them a 'lift' with an interesting and entertaining INSET day. A friend had been to one of Alistair Smith's sessions and I duly booked him for our staff development. I can only describe the input as inspirational and a revelation! We came away, as a staff, fired with enthusiasm with a number of staff saying to me that the day had reminded them why they had come into teaching in the first place!

Like all good INSET days it also provided answers, but for me it provided something else: questions – some of them uncomfortable. For example: could it really be true that, because I had little or no knowledge of preferred learning styles or Multiple Intelligences, I had excluded huge numbers of children from a worthwhile learning experience in my 23 years of teaching?

As it turned out I was not alone in this and at a staff meeting the week after our INSET it became apparent that we all felt that we had been given an insight into a way of working that could transform our teaching and our school.

It was important to me that the whole school community should understand what we wanted to do and why we wanted it so I embarked on a series of workshops that parents could attend with their children to find out more. We also looked carefully at the way our working day was organized and built 'break states' and 'brain gym' exercises into our day. Even the school tuck shop came under scrutiny with the traditional crisps gradually giving way to fruit bars and flapjacks! Music was introduced into the classrooms as a key-learning tool. These are all fairly low-key changes but ones that did make a real and observable impact on the attitudes and behaviour of the children. Our real challenge, however, was the adoption of the ALPS method in our teaching.

'What I learned when I was negotiating was that I until I changed myself I could not change others.' (Nelson Mandela)

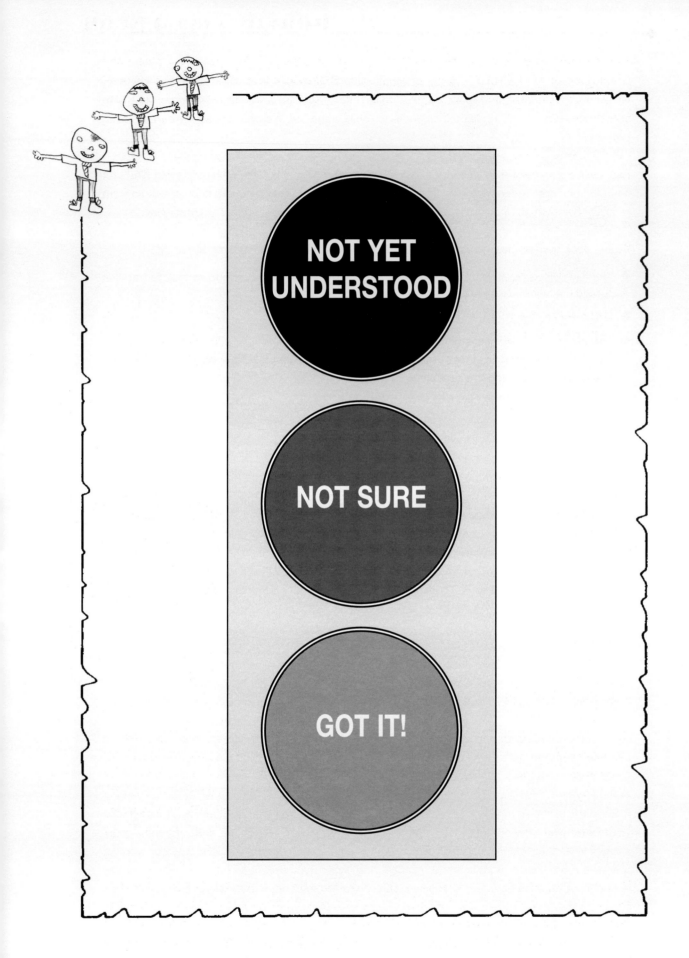

One of the beauties of the method is that so much of it simply reinforces or explains many of the good things that are happening in our classes already. But what we wanted to do was to give a commitment to the whole process and not just those elements that we were using here and now.

After a series of planning meetings between key stage co-ordinators, year groups and the whole staff our lessons quickly reflected the ALPS cycle and the impact was immediate:

◆ The classroom environment was transformed in many cases.

◆ Learning was connected so that children could see where they had come from.

◆ The class could see where the learning was going.

◆ Children could recognize when goals had been reached.

◆ A wide variety of teaching inputs [VAK] were used.

◆ There was greater interaction between the children with each member of the class, including the teacher, being seen as a learner and teacher.

◆ Plenary sessions that often 'dropped off the end' of lessons were prized and valued.

◆ The quality of teaching and learning rose.

As a result a new vigour was introduced into the school, which became evident in improved attitudes, behaviour and test results (moving in our KS2 SATs from low 60s [per cent] to between 85 and 92 per cent in the three key subjects) – all of which were monitored to ensure that we were getting a 'pay back' for all our hard work.

There were also other benefits that we couldn't foresee in 1997. The introduction of the Literacy and Numeracy Hour, which was a difficult experience for many schools, fitted easily into our way of working.

We also began to see the important part self-esteem played in the life and learning of our children. So important in fact that I established a post of 'Teacher with Responsibility for Self-Esteem' in the school and set aside one day a week for that teacher to work with children for whom self-esteem was a problem. That teacher is also responsible for promoting the use of circle time throughout the school and this too has had a significant impact on the life of the school.

There is still a lot for us to do and many more improvements to be made but the impact of ALPS has been great. Not only has it given us measurable successes in the classroom, it has also reminded us all that we can and should enjoy teaching and learning. We have become a learning community with our individual goals achieved through shared experiences and a common purpose.

'Those who know how to think need no teachers.' (Mahatma Gandhi)

Schools sharing success

For our final visit in the ALPS we go north to a cluster of schools in central Scotland. The Bo'ness Cluster consists of six schools: four primary and two secondary. Staff from the schools produced a resource pack for use in the six schools. We are indebted to them for being able to include excerpts from their pack.

The cluster took a quote from Woodrow Wilson as their starting point: 'I not only use all the brains I have, but all the brains I can borrow'. On this very sensible basis they have assembled information about learning from a range of sources and divide their pack into seven sections: personality and learning, classroom organization, positive ethos, early intervention, accelerated learning and target setting, teacher's survival kit and a bibliography. Here are four interesting ideas from their pack.

Seating

Two schools experimented with two classroom layouts and practised at changing between these layouts. Layout A, which was deemed ideal for predominantly independent work and was used in some maths activities and for some language activities, consisted of two 'U's, one within the other. In Layout A the smaller U of desks and chairs is positioned within the larger, with both 'U's facing a teacher table and whiteboard. In Layout B children are clustered around tables which are spaced evenly around the room. In Layout B there is more language interaction and collaborative work between pupils. The challenge is to be able to move between layouts! Can you designate six classroom furniture assistants to move the layout? Can they do it against the clock or timed to a piece of music? What would be good table shifting music? How about 'we like to move it, move it ...?'

Research from Nottingham Trent University (Hastings, 2000) suggests that changing layout can accelerate learning by 'allowing children to work in situations which support their learning'.

Practical ideas for circle time

Based on work by Jenny Mosley and others, the cluster lists ideas for improving circle time.

- ❋ Seat the children comfortably on chairs of equal height in a circle.
- ❋ Begin with a warm-up game.
- ❋ Agree the rules and behaviours that should operate in the circle.
- ❋ Have an agenda box in class where children and staff can jot down an issue for discussion and put it in the box.
- ❋ Having agreed the agenda, each person has the opportunity to contribute without interruption.
- ❋ This can be achieved by having a 'speaking object ' to pass around – koosh ball, teddy bear, glove puppet or a delicate object which needs to be passed carefully.

'The teacher is one who makes two ideas grow where only one grew before.'
(Elbert Hubbard)

❋ Use sentence openers to help the children: 'I like it in the playground because …; I enjoy working in class when …; I find it best to …; I feel annoyed if …'

❋ Help the quieter children to begin by a gentle prompt with some easy to convey information: 'My favourite time is …'

❋ Next can follow the open forum. This is a chance to discuss the issue for about five minutes, where children put up their hand to speak and listen to each other.

❋ This can be followed by a problem-solvers session where each person contributes to solving any problems which have been raised. This could be called problem page and you can either write to or respond to the problem page.

❋ If the problem is a shared one, then the circle can agree on a plan of action where each pupil knows what his role will be.

❋ Have special day by putting a child's name in a balloon. Burst the balloon to reveal the name!

Visual reinforcers

Visual ways of 'catching them being good, catching them being successful and letting them know', include:

✳ a large tree where each child puts on a leaf with her achievement

✳ a wall of achievements built brick by brick

✳ a peacock with feathers

✳ a starry sky with stars, suns and planets

✳ a flower bed

✳ a beach with pebbles and sea creatures

✳ a magic fruit tree with exotic fruits growing on the same tree

✳ under the sea

✳ into the sky.

Thinking tools

The pack describes how one school uses a step-by-step approach to developing questions. 'Kircaldy West Primary School recommends Robert Fisher's series – Stories/Poems/Games for Thinking – in talking and listening lessons. Teachers maintain that their national test results have improved markedly across the board as a result. The idea is children listen to a story, then they are taken through a carefully structured question and answer session. Initially, questions are of a literal nature, but this builds up to inferential-type questions that encourage learners to think at a progressively deeper level. The most able eight year olds are thinking metacognitively while the others are more confident about their ability to think. There is only one rule – OOPSAT – only one person speaks at a time – and thinking books, exercise books covered in white paper, then decorated by children are used for confidential notes/drawings of their own thoughts.'

Early intervention principles in early years classes (some excerpts):

✳ Use everyday packaging to create interactive displays.

✳ Use bottle tops with logos instead of counters for games.

✳ Use photographs from walks and visits in albums and displays as an opportunity for children to write captions.

'To teach is to learn twice.' (Joseph Joubert)

✳ Clearly label all materials, workbooks, resources, coat pegs, displays and trays.

✳ Scribe for the children when they tell their stories and encourage them to complete parts of the writing and take on more and more as you go.

✳ Encourage children to make, mark and talk about emergent writing.

✳ Be a model reader, writer and story-teller at every opportunity and encourage the children to take turns in mimicking you.

✳ Use authentic materials to set up opportunities within play situations for children to experience being a literate person. For example, recipe books in the baking area, writing tools and office materials, stamps and envelopes in the office area.

✳ Use large drawstring book bags containing the book and related items which can be brought out and discussed.

✳ Provide magnetic boards or velcro boards with letters, numbers, pictures and artefacts for the children to manoeuvre.

What the teachers said

The cluster also included the advice of teachers, again some of it too good to be omitted.

'Children like to know what's ahead of them for the day – their goals, also how they've done at the end of the lesson (or day). Have they achieved the goals? Gather them together to go over the main points.'
Jeanette Deans, Kinneil Primary

'Supply teachers – it's a good idea to get each pupil to make a name badge, perhaps with a picture which tells you something about them. It can be effective to bring in something which shows something about you such as a photograph.'
Pat Ballantine, Supply Teacher

'When I have written a comment on children's work, I ask that they initial the comment so I know they have read it and will act on it.'
Julie Borland, Grange Primary School

'Self-assessment diaries, endeavouring to involve parents and also to motivate pupils are sent home every weekend. Build up self-respect in children through positive comments and realistic aims in the diary and in verbal appraisal, where they too contribute.'
Marion Duncan, Kinneil Primary

The final word from the Bo'ness cluster of schools lies with Barbara Kilpatrick of Deanburn Primary. Her advice for staying on top of the job: 'Aromatherapy candles, massage oil and a chilled bottle of wine!'

'A single thought can revolutionise your life.'

The ALPS model explained

At the heart of the ALPS approach are classroom strategies that build and maintain a positive and supportive learning environment. Without such positivity, the other classroom strategies are worthless.

The Accelerated Learning Cycle provides the structure of every lesson in the ALPS. The seven stages needed for you to follow the Accelerated Learning Cycle are listed below.

1 Connect the learning
Begin every lesson by ensuring that the present learning experience can be situated between what has already been covered and what is to come. Do this with connecting activities that are child centred and involve a high level of participation. Connecting activities also allow children to establish what they already know about a topic before jumping into that topic.

Useful phrases:

* In the last lesson we …
* Three words that we remember were important are …
* Three things we learned about … were …
* Take turns with your partner to say three things you already know about …
* On last night's To Do list you were asked to …

2 Give the Big Picture
Provide an overview of the lesson. Explain how you will do it so that you give a summary of what is to come and provide an initial exposure to key ideas and key terminology. Write a précis of the Big Picture on the board or a flip chart to aid the visual learners. Embed open-ended questions to engage curiosity and challenge understanding. This means asking them early, perhaps writing them up and then constantly going back to them. Identify key terminology and reinforce it visually.

Useful phrases:

* On the whiteboard are the questions we will answer by …
* I'm holding up the poster that shows how in this lesson we are going to …
* Here are the important words that we will need today …

'Learning is not about consumption it is all about production.'

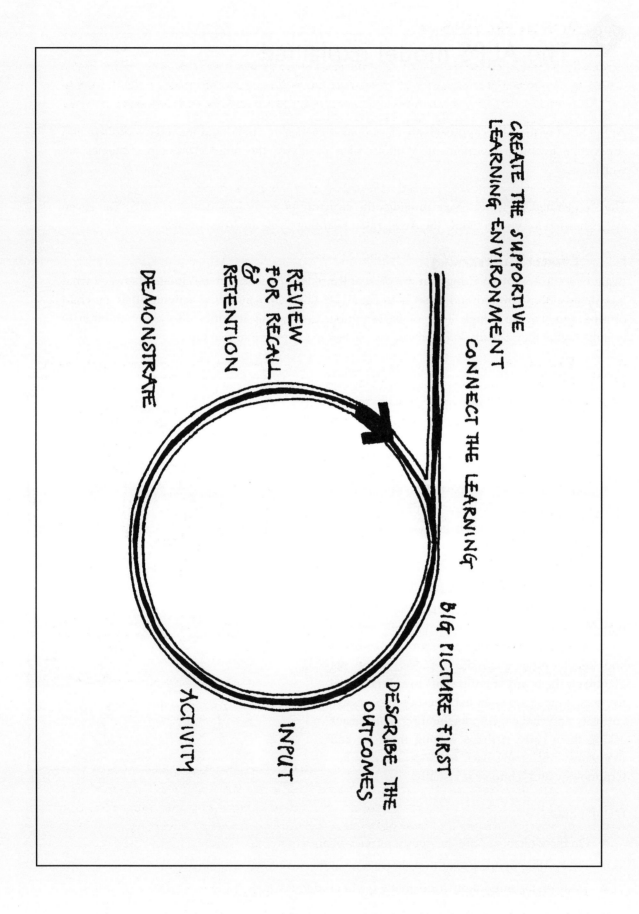

CREATE THE SUPPORTIVE
LEARNING ENVIRONMENT

CONNECT THE LEARNING

BIG PICTURE FIRST

DESCRIBE THE
OUTCOMES

INPUT

ACTIVITY

DEMONSTRATE

REVIEW
FOR RECALL
&
RETENTION

3   Describe the outcomes

This is our target-setting space. Sometimes it is appropriate to formalize it, often it is better done informally. Some targets can be specified whole class, some by table or group, some individually. Encourage students to think in terms of achieving a successful and specific outcome. Teach them to be able to describe that outcome in detail to themselves, on paper perhaps, and later to others. Make a note of expected class outcomes on the board or a flip chart.

Useful phrases:

* By the end of today you will understand that … and that … and that …
* Lets look at the targets we set ourselves last week for …
* Get out your target cards and place them in front of you …
* Read your targets quietly before telling someone else …
* When we have finished you will know you will have done a good job because…
* Up on the wall are some examples of good work done already in …
* Decide who you will show at the end of today how you can…

4   Give input

Ensure that input of information is, wherever possible, multisensory in order to engage different types of processing pathways in the brain. Provide experiences that exploit VAKplus – visual, auditory and kinesthetic learning preferences with plus for lots of challenging questions. This is where the teacher creates see, hear and do experiences.

Go to page 159 for move on VAKplus

Useful phrases:

* Shut your eyes and see the word you are trying to spell …
* Picture yourself being really good at …
* Say the word you are trying to spell in a whisper voice …
* Talk yourself through how you would …
* Draw the word you are trying to spell in the air or on your desktop …
* As you do it, talk yourself through it …

5   Activate understanding

Activating understanding involves going deeper into the learning. This may involve the learner re-presenting their understanding in some way. A good mechanism for choosing possible modes of re-presenting is via different types of intelligence or intelligent response. In our case we feel that Howard Gardner's modes of multiple intelligence is a friendly structure for doing this.

Useful phrases:

* Explain this to someone who may have difficulty understanding.
* Summarize in your head what, for you, are the most important things.

'We don't see things as they are, we see things as we are.' (Anais Nin)

* Select the five key new words and think of words with a similar meaning.

* Now take the five key new words we've just learned and try to put them to a memorable tune.

* What would be a good way to draw this for someone who needed to remember what it looked like?

* If you had to dance this, what would be your first three movements?

* Try to remember all the things we have done today and list them one at a time, now put them in order of importance for …

* At the zoo, which animals are best at the different school subjects? Why?

6 Ask children to demonstrate understanding

Provide frequent opportunities to show understanding and to test that understanding. Use pole-bridging – murmuring your thoughts aloud – and mapping techniques liberally.

Useful phrases:

* You have as long as this piece of music lasts to explain to your neighbour how …

* What is the most important word in this page/paragraph/sentence and why?

* With your partner, prepare a roleplay to show how …

* Invent a joke – 'what did the ancient Egyptian say to the …' – about what we have just learned.

* Make a poster to teach your friend about …

* If you have only got six words and you have to explain this, which six words would you choose?

* Reduce it to a sound bite by …

* Make cards with eight keywords for … and write their meanings on the back.

7 Give opportunities for review and recall

Make provision for regular review sessions during and at the conclusion of each learning experience in order to lift the level of simple recall and make each subsequent lesson more effective. Self-testing or testing in friendly pairs is an excellent and time-effective way of beginning this.

Useful phrases

* On your own hide the spellings and …

* In pairs test each other on the spellings for …

* 'In So You Want to be a Millionaire today we have … who will be answering questions on …'

* 'Nervous?' 'We don't want to give you that!' 'Final Answer?' 'I'll stick with what I've got.'

* Stand up and go to the next table, then tell that group two things that you know about …

* Decide in your group on one important thing to tell the class about …

* Write three new keywords on your memory map about …

* At your table devise ten quiz questions for another table on …

* For homework I'd like you to teach someone in your family how to …

'You have to leave the city of your comfort and go into the wilderness of your intuition.
What you'll discover will be wonderful. What you'll discover is yourself.' (Alan Alda)

An ALPS classroom is one free from intimidation, threat or put-down. It is a positive, supportive and safe learning environment where there is, nevertheless, high challenge. Challenge that jumps out in an unpredictable way evokes the same response as a tiger jumping out of the forest in an unpredictable way – you run for your life! When you pounce on children with an unanticipated question, when you have a sudden request, when you show a quick change of mood, you tip them into stress. Stress, long term, is not so good for meaningful learning. Short term it can be OK. Help your children to manage the risk of learning through the protocols you adopt and model. The ALPS classroom and the Accelerated Learning Cycle can help you do this. For example:

❋ Make your classroom a 'no put-down zone'.

❋ Take care in how questions are asked and responded to.

❋ Avoid the double jeopardy of 'hands up who doesn't understand?'

❋ Avoid pouncing on a child with a question.

❋ Avoid trampling over vital processing time. Allow processing time to hear the question, assimilate it, formulate a response and surface the response in language.

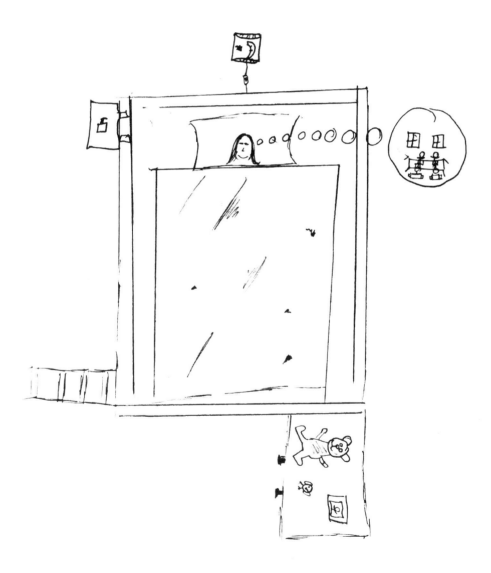

My dreams about school

'I forget what I was taught. I only remember what I have learnt.' (Patrick White)

A big journey begins with a little step

The children who journey with you

This chapter of the book differs from the others. Each of the other chapters contains a description. It can be a description of a school or a situation in a school, a model of learning, a stage in a cycle, some principles perhaps or maybe even a resource list.

This chapter sets out to describe the 'children who journey with you' – a rather pompous aspiration perhaps? We have never met the children with whom you work, so who are we to describe them? You may know them well but there will be some children of whom you are not so sure. The children will have their own friends and favourites, so they will not know each other that well. And in some cases, individual children are asking themselves big questions. Questions borne out of philosophical or spiritual intrigue: who am I? Questions borne out of temporary uncertainty: what mood am I in today? Questions borne out of desperation: will I struggle with my learning? Questions borne out of angst: will I have a friend today?

Self-questioning – learning a little over time, through experience, through interaction with others and through reflection – is part of individual growth. Asking questions of each other – learning about relative strengths and possible weaknesses and adjusting for those – is about human development. Asking questions of one's place in a community and one's place in a world is part of spiritual and social growth. Very powerful tools for learning – at whatever level and with whatever application – are those we can use ourselves. Questions are part of our self-discovery repertoire. What we have provided in our first questionnaire for children on page 34 and those in Part 4 is a very powerful set of tools for self-discovery. Rather than tell you what your children are like, or ought to be like, or how they compare with others, we provide tools for you to use to open up and explore the possibilities of becoming what they like.

The questionnaires provided throughout this book are designed to help teachers and children reflect on perceived strengths and weaknesses and grow as a result. They are not scientifically, psychologically or statistically proven. Their purpose is to open dialogue and to allow children to develop a sense of themselves as learners. Part 4 contains questionnaires that allow children to reflect on aspects of learning that relate to motivation, dispositions towards learning, learning preference and multiple intelligence. The brain-builder questionnaire over helps children understand that there are important lifestyle choices to be made. By completing it a wonderful dialogue about how we look after ourselves and our capacity for becoming a good learner can begin. Use it carefully. Use it in the fun spirit intended.

'A teacher is one who makes himself progressively unnecessary.' (Thomas Carruthers)

The brain-builder questionnaire
(strictly fun and only for children!)

The purpose of this questionnaire is to help you find out more about your brain, how it works and how you can help it work better. Your brain is very powerful. Did you know that you were born with about a hundred billion brain cells? Your brain cells are busy all the time, even when you are asleep. They send messages around your brain at great speed, telling you what to do, how to move, how to feel and what to think.

Your brain is totally different to every other brain in the world! We all have different ways of learning new things. If you want to be really clever, you need to know how your brain works. The questions below will help you to understand more about your brain, so that you can make the most of those billions of brain cells!

Do eight questions at a time then have a rest before going on.

		True	False
1	I enjoy doing exercise	☐	☐
2	I always go to bed when I am asked	☐	☐
3	I eat fresh fruit and vegetables everyday	☐	☐
4	I enjoy doing puzzles and things that make me think	☐	☐
5	When my teacher gives me a problem to solve I try to go straight to the answer	☐	☐
6	When my teacher gives me a problem to solve I work it out step by step	☐	☐
7	If I am shown something I can do it first time	☐	☐
8	I never get angry	☐	☐
9	I can throw and catch with both hands	☐	☐
10	I have dreams when I sleep	☐	☐
11	I like to drink water	☐	☐
12	I set myself targets	☐	☐
13	If I do a jigsaw, I look at the picture first	☐	☐
14	If I do a jigsaw, I never look at the picture	☐	☐
15	I can imitate other people's voices	☐	☐
16	I sometimes feel frightened	☐	☐
17	I do sport after school	☐	☐
18	I am never tired in the morning	☐	☐
19	I always eat breakfast before school	☐	☐
20	I never give up even when I'm stuck	☐	☐
21	I know if I'm going to like a TV programme before I watch it	☐	☐
22	I have to watch a programme first to know if I like it	☐	☐
23	I learn best if someone shows me what to do	☐	☐
24	I sometimes cry when I remember sad things	☐	☐
25	I can balance on a narrow beam	☐	☐
26	I have a television in my bedroom	☐	☐
27	Sweets are better for you than fruit	☐	☐
28	I learn best when I try it for myself	☐	☐
29	I have to do the whole computer game to get better at it	☐	☐
30	I practise little bits of the computer game to get better at it	☐	☐
31	I could teach someone else to do something	☐	☐
32	All my memories are happy	☐	☐

the alps approach resource book – Accelerated Learning in Primary Schools

Explanatory brain-builder text

The explanations below are for the teacher to read and discuss with the class. Once your learners have worked through the questions, have them read through their true or false answers. Then you are ready to read and discuss the explanations below.

The activity helps initiate discussion about all the things that are good and bad for learning. We suggest you do it a little at a time and allow lots of space for discussion. This is ideal for 'individual – pair – share' work. Start with children doing the questionnaire and looking at their answers. For children who may struggle, read them the question and explain it if necessary. Then put into pairs to discuss their answers; then into groups so the groups can discuss the implications of each question.

You can hang an entire 'learning to learn' or 'study skills' programme around this questionnaire and cover topics like lifestyle and learning, attitudes to learning, habits of learning and what makes us different learners. The explanations are complex but the questions deliberately easy!

1. Exercise increases oxygen and blood supply to the brain. This makes your brain more efficient at things like reacting quickly, concentrating for longer periods of time and remembering. Regular exercise helps the cells in your brain connect together more efficiently.

2. You need at least nine hours of uninterrupted sleep to be at your best. When you sleep you do so in cycles of 90 minutes with some of that time spent in a deep sleep that scientists call slow-wave and some in what they call REM. REM stands for Rapid Eye Movement.

3. Without the nutrients provided by a balanced diet your brain becomes less efficient. A balanced diet means fewer chips, fizzy drinks and sweets and more fish, chicken, rice, pasta, bread, fruit and vegetables.

4. The best way to develop the bits of your brain used in what is called higher order thinking is to stick at difficult problems and try and work them out over time and in different ways. This develops an area of your brain known as the pre-frontal cortex. Slap your hand on your forehead and it is under there!

5. Your brain is organized so that lots of different parts and lots of different chemicals come together when you try to solve a problem. Some people are good at trying to solve a problem all at once. Some are good at guessing or just have a 'sense of what is right'. Scientists believe that the right side of your brain acts as an 'organizer' and helps fit all the pieces together. Slap your right hand on the right side of your head and this part of your brain helps you with good guesses. Sides of the brain are known as hemispheres – why?

6. When different parts of your brain come together with different chemicals it means that your brain is working hard to help you solve problems. Your left hemisphere has more chemicals that help with 'selective attention'. This means it helps notice detail and does things step by step. Slap your left hand on the left side of your head and this part of your brain helps you with finding all the detail.

'Only the curious will learn and only the resolute overcome the obstacles to learning. The quest quotient has always excited me more than the intelligence quotient.'
(Eugene S. Wilson)

If you only look at what is, you might never become what you can be

7 When scientists watch large 'primates' such as chimpanzees or apes learning they notice it is done through mimicking. In other words, the baby chimp watches its mother then it does the same thing. It mimics. Humans also mimic and learn by this way and scientists think there may be parts of the brain designed to help us do this. Try sitting close with a partner, looking at each other and making different faces at the same time. Do opposites: happy and sad, angry and calm, fear and love. Is it easy? Try doing the same together. Is that easier? Why?

8 If you never get angry, then you are unusual! You have a part of your brain that helps with your emotions. Emotions are how you feel about yourself and about others. Emotions like joy, fear, envy and anger are controlled by chemicals in our brain. Some of the levels of these chemicals are set when you are young and depend on what emotions you experienced then. An area of your brain hidden away in the middle and known as the limbic system helps manage the emotions. It is good and healthy to develop your emotional brain by owning up to emotions when they occur. Your brain says it is OK to feel sad or happy, frightened or angry, jealous or proud. When your brain is not working properly you can get stuck in just one emotion. This does not happen very often and never when you are laughing happily!

9 Across the top of your brain running in a strip like an Alice band is something called the motor cortex. It is called motor because it controls movement. Put the tips of your fingers onto the tops of your ears. Now run your fingers across your head until they meet in the middle. This is where the control strip lies. The strip that is on the left side of your brain controls movement on the right side of your body, while the strip that is on the right side of your brain controls movement on the left side of your body. When you do movements that involve left and right, you use these areas.

10 When you dream you are helping store away memories and go over what you have learned from that day. When your sleep is disrupted it means you are not able to learn and remember as well as you would with uninterrupted sleep. Exercise, proper food, milk and a regular bedtime help you get the sleep you need.

11 Too much sugar and artificial colourings in drinks is bad for you. Your brain needs to be given sufficient water for it to function. You need to drink about six small glasses of water a day to help keep the chemicals in your brain nicely topped-up and balanced. Without being topped-up and balanced the chemicals do not work as well and you can become drowsy, not be able to pay attention or more forgetful.

12 To be really good at anything you need to be good at setting targets. When you set a target that you *really* want your brain works to help you get it. You cannot notice everything that goes on all around you. You certainly cannot notice everything and pay attention to everything at once. So your brain helps you filter out what is important and what is not so important. A filter stops everything that is important and lets everything else go. When you set an important goal your brain acts like this but only if it is important to you and you can imagine yourself being successful. The filtering mechanisms in your brain is called the RAS or Reticular Activating System.

'Tomorrow's employees will be doing what robots cannot do which means their work will call for sophisticated intelligence.' (Renata Caine)

You have never lost until you quit trying

13 When you start a jigsaw it helps to have a picture of what it should look like. Not everyone uses the picture, but your brain likes to have a sense of the complete thing. You can help your brain by trying to get into your mind a picture of what success is like. Do this before you start a new activity. Imagine yourself doing it really well. Practise being good at picturing success. When you do so you fool your brain because it uses the same brain cells for the imagined thing as it uses for the real thing. Brain cells are called neurons and they are organized to connect with each other in networks.

14 Some people learn by doing things a little bit at a time and then they look for patterns. With a jigsaw you might look for a shape to fit this one and try lots and lots until you get a match. This is like your brain making connections. Brain cells are called neurons and they are organized to connect with each other in networks. When they connect together your brain is learning. The more they connect together, the more likely they are to remember they have connected and the easier it becomes to learn. With brains it is a case of use it or lose it. Lots of practise when you make connections helps activate your brain. The more you use it, the better it becomes.

15 Every child across the world learns to speak in the same way. We do not all speak the same language, but we learn to speak in the same way. In your brain there are places for recognizing sounds, places for making sounds and places for organizing sounds into proper speech. Your brain needs to be taught to do this. This is called instruction. When you practise making different sounds you use different parts of your brain.

16 There is a small pea-sized area of your brain called the amygdala. This is the part of your brain that associates some things that happen with fear. This is very useful. To have no fear at all is dangerous. To have no fear of traffic would lead to a messy end. Sometimes when the amygdala does not work properly, fear 'kicks in' too often, or at the wrong time or with a bad memory.

17 Scientists have found that exercise helps your learning. They have also found that fewer and fewer children in the Western countries get enough exercise. When research is done with rats running on a wheel their brains get more chemicals to help with learning. Scientists think the same thing happens with humans.

18 Some people have high energy levels in the mornings and others have high energy levels later in the day. You have a body clock that remembers the difference between night and day. It works roughly on a 24-hour cycle and during that time you have changes in your levels of energy. If you alter your inner clock by, for example, travelling to a far away country with different time zones, you need a long time to adjust.

19 If you miss breakfast, your learning and memory suffers. If you have the wrong sort of breakfast, say sweets and crisps and fizzy drinks, then you will find it more difficult to concentrate and to remember things.

20 'Sticking at it' is good for learning. A little bit of stress is good for your learning but not too much. Experiments with rats and mice have shown that injections of a stress hormone called epinephrine into the brain improves their ability to run mazes. Challenge is good for your learning. If it is too easy, learning is not as successful. If it is too hard, then you are tempted to give up. Coming back to a problem after a break is a good learning habit.

'If information doubles on the Internet every 58 days, how are you going to keep up to help pupils keep up with it?'

21 Some very recent research suggests that 'intuition' can play an important part in learning. Intuition is when you have a feeling that something is right without being absolutely certain. Informed guesswork is another way of describing 'intuition'. The brain works in what are called conscious and sub-conscious ways. When you are conscious of something, you are aware of it. When you are not aware of something then it may be sub or below consciousness. For example, if a shelf of books toppled suddenly and fell towards you, it may be that you would start to jump out of the way without thinking about it. At the same time your heart would go faster, your blood pressure would go up and chemicals would flood into your body. This is a good example of a 'survival' response and one that operates sub-consciously.

22 Some people need more convincing before they begin to believe in something. This is natural and we all differ in how much we need to be persuaded. For some people they need to do things again and again before they become confident they will like it or enjoy it. It is as though a bit of your brain will not let go until it is ready to. When you get really used to doing something, you no longer notice you are doing it. You just seem to do it anyway. It is when you get used to doing things in just the same way that it becomes difficult to undo it. Try folding your arms. Now unfold your arms and try it in the opposite way. See what I mean! You do not have to believe that you will always have to do things the same way but you have to be prepared to undo it. It takes effort.

23 Large animals like lions and chimps learn by imitation and through play. Sometimes when you play you pretend you are someone else. This is a natural way to learn and a good way to learn. Mimicking and taking risks are good ways to improve. Find the person who is best at something and ask them how they do it. Watch them and try it like they do. Find the best speller in the class, or the best at doing sums, or at drawing, or at football. To be good they practise and the best way to practise is by imitation and play. Brain scientists now think that imitating is something we do naturally. Watch adults talking together and see if they imitate each other. Watch for them nodding heads together or shaking their heads or changing the way they speak to be more like each other.

24 It is natural to have changes of mood. To stay stuck in one mood all the time or to change quickly from one to the other is unusual. Some people, who are always sad, have a different balance of chemicals in their brain, which makes it harder to be other than sad. This is very unusual and can sometimes be treated by doctors giving legal drugs that change the chemicals in the brain slightly, making it possible for the person to be happier. In learning you do remember things better when there is a very strong change of mood associated with it. For example, if you did something that made you very, very happy or something that frightened you a little, you will remember how you felt at the time for a long time afterwards. We remember when there is a strong emotion. That is why your teacher will sometimes ask you to do unusual or risky things, or things that make you feel a little silly. What can you remember really well that had a strong emotion?

25 There is a part of your brain at the base of your skull called the cerebellum. The cerebellum helps with balance and controlling movements. When you balance on a narrow beam you activate the cerebellum.

'In teaching others we teach ourselves.' (Proverb)

Lots of artificial light late at night confuses your body clock. You might find it difficult to get to sleep after a late night of watching television. Sometimes you wake feeling tired. Your brain has a part that acts like a clock. It responds to daylight and to darkness. Your body clock begins to think that night is starting later and shifts round. Too much television can shift it a little further. It is a good idea not to have television on late at night.

 Fruit contains natural sugars that your body and your brain can absorb easily. Lifestyle – what you eat and drink, what you watch, what you do in your spare time, how much hard exercise you get, how much uninterrupted sleep – can affect your ability to pay attention. Scientists now believe in a disorder of attention and it is called Attention Deficit Hyperactivity Disorder or ADHD. Symptoms include being easily distracted or bored, rushing about a lot, difficulty in completing things, getting angry with friends quickly, talking too much and sometimes being disorganized. Lots and lots of people who do not have any sort of disorder do these things!

 When you try something for yourself and you experiment with little changes to help you get it right, that is good for learning. The best ever learning is through self-discovery. Testing yourself is good. Setting yourself targets, that are just a little more difficult than before, is good. Practising different ways of doing something is good. There is a saying among brain researchers that 'brain cells that fire together, wire together and survive together'. This means that the billions and billions of brain cells you have get excited when you do something for the first time and make connections with other excited brain cells. The more you do things in different and challenging ways the more connections between these cells are formed. Do it often enough and the little connections are there forever. If you do not do it at all, then the connections never get made.

 Some people learn best by completing all the puzzle or task in one go. This would be like practising a sport – say tennis – by always playing matches. Or it could be like writing up a diary at the end of the month and not day by day. This is a very personal thing and there is not a right or wrong way to get better but it may be better for learning to be able to adapt. In tennis, practising serve after serve and trying to correct little faults is also a good way to improve. Your brain will be improved by testing your adaptability. Try different methods. Experiment and take risks.

 Some people like to learn in little chunks. Some classroom lessons are best approached in a step-by-step way with lots of focused concentration. When you learn to do something step by step, you activate different parts of your brain and use different chemicals than when you try to do it all at once. Sometimes it is good to try the other way. It is like proving how adaptable your brain can be! Say things like 'I'm deliberately going to try to do this a different way!'

'Children are the messages we send to an unknown future.'

Teaching someone else to do something is an excellent way for you to learn. Rehearsal is important in learning. Rehearsal means going over something again. When you rehearse you use similar parts of the brain and similar neural networks. Remember our rule that 'brain cells that fire together, wire together and survive together'? When you deliberately attempt to do something well your brain begins to alter and the more you deliberately try to do that thing really, really well then the more permanent those alterations in your brain become. So the next time you are ready for it! The more you rehearse or practise, the more likely your brain will become super efficient at doing it.

 There is no doubt that how you feel about something affects your attitude to doing it. Learning with strong emotions seems to be more memorable. You remember better when you feel personally involved. Your brain is coding the memory of the event as 'more significant than others like it'. You will remember experiences that are emotional – the first time you did something or when you took a risk or when you felt that everyone was watching you. Emotions affect your memory.

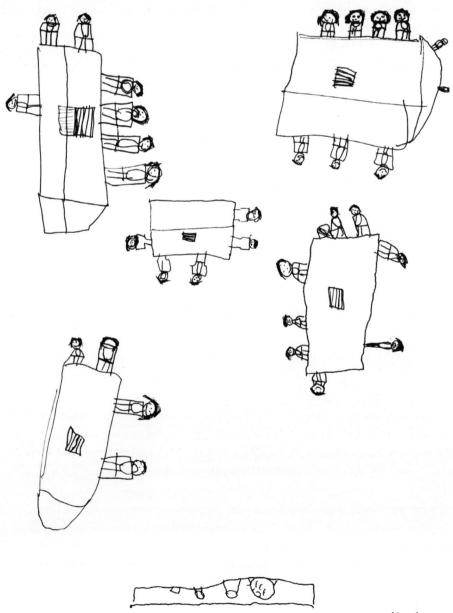

My class

42

'We must view young people not as empty bottles to be filled, but as candles to be lit.'
(Robert H. Shaffer)

Nine 'brain-based' principles

In our original ALPS book we tried to explain our methods in terms of nine 'brain-based' principles. At the time we pointed out that these were broad and aspirational. Although loosely based on emerging research into what helps, and what hinders, a brain's capacity to 'learn', they were not offered either as a succinct summation of neurological research or as a set of absolutes legitimized by science. Use the principles to explore further what different disciplines can offer our understanding of learning. Use the questions to reflect on your own classroom structures and methods. Be open minded to where the arts and the sciences meet and what they can offer to you as a professional educator.

The nine 'brain-based' principles on which the ALPS approach is based are detailed below. Also detailed are some prompt questions for you to consider and to which we provide answers in the sections to come.

Principle One. The brain develops best in environments with high levels of sensory stimulation and sustained cognitive challenge. Accelerated Learning teachers create environments for learning with high levels of learning-related sensory stimulation.

- In what ways does your classroom appearance convey positive messages about learning and about the relationships therein?
- What is the balance between natural and artificial light in your classroom?
- How warm or cold is your classroom?
- How 'distracting' is any surrounding noise coming into the class?
- Is there space to get up and move around?
- Could a child learn something about content from the surroundings?

Principle Two. The optimal conditions for learning will feature sustained levels of cognitive challenge alongside low threat. Accelerated Learning teachers make it safe to take risks and to experience and learn from those risks. They help children to develop the lifelong learning quality of persistence.

- What are the stressors affecting your teaching?
- What are the stressors from home that may affect the children?
- What experiences within a class lesson may provide stress for you or for the learners?
- Is stress differential?
- What direct interventions would we see in your classroom to help children manage stress?

'What we want is to see the child in pursuit of knowledge, and not knowledge in pursuit of the child.' (George Bernard Shaw)

Principle Three. Higher-order intellectual activity may be diminished in environments that are emotionally or physiologically hostile or are perceived to be so by the learner. Accelerated Learning teachers pay attention to the emotional and physical readiness of the child for learning.

- **Q** In what ways do you generate a sense of belonging? (Belonging)
- **Q** How would a child know that his aspirations will be identified, developed and worked towards? (**A**spiration)
- **Q** Is the learner free from put-down or physical intimidation in your class? (**S**afety)
- **Q** How is the learner's individuality affirmed and accommodated? (**I**dentity)
- **Q** How are learners encouraged to take the risk of learning in your class? (**C**hallenge)
- **Q** In what ways do you guarantee the experience of success? (**S**uccess)

Principle Four. The brain thrives on immediacy of feedback and on choice. When reflectivity is encouraged reflexivity occurs. The Accelerated Learning teacher knows that when learners engage in what is described as 'pole-bridging' – a method for internalizing feedback – improvements in reasoning powers are dramatic.

- **Q** Do you distribute your attention and thus your feedback equitably? What governs who gets what sort of feedback on their learning?
- **Q** How do you structure positive and purposeful self-talk among learners?
- **Q** Might negative self-talk have an adverse affect on our brain?
- **Q** In what ways is your marking educative? Does it encourage reflectivity and choice?
- **Q** What is pole-bridging? Why might it help long-term learning?

Principle Five. There are recognized processing centres within different structures of the brain. These centres are highly integrated, complementary and capable of change. Accelerated Learning teachers use this knowledge as authority for structured variety in classroom input. They also notice and exploit different attentional states.

- **Q** In what ways do you affirm the overview and make connections explicit? (Aggregating)
- **Q** With what frequency would you expect to go through things in small chunks, a bit at a time? (Dis-aggregating)
- **Q** How do you enhance visual aspects of learning? (V)
- **Q** How do you structure variety in oral input? (A)
- **Q** How would movement be used to enhance learning in your class? (K)
- **Q** In what ways do you provide for changes in physical state? (Focus-diffuse)

Principle Six. Each brain has a high degree of plasticity, developing and integrating with experience in ways unique to itself. The Accelerated Learning teacher also understands the significance of operating from models or assumptions about intelligence. She has at her disposal an understanding of different models, including those that argue for intelligence being multiple and modifiable and capable of being taught.

- **Q** What are your underlying assumptions about intelligence? Is it shaped by inheritance? Can it be taught? Are there limits? If so, how are they defined?
- **Q** If you changed your assumptions about intelligence, would it change how you taught?

'When teaching, light a fire, don't fill a bucket.' (Dan Snow)

Q One of the ways a child cues her sense of how intelligent she is, is through her teacher. Others in the class pick up on this cueing and act accordingly. How specifically do you let each child know they have the possibility of a range of intelligences?

Q How might the underlying assumptions impact on your classroom practice?

Q In what ways do you structure for different intelligent responses in your classroom?

Principle Seven. Learning takes place at a number of levels. An Accelerated Learning teacher engages both conscious and unconscious processing through suggestive methods, variety in questioning strategies and personal goal setting. She integrates learning challenges.

Q Learning occurs as connections are formed. How do you make connections explicit?

Q How do your learners know what success looks like?

Q Do your learners own their own targets?

Q Does the complexity of your language help or hinder their learning?

Principle Eight. Memory is a series of processes rather than locations within the brain. Accelerated Learning teachers recognize that the processes to access meaningful long-term memory must be active rather than passive and ensure that activities are engaging, accessible and rich in context.

Q Which memory methods do you teach? How?

Q To what extent is regular participative review part of your classroom repertoire?

Principle Nine. Humans are 'hard-wired' for a language response. They may also be hard-wired for a musical response. The Accelerated Learning teacher exploits this by maximizing purposeful language exchange and musical responsiveness.

Q How do you develop questioning skills in your learners?

Q Can you, or do you, use music for different learning purposes?

Q In your class do you utilize movement to aid learning?

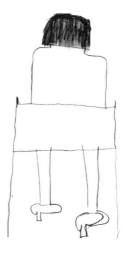

Numeracy hour

'The secret of teaching is to appear to have known all your life what you just learned this morning.'

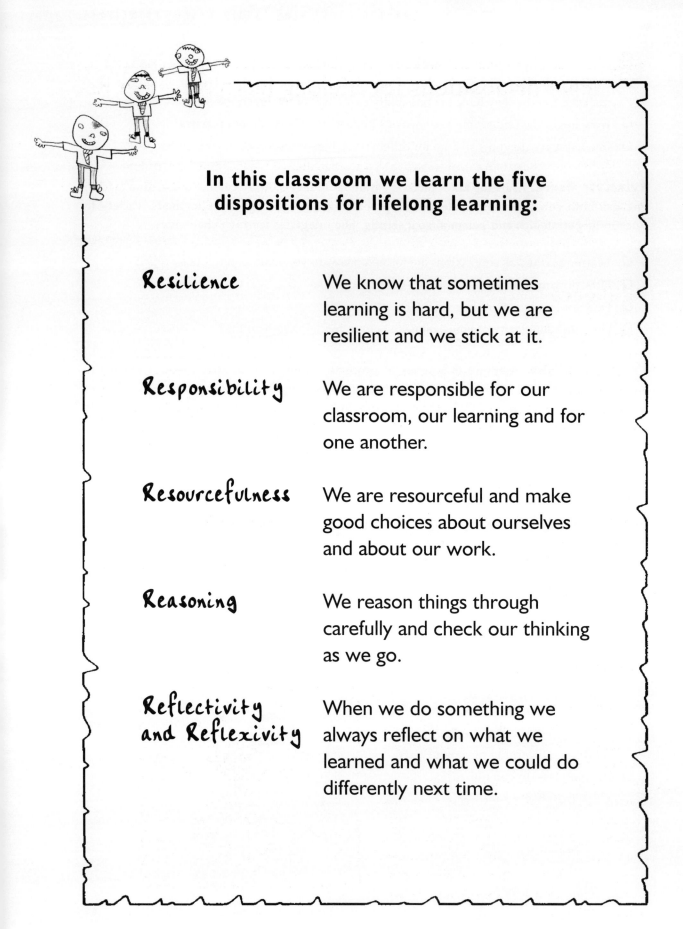

In this classroom we learn the five dispositions for lifelong learning:

Resilience

We know that sometimes learning is hard, but we are resilient and we stick at it.

Responsibility

We are responsible for our classroom, our learning and for one another.

Resourcefulness

We are resourceful and make good choices about ourselves and about our work.

Reasoning

We reason things through carefully and check our thinking as we go.

Reflectivity and Reflexivity

When we do something we always reflect on what we learned and what we could do differently next time.

Five dispositions for lifelong learning – five Rs

The outcome of ALPS is more than an ability to perform better within the formal curriculum. ALPS teachers foster the lifelong learning attributes of the five dispositions for lifelong learning: resilience, responsibility, resourcefulness, reasoning and reflectivity–reflexivity.

Below are definitions of the five dispositions for lifelong learning in the context of the ALPS model.

Resilience

Resilience means being able to persist in the face of frustration or setbacks, or when complexity is seemingly overwhelming. Metacognition – the ability to engage with and be curious about your own thinking – is the sign of a resilient learner. The resilient learner has developed a range of coping strategies and does not either internalize or externalize blame. The coping strategies of a resilient learner are bolstered by a positive self-image, which in turn emerges from high self-esteem. This allows the resilient learner to be able to place failure in context and to be able to see possibilities for learning within the experience. To a child with resilience 'there is no failure, only feedback'.

Responsibility

Responsibility is the recognition that actions have consequences, and the ability and willingness to consider fully those consequences before taking action. Managing impulsiveness, delaying immediate gratification and thinking in terms of success outcomes are characteristics of the responsible learner. So too is the ability to empathize and to see things from multiple perspectives. Responsibility is also about locating your own actions within a larger scheme of things.

'The mediocre teacher tells. The good teacher explains. The superior teacher demonstrates. The great teacher inspires.' (William A. Ward)

Resourcefulness

To be resourceful is to be able to adapt to different learning challenges. This is about having the tools of a good learner and the skills with which to deploy those tools. A child who is never involved in positive decisions about her own learning will not have the attribute of resourcefulness. If, for whatever reason, a child develops a presupposition that learning is a passive activity, then the ability to make autonomous decisions about applying skills and utilizing learning tools will be significantly diminished. To be resourceful is also to be willing to take the risk of learning, which may involve revealing ignorance or making mistakes.

Reasoning

To be capable of reasoning is to be able to see problems through in self-managed, considered and systematic way. Complex problems are broken down into their elements, their essential features described and the relationships between such elements defined. Reasoning thus involves seeking patterns of relationships, describing those relationships and then reconstituting those relationships. Children who can reason discern patterns in everyday experience and can also originate patterns. A teacher who develops the capability of reasoning in a child therefore endows that child with a range of tools that are capable of

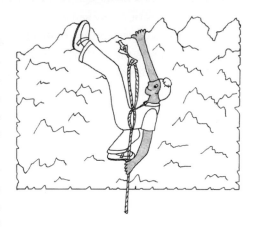

enduring transfer into a range of everyday challenges. The disposition to reason does, however, differ from the ability to reason. This is why reasoning of its own without resilience, without responsibility and resourcefulness, does not have the same enduring transfer.

Reflectivity–reflexivity

Reflectivity–reflexivity is the capability of reflecting on experience – making comparisons with similar and dissimilar experiences – to infer or draw conclusions. Reflectivity–reflexivity is an active and dynamic process. By reflecting backwards, patterns of response are located and can be reinforced. The more we reflect, the more likely we are to be able to and to want to. Thus reflection itself becomes reflexive. As we reflect on experience we begin to open the possibility of acting on experience and thus learn. Reflexivity is the consequence of reflectivity practised, or distributed, over time. A teacher develops this capability in her children by reflective questioning, by review, by distributed rehearsal, by educative feedback.

'Teaching is the greatest act of optimism.' (Colleen Wilcox)

The five dispositions for lifelong learning teacher's questionnaire

On page 50 we provide a teacher's questionnaire for the five dispositions for lifelong learning. To complete this questionnaire you need to consider each child in your class in turn. For each question give the child a score between 1 and 10. A score of 1 means that the child does not resemble the description, a score of 10 means that the description is extremely accurate. Each child's total score will give you a sense of how far he displays each of the five dispositions for lifelong learning. You may then wish to analyse the group strengths and weaknesses of your class and use the suggestions in the next section for promoting the five dispositions for lifelong learning in your class.

Five ways to promote resilience

1   Give team activities with no 'correct' answer, such as building structures to fulfil set criteria.
2   Create 'have a go' times and model 'having a go' yourself.
3   Organize outside speakers to talk of the necessity of resilience in their field of work or sport.
4   Set challenges based on improvement not overall scores and draw attention to the improvements.
5   Explore the idea of failure and show children alternative ways of managing it.

Five ways to promote responsibility

1   Ask the children to consider 'what if?' questions.
2   Do exercises that involve considering the outcomes of various scenarios.
3   Involve children in writing the week's To Do list.
4   Distribute the responsibility roles – furniture monitor, book monitor – throughout the class.
5   Set up a buddy system and give paired assignments.

Five ways to promote resourcefulness

1   Set tasks that involve children thinking of lots and lots of really good questions.
2   Play test the teacher, test each other, test yourself.
3   Set homework assignments that necessitate asking other people questions.
4   Volunteer for your class to organize an aspect of each school function.
5   Set assignments that involve teaching or producing resources for younger children.

'Learning is not compulsory but neither is survival.' (W. Edwards Deming)

The five dispositions for lifelong learning teacher's questionnaire

Child's name:	Score 1–10
Resilience	
1 Only asks the teacher for help after a reasonable amount of independent effort.	
2 Responds positively to challenges and new activities.	
3 Responds to failures calmly and is willing to continue to try.	
4 Does not externalize blame; for example, 'it's not my fault, it's because ...'	
5 Contributes to group activities enthusiastically even when the work is a challenge.	
Responsibility	
6 Always volunteers for errands.	
7 Can be sent to do an errand alone.	
8 Completes the task in the midst of distractions.	
9 Meets deadlines.	
10 Can work in a group and take the lead when necessary.	
Resourcefulness	
11 Works independently and finds own resources when necessary.	
12 Is inventive and creative in her use of materials.	
13 Is confident in asking questions.	
14 Is happy in exploring alternative approaches or solutions.	
15 Uses classroom resources or peer support to help with tasks before approaching the teacher.	
Reasoning	
16 May be slow to get started.	
17 Can sometimes respond with eccentric solutions.	
18 Shows understanding of cause and effect.	
19 Can appear so absorbed in an activity they are oblivious to what is around.	
20 Is excited by challenging problems.	
Reflectivity–reflexivity	
21 Checks his work before handing it in.	
22 Curious about improving the quality of his work.	
23 Participates actively and positively in review activities.	
24 Seeks to make connections between performance improvement and what was done differently.	
25 Believes she can improve.	

Five ways to promote reasoning

1   Give challenges such as 'Write three facts about x, now find out one more'.
2   Explain your own reasoning when you describe everyday experiences.
3   Get the children to talk themselves through solutions to problems.
4   Use problem-solving templates in and around class – put the templates on large posters and use them for class activities.
5   Encourage participation in clubs like Scrabble, Go, Chess and even Pokémon Exchange that develop sustained concentration.

Five ways to promote reflectivity–reflexivity

1   Spend an hour on Friday afternoon in actively reviewing the work of the week.
2   Insist that children read their work before moving on or handing it in.
3   Practise planning, drafting and redrafting.
4   Use circle time for reflection on learning attributes not just on behaviours or relationships.
5   Use target-setting activities and encourage discussion on progress on the targets.

Playground

'You play the way you practice.' (Arsene Wenger)

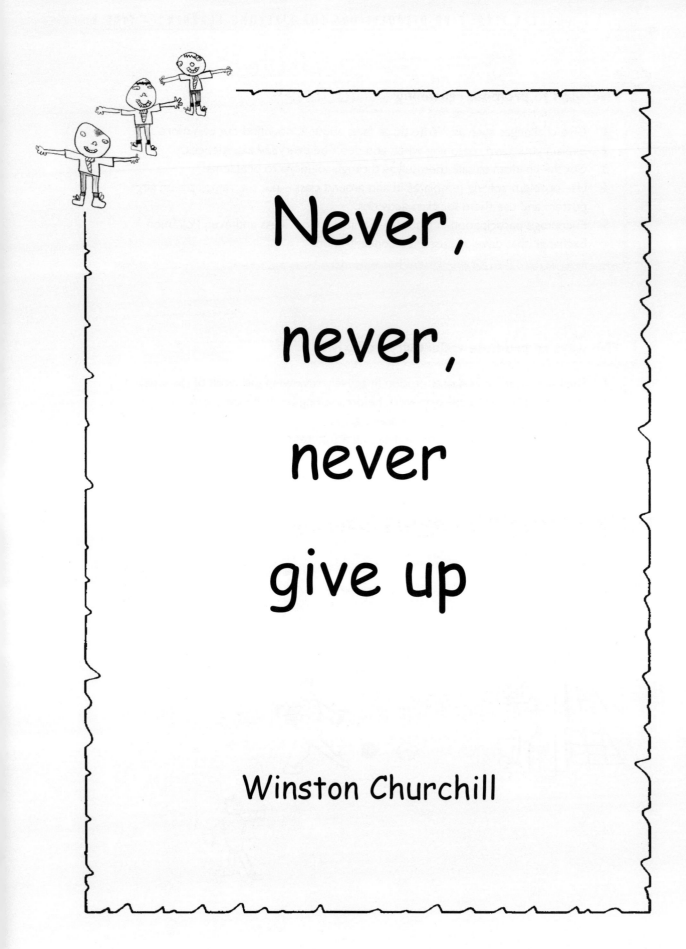

Never, never, never give up

Winston Churchill

6 Take a map on your journey

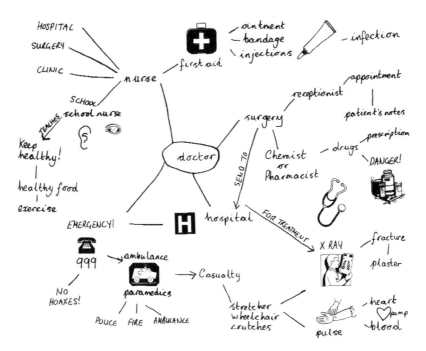

Jumoke's notes from a talk given to the class by a doctor

Using memory mapping for planning

Below is Jimmy's memory map as he planned his story, 'The Rescue'. The class had initially done the 'Private Cinema' activity described in *The ALPS Approach*. Individual children then drew a memory map of their story plan. Following this, they talked through their map with a partner and added any additional ideas. Finally, they kept their map beside them as they wrote their story.

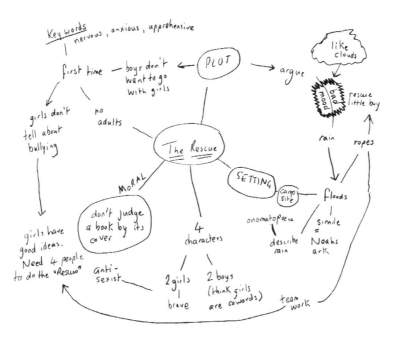

Jimmy's memory map for 'The Rescue'

'In the end we retain from our studies only that which we practically apply.'
(Johann Wolfgang Von Goethe)

Four STEPS to teach young children to map

1 Group the children around you sitting on the floor. Remind them of a topic that you have recently learned about, such as 'toys', 'homes' or 'living things'. Write the title of the topic on a large piece of card, or wherever you intend to build your memory map. If you build it on the board, you must later transfer it onto paper or card for display.

2 Write keywords about the topic, such as 'wooden toys' or 'cement' or 'oxygen' on small pieces of card or post-it notes. As you write each one, stick it onto the large piece of card, starting to build a memory map. Draw lines to connect ideas and use symbols to represent key concepts. Pictures from clip-art or magazines can be added.

3 As children begin to see what you are doing, ask them for suggestions then allow them to stick the words up and help to build the memory map. Alternatively, hand children pictures or symbols and ask them to place them in a logical position on the memory map.

4 Display the memory map in the classroom and add new ideas to it as you continue to learn about the topic. Even after the topic is finished, refer to the memory map for some time for revision and to make links to new topics and concepts.

Seven STEPS to teach older children to map

1 Sit children in groups of four. Friendship groups work well for this activity. Give each group of children about 20 pieces of card or post-it notes and a selection of coloured pens.

2 Choose a subject that you have studied very recently, such as 'Tudors', 'Forces' or 'The Water Cycle'.

3 Ask each group of children to think of keywords, names, or short phrases about the subject, which they must write on the cards or post-it notes. Examples might be 'six wives', 'buoyancy', or 'evaporation'.

4 When each group has filled in at least ten cards, stop the class. Working around the room from one group to the next, invite children to the front in pairs to stick their notes onto the memory map on the board, drawing lines to make connections to other concepts, pole-bridging – talking their thoughts aloud – as they do so.

5 Talk through the evolving memory map as the children work and contribute, drawing attention to links between concepts, correcting any misunderstandings and making suggestions for further keywords or phrases. Use the remaining cards for new ideas as they arise.

6 Draw symbols to represent lengthy phrases and teach the class how to précis their sentences.

7 Finally, you can allow individuals to copy the memory map onto paper, adding to it as they think of more ideas, or you can produce a neater version of the memory map to display in the classroom.

'In a time of drastic change it is the learners who inherit the future. The learned usually find themselves equipped to live in a world that no longer exists.' (Eric Hoffer)

Using memory maps for assessment

Memory mapping can be one of your most valuable tools for assessing children's levels of conceptual awareness. It is more useful than many other forms of testing, as it allows you an insight into what and how a child thinks rather than simply finding out if she can answer a series of questions. Misconceptions can often be picked up through memory mapping, as can higher order levels of thinking that may otherwise never have been tested.

Five STEPS for using memory maps for assessment

1   The effectiveness of your teaching of a topic could be assessed through a whole class mapping session where you invite children to contribute ideas to a large memory map. The children's responses, confidence, selection of language and enthusiasm will give you a guide to how effectively you have covered the material from your lesson plans.

2   After you have mapped as a class, individual memory maps will give a more accurate picture of each child's progress. If you make individual memory maps at the beginning of a new topic and again at the end, comparisons of the child's two maps can be a powerful tool for measuring success and building self-esteem and confidence. Be careful, however, never to call memory mapping a 'test'. You do not wish to create anxiety about the activity. Instead, call it a 'revision exercise'.

3   As children create their individual maps, encourage them to include a variety of arrows, lines and symbols. Ask them to explain the connections with short phrases written along the lines. These explanations will help you to assess the memory maps later for their sophistication and depth of understanding.

4   When you collect in the individual maps, you may find that some are difficult to understand and assess. In such cases, you may wish to sit individually with the child and ask him to talk through his memory map with you. If you find that there are levels of understanding that he has not shown on the map, teach him how to include the information so that next time his map is easier to assess. You may wish to make a list of the key vocabulary and concepts that they would wish to see on the map and 'mark' the maps according to these criteria. However, never write on the map itself – record your assessment elsewhere.

5   After assessing the memory maps, plan how to address any gaps in understanding. You may use the information gathered from the memory maps for school records, target setting or reports to parents. However, your most important task now is to decide how to use the information that you have gathered to challenge your class still further. Memory mapping can be the most informative method of checking understanding in order to inform the planning of your next series of lessons.

'Whatever games are played with us, we must play no games with ourselves.'
(Ralph Waldo Emerson)

Examples of using memory maps for assessment

Mandeep

This is Mandeep's map showing her understanding of the topic 'Temperature'. Her teacher encouraged her to include arrows and notes to explain her thought processes.

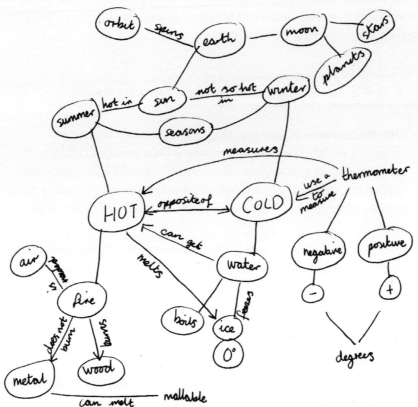

Mandeep's temperature map

Samuel

Samuel, who is five years old, worked with his mother to create the memory maps opposite. They mapped Samuel's ideas about the topic 'Living Things' using Power Point on the computer. The first map was done before Samuel's class began work on the topic and the second was done at the end of term. His mother was interested in knowing how much Samuel already understood about living things and wanted to assess what he had learned by the end of the topic. She was astounded by the amount that he had learned and the connections that he had made. This is what she told us:

> I knew that Samuel had covered work on the life cycle in school, and that he'd looked at frogs and caterpillars. My husband and I make an effort to relate things to the work that we know Samuel is doing in school, so we did activities such as reading 'The Hungry Caterpillar' and talking about how to care for Samuel's rabbits, Smudge and Dippy. However, some of the items and connections that Samuel made on the second memory map four weeks later amazed me. For example, he connected the things that he had seen at the Body Exhibition at the Millennium Dome to the work he'd done in school. His concept of food and our basic needs had linked in his mind to what he'd learned on a school trip to a farm, but he also connected an experience last weekend when we visited a friend who had a horse. He realized

'He that undervalues himself will undervalue others, and he that undervalues others
will oppress them.' (Johnson)

that her horse was a pet, whereas the horses on the farm were working animals. As the map unfolded I could see how a wide variety of experiences, both at home and at school, had interconnected in his mind to make a map that was infinitely more sophisticated than the original.

'I am very clever at knowing about animals and stuff. I put it all on my map and I showed Mummy and Daddy how clever I am.
Samuel, aged 5'

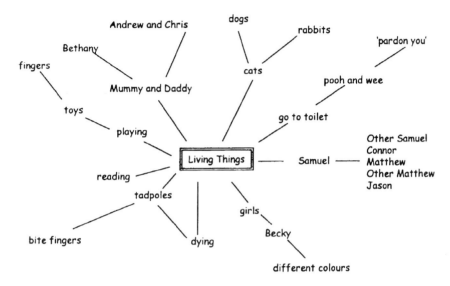

Memory map by Samuel before doing a topic on 'Living Things'

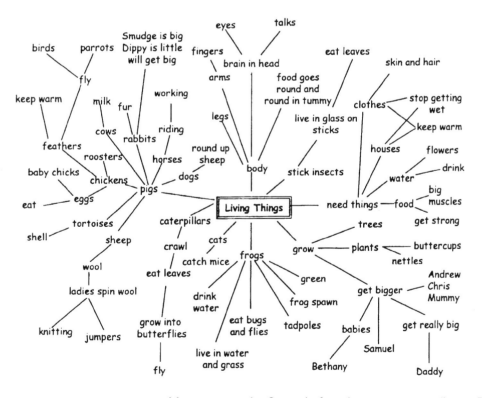

Memory map by Samuel after doing a topic on 'Living Things'

'Learning is what most adults will do for a living in the 21st century.'
(Sydney Joseph Perelman)

Using memory maps for connecting concepts

While class maps should be used for visual display to reinforce the learning done in class, individual memory maps can be collected in files or glued into the covers of children's exercise books. They are working documents and as new concepts are learned, they should be added to the map. No single concept should be learned in isolation. Memory mapping can be a useful way to help children to make connections between two lessons or subjects. This can be done in a variety of ways: as a class, as groups, or as individuals.

As a class activity

Put the memory maps for two separate topics on display. For this activity it can be simplest if you use the original maps that you made with post-it notes or small pieces of card. Between the two memory maps, pin up a new blank chart for the joint memory map, and write the key concepts in the centre. If your class are experienced mappers you may wish to challenge them by giving your new map a different title.

For example, one ALPS teacher, having covered the topics of 'Habitats' in geography, 'Space' in science and 'Diet' in PHSE, pinned up all three memory maps and asked the class to create a new map with the central theme 'Conservation'. It is easy to imagine how the children were challenged towards higher order-thinking. The teacher reported that:

> The discussion in the classroom was highly charged. I could feel the energy and passion of the children, as they saw how the learning that they had done in three separate curriculum areas connected. Feelings ran high, especially among the three children who were strict vegetarians, who felt strongly that those classmates who spent Saturday lunchtimes at fast-food restaurants were irresponsible! The discussion as the memory map built up startled me with its maturity. Memory mapping gave the children the opportunity to link concepts and to verbalize as they did so – often rather loudly and passionately! We all went home in a thoughtful mood that evening.
> Year 6 teacher

As a group activity

Give each group of children copies of two maps that have been made previously in class. These could be the same two maps for each group, or you may choose to vary them. Ask the children to work as a group to make one joint memory map, either with a joint title, for example 'Toys and Materials', or with a new title such as 'Leisure'. The advantage of a new title is that children are challenged to think beyond simply combining the two memory maps and have to make connections to a new concept while drawing on the content of the two original maps.

Once each group has created a new map, invite them to the front of the class to display their map and to talk through their reasoning. Encourage other children to make contributions and interact with the group.

At any stage during this activity, you may wish to give the class, or an individual group, a list of additional words or phrases that you would like them to add to their maps. Alternatively, you may

'Learning is a treasure that will follow its owner everywhere.' (Chinese Proverb)

wish to give the class some time after all the groups have reported to add any details to their maps that other groups may have included, along with a list from you that you feel are essential elements for everybody's map. Finally, you may choose to make either one large map incorporating everyone's ideas, or you may ask each individual child to make their own map either then or as a homework activity.

As an individual activity

Ask each child to spend some time looking at two of their individual memory maps from previous lessons, or at two large class maps. You may choose to select the maps yourself, or you may allow children to self-select according to their own interests. Give them paper and pens to make their own single map and ask them to try to include every aspect of both maps, adding in ideas that occur to them as they work to connect the two sets of concepts.

Alternatively, give each child a selection of small pieces of cards on which to write key phrases, words or symbols. Ask them to do this and then arrange their cards on a large piece of paper. The advantage of working this way is that words can be moved around while the child processes his thoughts. At any stage you may choose to give out a list of other keywords, symbols or phrases that you would like added to the maps. Once children are satisfied with their maps, they can tell their neighbour how they linked three important things from the two original maps. They can then add their neighbour's ideas to their own map, then swap partners to find out another three, and so on. To finish, they can draw up a final copy of their map, or a class map can be made. This activity does not have to be completed in one session, and can be revisited at any time. Mapping is not a lesson, it is an activity that fosters higher-order thinking. It should not be strictly timetabled, but rather should become an integral part of learning in the ALPS.

Using memory maps for revision

The best way to commit information permanently to memory is to revisit it and to use it in different contexts over a period of time. Many children hold information with little difficulty in their short-term memory, but find committing knowledge to long-term memory more challenging. Therefore continual revision activities are essential if learning is to be made secure. Memory mapping, again, can be the answer.

Seven ways to use memory maps to revise

1 Keep memory maps in plastic wallets on the children's desks.

2 Use as a weekly review activity.

3 Encourage children to display memory maps at home.

4 Set homework tasks of creating new memory maps combining two concepts.

5 Challenge children to reproduce their map after two minutes studying the original.

6 Ask children to reproduce a map for homework, without referring to the original.

7 Ask children to tell their partner the five most important things on their map.

Life mapping

'Life mapping' is a technique that helps you to discover the aspirations of every child in your class. A 'life map' is a memory map of an individual person's ambitions and goals.

Christopher is 11 years old. This is his life map at the start of step 3. He had not yet begun to consider what actions he was going to need to take in the immediate year ahead to help him to fulfil his goals. We show the next stage of his life map on page 62.

Christopher's first life map

'It is best to learn as we go, not go as we have learned.' (Leslie Jeanne Sahler)

Five STEPS to creating a life map

1   Begin a class discussion about ambitions and allow all the most creative and ambitious thoughts to surface. Tell the class that you are going to map out where you each wish to be in ten and 20 years time, then you are going to help them decide what you need to do as a teacher to ensure that they fulfil their dreams.

2   As the children share their ambitions, begin to direct the discussion. Steer the conversation towards higher aspirations and do not allow 'ambitions' that are reinforcements of poor self-image. If necessary, plant ideas, but on no account allow anyone to opt out. Introduce the language of further education and personal development. Deliberately use the language of achievement. If children mention only ambitions such as being sportsmen or popstars, support them in their ambitions, while retaining a motivation towards high standards of achievement in school.

3   At a point when the discussion is still vibrant and enthusiastic, give each child a piece of blank paper and a selection of pencils and ask them to memory map their ambitions individually. When they have done this, ask them to fill in the details of what they think they will need to do in order to achieve their goals. Encourage them to think of the academic learning that they must do in the year ahead. Next, begin to reflect on these individual life maps. Ask what commitment they must make and decide what help you should give.

4   Now begin to create a whole class life map on an 'aspirational wall'. Agree with the class on the common factors on all their life maps, such as improving spelling, mental arithmetic, or developing skills in group-work. Beginning in the centre and working outwards, stick up captions, symbols or pictures to show the actions you will all take that year. These could include increasing access to computers, setting up high achiever groups, lunchtime help groups, home reading schemes or home study groups. Put whole class actions in the centre, then work out towards the border, where each child's future should then be represented with a clear, four- or five-word sequence, such as: Samantha – Inventors' Club – University – Computer Science – Engineer.

5   Throughout the year, refer to the individual life maps and the aspirational wall frequently and allow for changes of focus and needs. Add new challenges as they arise, celebrate when an area is completed and allow children to review their ambitions. Encourage each child to show the completed maps to his parents and make the maps available on consultation evenings. Life mapping encourages students not only to reach for the stars, but also to see how they will get there.

'You cannot achieve a new goal by applying the same level of thinking that got you where you are today.' (Albert Einstein)

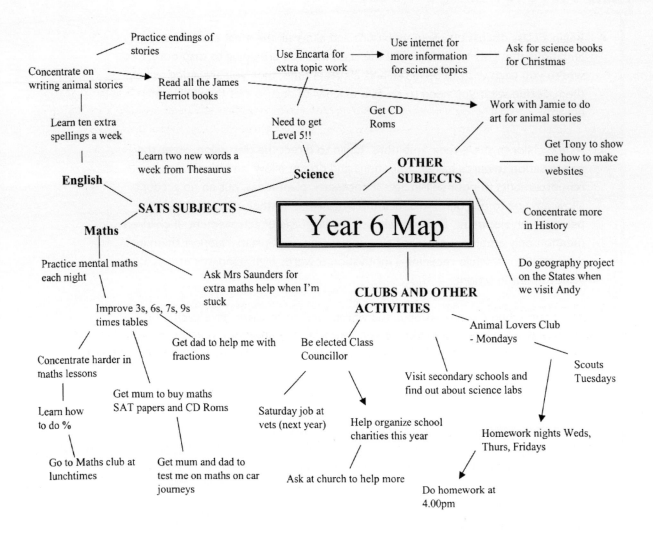

Christopher's revised life map

'That is never too often repeated, which is never sufficiently learned.' (Seneca)

Review of Introduction

✔ Read the three case studies provided. List five ideas that you can take and use in your class tomorrow.

✔ In our original ALPS book we discussed how the brain operates under stress and the importance of positive, supportive learning environments. Write down anything that may cause stress for your class. For example, testing or taking timed challenges may be stressful. Worrying about grades or overall marks may cause children stress. Discuss your list with a colleague. Next to each possible cause, note the actions that you could take to alleviate the causes of stress.

Possible cause of stress for the class	Action plan

✔ Note the names of children whose learning may be particularly impacted by individual issues that cause them stress. Make an action plan of how you could minimize the impact of stress upon their learning.

Name	Cause of stress	Action plan

✔ We discussed the many uses of memory mapping. How might you use memory mapping in your everyday life? How might it be useful in your classroom? Make a plan about how you could teach the skills of memory mapping in your school.

✔ Life mapping is an essential element of the ALPS approach and links closely to target setting. How and when might you use the life mapping activity with your class?

✔ Look at the Accelerated Learning Cycle poster. What elements might be missing in your lessons? How could you ensure that you remember the cycle as you teach each lesson? Can you consider the Accelerated Learning Cycle as you draw up lesson plans?

✔ What could you do to ensure that your teaching addresses each of the brain-based principles? Which of our suggestions could be incorporated into your teaching? How far do you:

♥ understand current theories of learning and brain development;

♥ create the right environment for learning;

♥ pay attention to the physiological needs of students;

♥ exploit VAK learning in every lesson;

♥ encourage pole-bridging;

♥ use memory mapping extensively;

♥ provide frequent opportunities for brain breaks;

♥ use music, rhythm and rhyme for multiple purposes;

♥ plan for activities to build self-esteem;

♥ use RAP to develop self-motivation;

♥ plan for the multiple intelligences;

♥ set clear and ambitious targets;

♥ develop the new 5Rs: resourcefulness, resilience, responsibility, reasoning and reflectivity–reflexivity;

♥ teach relaxation techniques and use music to enhance learning;

♥ teach children to be metacognitive – to understand how they learn.

✔ Decide which of the above are priorities for you and make a note of the sections of this book that you will wish to visit to help you.

✔ How might you promote the five dispositions for lifelong learning? List three ways that you could further promote resilience, resourcefulness, responsibility, reasoning and reflectivity–reflexivity in your classroom.

Part One

Establishing base camp

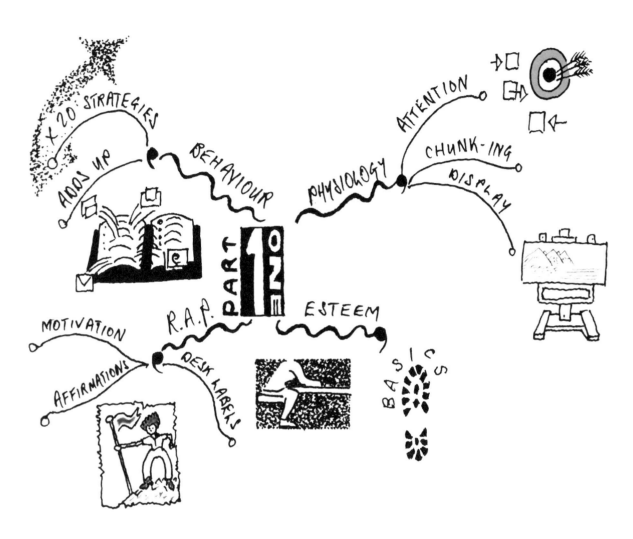

In Part One you will:

* find out about physiology and learning, chunking, how to manage noise levels and how to get the best out of display;
* be given an update on the best ways to build and maintain positive self-esteem through the BASI(C)S model;
* learn about the motivational loop, about affirmations and be given a desk label activity;
* be able to check if your school behaviour strategy ADDS UP through our 20 strategies.

Key vocabulary for Part One:

ADDS UP	Focus and diffuse	Noise levels
Attention and chunking	High 'can do' talk ('I can do'	Recognition, Affirmation,
BASI(C)S	talk)	Praise
Display for learning	Language of progression	

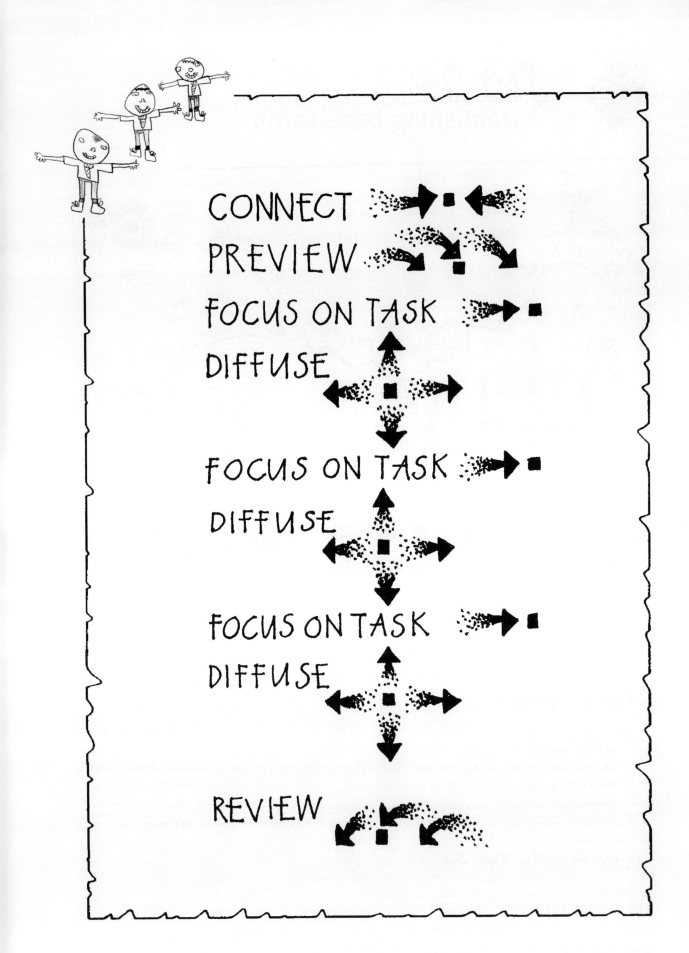

CONNECT

PREVIEW

FOCUS ON TASK

DIFFUSE

FOCUS ON TASK

DIFFUSE

FOCUS ON TASK

DIFFUSE

REVIEW

Assembly

Here are some guidelines for you on chunking. They are expressed in very general terms and will, of course, vary by child and by topic. Crudely put, the younger the child, the fewer the chunks of novel and dissociated information they can hold. Use these guidelines when presenting steps to follow, class rules or factual information for the first time:

Up to 5 years	2 chunks
3–7 years	up to 3 chunks
7–10 years	3 plus chunks
10–14 years	5 chunks
14–16 years	5 plus chunks
16plus	7 chunks

Model chunking in class. Help children practise at home.

Exercise

Physical activity releases natural neural growth factors in the brain. In 1996, University of California at Irvine researchers discovered that exercise may be the best brain food. Rats that had exercised on a wheel had elevated expression of BDGF (brain-derived growth factor), which enhances the ability of neurons to connect with another. We need to move.

'Low self-esteem is like driving through life with your hand-break on.' (Maxwell Maltz)

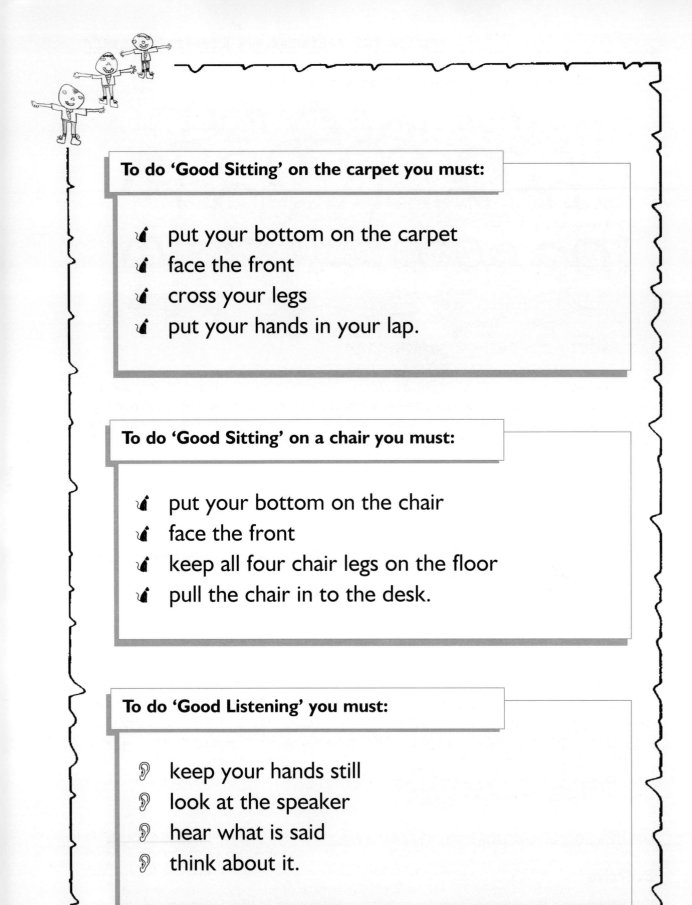

To do 'Good Sitting' on the carpet you must:

- ☝ put your bottom on the carpet
- ☝ face the front
- ☝ cross your legs
- ☝ put your hands in your lap.

To do 'Good Sitting' on a chair you must:

- ☝ put your bottom on the chair
- ☝ face the front
- ☝ keep all four chair legs on the floor
- ☝ pull the chair in to the desk.

To do 'Good Listening' you must:

- 👂 keep your hands still
- 👂 look at the speaker
- 👂 hear what is said
- 👂 think about it.

To enhance learning through improved attitudes to exercise you could:

- teach playground games;
- use the brain-builder questionnaire on page 34 to initiate discussion about lifestyle and learning;
- develop brain-break activities that involve smooth controlled cross-lateral movement;
- organize your classroom to ensure freedom of movement around desks and have a furniture movers' rota to change room layout;
- use music to accompany vigorous physical activity to energize children;
- monitor the PE curriculum and ensure that all children participate;
- provide sport activities for break times and after school.

Teaching the skills of attention

ALPS teachers do not leave it to chance that children will develop good listening skills; they actively teach attentional skills from the earliest age. They continue reinforcing these skills throughout the primary age range. Listening is not the same as hearing, and sitting is not the same as remaining still. The ALPS rules for 'Good Sitting' and 'Good Listening' are provided opposite.

Many ALPS teachers also specifically teach the skills of 'Good Looking' and 'Good Asking'. Some children find it hard to give eye contact. Often these same children also find it difficult to ask for help. Usually a reluctance to give eye contact or ask questions is due to a lack of confidence, but, once practised, the very acts of giving eye contact and asking questions will increase the confidence of the child. The ALPS rules for 'Good Looking' and 'Good Asking' and also 'Good Answering' are provided on page 72.

The appropriate noise level

What is the appropriate noise level in a classroom? What is appropriate depends on the activity being undertaken, the age of the children, the groupings within the class and, to a certain extent, the personality and preferences of the teacher. It would be ridiculous to expect that every group-work lesson should have a certain level of noise, or that every sentence-work session should be done in silence. Each lesson must be taken as an individual unit and the appropriate noise level determined from the criteria above. What is essential, however, is that the teacher is clear with her students about the noise level that she expects.

The teacher's expectation should be made clear at the start of each activity and children should be reminded before the noise level rises significantly above acceptable levels. It should never be allowed to rise to the point where the teacher has to make major efforts to re-establish the required level. Some methods that the ALPS teacher uses to communicate her expectations might include:

- a noise wheel in the front of the class;
- a scale of noise level from 0 to 3 where 0 = silence, 1 = whispering, 2 = talking and 3 = celebrating;

'The most mature person in any social setting is the one who is most adaptable to other peoples needs.' (John Dewey)

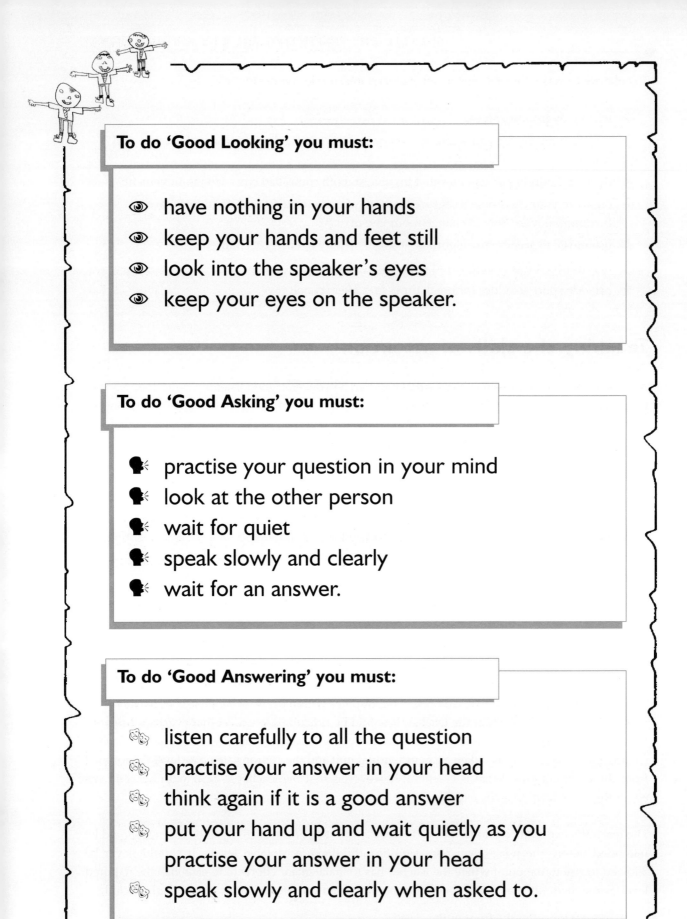

To do 'Good Looking' you must:

- 👁 have nothing in your hands
- 👁 keep your hands and feet still
- 👁 look into the speaker's eyes
- 👁 keep your eyes on the speaker.

To do 'Good Asking' you must:

- 🗣 practise your question in your mind
- 🗣 look at the other person
- 🗣 wait for quiet
- 🗣 speak slowly and clearly
- 🗣 wait for an answer.

To do 'Good Answering' you must:

- 🎭 listen carefully to all the question
- 🎭 practise your answer in your head
- 🎭 think again if it is a good answer
- 🎭 put your hand up and wait quietly as you practise your answer in your head
- 🎭 speak slowly and clearly when asked to.

◁)) hand signals where hands touching means silence, close means whispering but far apart means talking;

◁)) pieces of music that indicate levels of acceptable noise;

◁)) writing the expected noise level on the board when giving the Big Picture.

How to engage attention in the classroom

One of the greatest challenges to inexperienced teachers is how to gain and hold students' attention. This is a skill that has to be learned.

The golden rule used by all successful teachers is never to continue to speak when the class is not paying attention. To accept background noise and continue to speak is to give a clear signal that background noise is acceptable, even when you have requested silence. Clarity about your expectations is vitally important. If you ask for silence, you must settle for nothing less. For the time that you are addressing the class, it is quite reasonable to expect silence, even from very young children. Obviously, the length of time that you expect the class to maintain the quiet must be structured to be appropriate to their age and developmental stage.

Ten ways to obtain students' attention

1 Keep a tiny bell on your desk and teach the class to recognize it as cue to fall silent.

2 Teach the children to recognize a piece of 'Quiet Music' as a cue for silent time.

3 Start by clapping your hands, quickly becoming quieter and quieter until you are tapping three, then two, then one finger on your palm. Teach the class to copy until you silently put your hands in your lap and are ready to speak.

4 Use your arms as a slider scale – as your arms move together so the noise level should diminish.

5 Start by clicking your fingers in a rhythm, encouraging the children to copy. Move your hands in circles as you do so, from side to side and up and down, growing slower and quieter until you cease and are ready to speak.

6 Tap your chin with a finger, then make a circular motion, tapping your ears, head, mouth, nose and so on, while the children copy until you put your hands down and start to speak.

7 Use a prop such as a magic wand or a soft toy as a signal to gain silence without needing to use your voice. Encourage the children to recognize the signal and respond immediately.

8 Teach the class some magic signals for silence, such as rubbing noses with palms or tummies with thumbs. Ask children to invent new signals and make posters to remind the class what the magic signal means.

9 Tap the nearest child and give him the magic signal. He then taps the next child, who passes the signal on around the classroom.

10 Teach the class a variety of action rhymes for silence, such as those on page 74.

'Until you make peace with who you are, you'll never be content with what you have.'
(Doris Mortman)

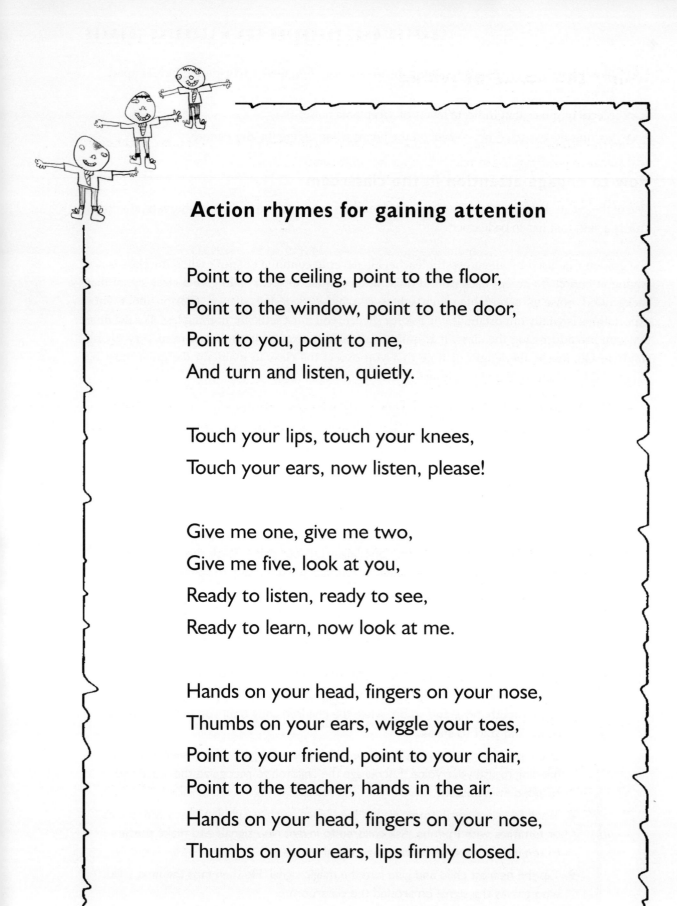

Action rhymes for gaining attention

Point to the ceiling, point to the floor,
Point to the window, point to the door,
Point to you, point to me,
And turn and listen, quietly.

Touch your lips, touch your knees,
Touch your ears, now listen, please!

Give me one, give me two,
Give me five, look at you,
Ready to listen, ready to see,
Ready to learn, now look at me.

Hands on your head, fingers on your nose,
Thumbs on your ears, wiggle your toes,
Point to your friend, point to your chair,
Point to the teacher, hands in the air.
Hands on your head, fingers on your nose,
Thumbs on your ears, lips firmly closed.

Using the space provided

Building base camp

In order to follow the principles of the ALPS method™, you need to create a secure environment within which your pupils can work. We call this 'base camp'.

Here are some simple methods that could help you to achieve each step.

Step 1: create a base for each student.
- Allocate a main seat for each child.
- Label each desk with the child's name.
- Take a photograph of each child at the start of the year and stick it next to his name on the desk.
- Colour code name labels for different activities, such as blue for literacy sessions and pink for maths sessions.
- Display a classroom plan with group lists and a diagram of seating arrangements.
- Fasten a plastic wallet to each desk for the display of personal targets or memory maps.
- Stick desk labels onto the desk of each individual following the desk label activity (see page 92).

Step 2: create your own personal base.
- Use fabric, plants and coloured card or paper to soften the look of your base.
- Display photographs of your family.
- Display photographs or information about your hobbies and interests.
- Agree rules for children about coming to your desk.
- Display the rules in words and pictures.
- Play games where the class roleplay how to follow the rules.
- Display lists of what children should check before approaching your desk.

Step 3: create a focus area around the board.
- Ensure that there is space around the board for groups of children to gather.
- Create a space on or near the board for displaying the Big Picture.
- Create a space for To Do lists.
- Display the Accelerated Learning Cycle (see page 28).
- Display a noise wheel and a method for checking understanding, such as the traffic light.
- Store pieces of card, blu-tac and coloured pens and chalks near the board.
- Keep a box of props for whacky activities near the board (see page 137).

'The greatest success is successful self acceptance.' (Ben Sweet)

Five STEPS to creating an ALPS base camp

1 **Create a base for each student** — ensure that they have their own recognized space.

2 **Create your own personal base** — demarcate your space and the protocols for pupils to access it.

3 **Create a focus area around the board** — around the board becomes a place for a special sort of learning.

4 **Clear out the clutter** — get rid of rubbish that does not enhance learning.

5 **Organize the space that you have created** — use different spaces for different activities.

Step 4: clear out the clutter.

- Spend some time with children deciding what should stay and what could go.
- Organize a 'clear out the clutter' session with colleagues.
- Decide where items could be centrally stored and shared.
- Log for a week the items that are used and then decide which could be discarded.
- Ask a colleague to help you brainstorm how to create space by being creative.
- Clear out items for a week and see if you miss them.
- Work with parallel classes to decide where shared resources could be stored.

Step 5: organize the space that you have created.

- Create enough space around each table for kinesthetic activities and brain breaks.
- Agree rules with children about moving around the classroom.
- Label drawers, cupboards and shelves, using picture cues for younger children.
- Draw diagrams on or above tables to show where items should be placed.
- Create areas for types of learning based on multiple intelligences or different activities.
- Display the rules and expected noise levels for each area that you create.
- Practise 'tidy up time' with children and play games where they have to find and replace resources.

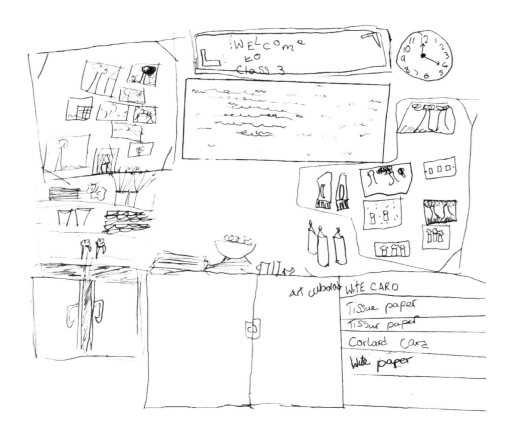

My class

'Theories and goals of education don't matter a whit if you do not consider your students to be human beings.' (Lou Ann Walker)

Twenty useful items for setting up your base camp

1   A copy of the Accelerated Learning Cycle.

2   A class traffic light for checking understanding.

3   Individual traffic lights for checking understanding.

4   A set place for displaying the Big Picture.

5   A 'noise wheel'.

6   A cassette player or CD player.

7   A number of music cassettes or CDs.

8   A set of scripts for relaxation and visualization exercises.

9   A large amount of blu-tac for sticking up keywords, posters or memory maps.

10 Sets of coloured pens or chalks for brainstorming sessions.

11 Pieces of card and paper of various colours and sizes for posters and memory maps.

12 Sets of affirmation posters.

13 Award certificates for achievement.

14 A Brain Box.

15 Props for whacky activities (see page 137) and brain breaks, such as balloons, baseball caps and soft toys.

16 A brain-break menu or cue cards.

17 Group charts and wheels.

18 Numbered cards for selecting groups by bingo.

19 Lengths of string and coloured pegs for displaying posters from the ceiling.

20 Plastic wallets for displaying keywords or memory maps on desks.

Display

ALPS teachers argue that displaying large amounts of children's work in classrooms that does not directly support learning is an out-of-date tradition. While in the early years displaying children's work can lead to a sense of security, pride and belonging, experienced ALPS children do not need to see their work double-mounted on the walls in order to gain self-esteem. They gain self-esteem from the ALPS method of RAP, from the relationships they form and maintain and from the learning process itself.

In ALPS schools display is used primarily for the purpose of accelerating learning.

Look on page 87 to learn more about RAP

'The person we believe ourselves to be will always act in a manner consistent with our self-image.' (Brian Tracy)

Ten extra places for display

1 The areas between display boards – use hooks, washing lines, or blu-tac.
2 The ceiling – attach lines up high and use pegs to hang posters, targets, rules and affirmations.
3 The cloakrooms – attach affirmations or individual messages above children's pegs.
4 The door – use the door for positive messages or your class life map.
5 The toilets – use these areas for positive messages and affirmations.
6 The corridors – use these areas for affirmations, key vocabulary, and phonics or spelling cue cards.
7 The hall – display affirmations, spellings, quotations and number facts where children sit for assemblies.
8 The dining room – display information where children will gaze at it while relaxing at lunchtime.
9 The office areas – put affirmations where both adults and children will absorb the messages.
10 The desks – attach plastic wallets in which children can put memory maps, cue cards, or targets to each desk, and make tent cards for rules and key information.

In the ALPS display should:

❖ be interactive and capable of enhancing learning
❖ aid recall
❖ stimulate further thinking
❖ make connections between concepts
❖ remind of rules and targets
❖ celebrate and affirm success
❖ motivate towards further learning.

Sixteen questions to ask when drawing up a Display Policy

1 What is the purpose of display in our school?
2 In what way does display enhance the learning of children in our school?
3 In what circumstances should children's work be displayed?
4 Where are the key areas for display?
5 Who is the audience for displays in each area?
6 Who is responsible for the displays in each area?
7 What areas of the classroom should be used for display?
8 How might a teacher create additional areas and space for display?
9 What aspects of display are mandatory in every classroom?
10 How might a teacher use key colours, codes or symbols for display?
11 How might memory maps contribute to displays?
12 When should displays be created and by whom?
13 What types of questions might feature on displays?
14 How might children become involved in creating and developing displays?
15 Does the language of display ensure that our target groups can access the display?
16 How do we ensure that all the communities within our school are represented in our display?

'We do not deal in facts when we are contemplating ourselves.' (Mark Twain)

Audit forms for classroom and whole school display

Assess your displays against the ALPS criteria. Analyse how far your displays:	
reinforce learning and aid recall	
challenge ideas	
stimulate further thinking	
inform and give new information	
make connections between concepts	
remind about rules and targets	
celebrate and affirm success	
share ideas and interact	
motivate towards further learning	

Assess the use of available display space in your classroom. How much use do you make of:	
display boards	
areas around display boards	
the doors	
the windows	
the ceiling	
hanging space	
the board	
flipcharts and boards	
backs of cupboards	
children's desks	
other: 1	
2	
3	

Consider how far you use these tools in your displays:	
colour	
codes	
symbols	
memory maps	
keywords	
mnemonics	
rhyme	
the whacky or obscure	
words of songs	

Exceeding expectations

BASI(C)S: the (six) essentials of positive self-esteem

The ALPS model stresses the importance of building positive self-esteem in children. Children are not born with good self-esteem. A wide range of previous experiences will have created a self-image for each child in your care. It is up to you to ensure that any negatives are balanced while the child is in your class and that positive messages are emphasized.

In the original ALPS book we used the mnemonic BASIS as the ALPS checklist for positive self-esteem. We would now like to add a sixth element that, we feel, on retrospect was missing. The six elements of BASI(C)S are now:

☺ Each pupil is part of the group and his contribution, whatever its nature, is valued – he feels a sense of **belonging**.

☺ Every pupil is encouraged to work towards his own achievable goals and reflect on his progress as he does so – pupils are learners with **aspirations**.

☺ The classroom and the learning environment are safe havens for learning where there is consistency in expectations and standards – pupils learn with **safety**.

☺ A realistic level of self-knowledge is supported by the belief that individuality is not threatened by undue pressure to conform – pupils build an **identity** and a recognizable individuality.

☺ Acquiring coping strategies are an important part of development and of learning – pupils experience, and learn to manage, **challenge** and in doing so develop a range of coping strategies.

☺ Mistakes are valuable learning tools in an environment where pupils can take risks and achievement is valued – teachers reinforce **success** and everyone learns from 'failure'.

How to build a good BASICS for learning in your classroom

Belonging

Many children do not experience a strong sense of belonging in their lives. Children, like adults, need a site to which they can attach their affiliations. To be outside the peer group is an isolating experience. Teachers should provide alternative channels to connect with different class groupings. Children can then find ways in to different class and peer groupings. Interventions for generating a sense of belonging include:

♥ using the child's given name frequently and positively

♥ equitable distribution of positive attention

♥ structured turn taking and use of different responsibility roles

♥ use of home or 'safe' pupil groupings

♥ use of away or 'challenging' pupil groupings

'Think highly of yourself, for the world takes you at your own estimate.'

♥ using circle time or similar whole class sharing activity

♥ collective celebration of success

♥ involvement in non-academic after-school or lunchtime clubs.

Aspirations

Just as adults work best when they understand the purpose of the task and the benefits of participation, so children attain more highly when they feel more in control of their learning. When pupils are encouraged to set and work towards their own achievable goals and reflect on their progress, they become learners with aspirations. The ALPS teacher develops aspirational thinking by:

✩ modelling positive behaviours as a teacher;

✩ modelling outcomes thinking as a teacher; for example, 'as a result of this we will all be able to …';

✩ building in the use of personal performance targets as part of lessons;

✩ using exemplar material as part of interactive classroom display;

✩ using the language of progression and thus selling 'benefits' not 'features';

✩ using rolemodels from the school and local community to promote positive views about what can be achieved;

✩ catching limiting self-talk and helping re-frame it – turning 'I can't' into 'I can';

✩ using the aspirational wall technique of sharing 'life-maps'.

Page 109 has more on positive talk

Safety

The child needs to 'feel' free from physical and psychological intimidation and threat. Teachers who exist on a diet of frequent criticism, emphasis of sanction over reward and isolation of failure rarely make lessons feel safe. The ALPS teacher creates a safe environment by:

✚ structuring work so that children can make small but perceptible improvements;

✚ taking care in how we ask questions and how we manage oral feedback in open class;

✚ making it safe to get something wrong by emphasizing how we need feedback in order to progress;

✚ marking 'educatively' – with positive targets for improvement;

✚ using trust-building activities to get pupils to 'know' each other in different contexts;

✚ applying class and school rules fairly and consistently;

✚ reinforcing positive behaviours by deliberately praising children for them;

✚ anticipating disruption, dealing with it immediately or signalling when and how it will be dealt with calmly.

'I would live to study, and not study to live.' (Francis Bacon)

Identity

Children need to feel that they are valued as individuals. When a child has the beginnings of the knowledge of their own strengths and weaknesses, and an emerging set of values and beliefs, she develops a strong sense of identity. Children with such a strong sense of identity are, in some senses, 'freed up' to focus on other challenges in their lives. The ALPS teacher helps children to develop a sense of identity by:

! knowing who the child is, her name and a little about her background, interests and habits;

! isolating and drawing attention to small successes, contributions to group and class activity and to social relations in the class;

! using the desk label activity;

! finding something unique and positive about every child that can be drawn on in everyday class life;

! individualizing targets;

! sharing targets with parents or carers on consultation evenings;

! encouraging individuals to take on responsibilities within the school;

! class activities such as photo displays, classroom passports, circle time and life mapping.

Challenge

It is through challenge that we test the shape of our comfort zone. The comfort zone feels secure. It is where familiarity is reassuring. If we spent our learning lives in nowhere other than our comfort zone, then how would we ever obtain an authentic view of who we are and what we are capable of. Children do not develop a meaningful self-concept in a 'cocooned' environment. Teachers who make challenge part of their learning regime extend the comfort zones of their children. The ALPS teacher helps children to accommodate challenge by:

See more about targets on page 103 and grades on page 118

❖ encouraging 'self-test' as a fundamental to independent learning;

❖ using a variety of frequent and informal in-class testing regimes;

❖ focusing on personal performance improvement via target setting and discouraging comparisons with other pupils' work as the primary means of performance measurement;

❖ avoiding grading for effort without discussing, describing and agreeing what possible different meanings there might be for this – and then negotiating effort grades directly with the child;

❖ breaking down steps to improvement into small realizable chunks;

❖ using a variety of academic and non-academic competitions between home and away groupings;

❖ distributing roles and responsibilities within class and rotating these;

❖ 'talking up' achievement of different sorts in class and in assemblies and encouraging individual and team sports (with a broad definition of sports).

'Our chief want in life is somebody who will make us do what we can.'
(Ralph Waldo Emerson)

Success

It is not possible to go through life without experiencing failure. Children need to learn that failure is normal and is a part of the learning process. However, many children only ever get their failures noticed. For many, success is perceived to be something so large and so extraordinary it is beyond them. Yet, each and every one of these children has a series of small but definable successes patterned throughout their tender years. Often they are overlooked. Eventually they are overlooked by the child herself. To constantly see oneself and one's life to date only through an accumulation of failures is surely wrong. The ALPS teacher captures success by:

✓ taking time to capture small and recent successes from out of school and listening to the stories behind them;

✓ distributing the basic currency of motivation – human attention – equitably, and to success before failure; catch them being good, catch them being successful, let them know;

✓ using targets as a basis of improvement measures;

✓ using a light and humorous touch with class and school rewards and using individual, group and class rewards;

✓ audit the distribution of the rewards continuum – from your attention, through peer attention, through recognition to group and class recognition – to ensure everyone gets something;

✓ breaking down steps to improvement into small realizable chunks;

✓ fostering an identity within your class by emphasizing collective achievements;

✓ explaining the effects of negative self-talk and teaching children how to deal with it.

Playground

'To keep a lamp burning we have to keep putting oil in it' (Mother Teresa)

Some further BASICS activities for your classroom

Belonging
Create a photo board of pictures of the class at work, at home and at play. Encourage them to bring in photographs of themselves playing sports or participating in their hobbies. Put up captions with the photographs and ensure that every child features equally. Keep the display vibrant and add to it continually, using it as a tool for RAP (see page 87) and celebration of achievements.

Aspirations
Ask each child to prepare a three-minute speech about himself and his aspirations. This is a useful exercise after completing the life mapping activity on page 61. Ask one child a day to deliver their speech to the class. Invite the headteacher to listen, or send children individually to practise their speech to her, or to another teacher or class.

Safety
Have every child make a paper flag printed with the letters 'SOS'. Explain the meaning of 'SOS'. Set up practical group activities that are difficult enough to really challenge the class. Tell children at the outset that they will probably get 'stuck' at some point and that if this happens they are to hold up their flags. Whenever anyone raises an SOS flag the class will stop and discuss possible solutions to their 'stuckness'. You may then wish to keep SOS flags in a pot in the classroom or on desks so that children can use them with a feeling of safety.

Identity
Take a photograph of each child in the class. Glue it in the middle of a poster. Over several lessons build it into a personal mind map. Include names of family members, adjectives that describe that child, pictures and symbols that represent his hobbies, skills and interests. Add details from his life map. Display the children's posters and refer to them regularly.

Challenge
Have a high challenge week where a range of testing activities – including testing each other, testing yourself, testing the teacher, teacher testing the class – occur through class activities but also through games and puzzles. Then debrief at the end of the week starting with the word 'challenge'. What does it mean? Where does it come from? What sorts of challenges do we see in everyday life? Is challenge good? Or, is it bad? When does a good challenging experience begin to be a bad one? Who liked what challenges from the week and why?

Success
When the class has worked hard in a lesson, ask them all to stand up, with boys in one line, facing the girls in another line. They all raise their right hand and walk past one another. They do a 'high five' with each child as they pass him or her, saying 'Well done!' and giving eye contact as they do so.

'Genius is one per cent inspiration and ninety-nine per cent perspiration.'
(Thomas Alva Edison)

Have you exercised your brain today?

The motivational loop

RAP

A fundamental tool for the development of positive self-esteem in the ALPS classroom is the motivational loop that we call RAP. ALPS teachers always RAP their response! RAP stands for:

R ecognition

A ffirmation

P raise

Recognition

We use the word recognition rather than reward due to our concern that overuse of reward can create a situation where reward becomes an end to itself, so diminishing intrinsic motivation. We want children to discover that learning itself is its own reward and that they do not need to receive stickers, stars or team points in order to gain satisfaction from learning. Recognition simply recognizes and acknowledges success. It confirms in the child's mind that they are on target and that their actions were appropriate.

Affirmation

An affirmation is a statement. It assumes the positive. Affirmation is one of the most powerful tools belonging to the ALPS teacher. An affirmation states that the class, a group or individual children are being successful. Affirmations are used to reinforce desired behaviours. They state the behaviour that the teacher wants, even if maybe she is not witnessing it with every child. Eventually, children become living, walking proof of an affirmation. Affirmations are the ALPS teacher's antidote to negative thinking. She tells children frequently that they are good, polite, intelligent and successful.

'I am my message.' (Gandhi)

Winners don't quit

quitters don't win

Praise

Specific praise should be given to every child at some point in every lesson. Praise is a verbal or non-verbal recognition of achievement. Praise should relate to understood targets or rules or expectations. It should give the child a clear idea of what she is doing well and why you are pleased. It must be Precise and Personalized as well as related to Performance. There ought to be lots of 'P's in praise! As important as verbal praise is the approval or disapproval that can be exhibited through body language. The non-verbal is as important as the verbal. The ALPS teacher gives non-verbal cues that are as positive as her verbal praise. When the teacher is able to give effective praise, she then becomes capable of jettisoning extrinsic reward and the notion of consequence or punishment. Consequently she can develop intrinsic motivation on the shared journey of learning.

Twenty fun ways to recognize attainment

1 Pats on the back from every member of the class.
2 A drum-roll, made on everybody's knees or the desks.
3 Three cheers!
4 A round of applause.
5 An official pat on the back from the teacher.
6 A balloon tied to the child's chair for the day.
7 A class chant or celebration poem or song.
8 Taking a bow at the front of the class to the sound of an uplifting piece of music.
9 Being given the class mascot such as a teddy bear to sit on the desk for the day.
10 A class celebration dance to a familiar piece of music.
11 A trip to the Brain Box.
12 A laugh-a-minute brain break from pages 138–141.
13 A poster displayed in the classroom for the day that is then taken home.
14 An award such as 'Boffin of the Day', 'Brain of the Week' or 'Mastermind'.
15 Wearing a bow tie for the lesson.
16 A trip around the class to shake hands with a silly glove, to a slow 'hand clap' chant.
17 A high-five with everyone in the group.
18 Wearing the Brains Hat for the next lesson.
19 Conducting the class with a silly prop in singing a favourite song.
20 The singing of a class recognition song to a well-known tune such as 'Yankee Doodle'.

'No problem can stand the assault of sustained thinking.' (Voltaire)

Use it

or

Lose it!

Twenty class affirmation phrases

1   We do good listening!
2   Everyone in our class lines up beautifully at playtime.
3   We are always the first to be quiet and ready to leave assembly.
4   Everybody in this class completes homework on time.
5   We all know the best questions to ask in science.
6   We always remember to put up our hands before asking a question.
7   Everyone in this class knows how to open doors to visitors.
8   We do good looking!
9   Our partners always remember to wait for us to finish before speaking.
10 We have excellent group-work skills in this room.
11 We know our roles in group-work and we always work as a team.
12 Everyone remembers to do good listening when I give out homework assignments.
13 We are fantastic mathematicians!
14 We all know how to relax when we take tests.
15 Everybody in our class is caring and kind.
16 We are all gentle with the class pet.
17 We are all respectful of one another's feelings.
18 Everyone in our class is welcoming to new children or visitors.
19 We are all good at using our brains to solve problems.
20 We all have powerful brains!

Ten ways to turn negative self-talk into positive self-talk

Negative thinking is often simply a mindset. The phrases 'just my luck' and 'how typical' demonstrate the negative mindset when people choose to believe the worst of a situation and take an apathetic stance to managing their own future. Adults can do it and many children are experts by the time they leave primary school.

Here are ten negative phrases that could be used by a primary aged child, along with ten positive responses that the ALPS teacher could make:

1 I can't write my name	You can write the first two letters of your name!
2 I'm a slow runner	You're a great defender in football!
3 I can't swim	You're brave and can put your face under the water!
4 I'm shy in large groups of people	You're very good at communicating one to one!
5 I'm not confident being the group leader	You're great at working in a group!
6 I take a long time to understand new maths ideas	You're persistent and you always succeed!
7 I find new science concepts hard to understand	You ask the best questions in science!
8 I'm on the lowest reading book in the class	You've made good progress in reading this year!
9 I can't read long chapter books	You read with great expression!
10 I can't write long stories	You tell stories that are imaginative and exciting!

'There is no upper limit to what individuals are capable of doing with their minds.'
(H.G. Wells)

The desk label activity

A simple but very effective activity to start building an expectation of success for pupils is the 'Desk Label' activity. It takes ten minutes to complete in the first instance and can then become an integral part of classroom practice, being repeated as often as necessary.

Five STEPS to the desk label activity

1   Copy and cut out labels bearing positive adjectives such as those opposite, with at least one appropriate label for each pupil. Tell your class that you are going to celebrate and recognize all their best qualities as individuals. Read out the adjectives on the labels and display them so that the class can see them. Explain the meanings as you do this and give examples of children who best match each adjective.

2   Start to give out the labels, through discussion and deciding which labels best suit which children. Encourage the class to help by making suggestions. In some cases one word may suit two or three children, but in this first session ensure that a wide range is used and that children feel individually recognized.

3   Continue until each child has at least one label. Attach them to the corner of their desks neatly. Ensure that the labels are valued in the way that you want the children to value themselves and one another. Tell them that you will repeat the activity until they all have many labels. Allocate labels to the adults who work with the class also. This creates a feeling that everyone has attributes that are worth celebrating.

4   Refer to the children's labels frequently. Think of different ways to work the adjectives into your daily routine. For example, try to remember each one when calling the register, such as, 'conscientious Amy' and 'patient Andrew'. Use the adjectives when you mark work and use them for affirmations. When another adult asks for a child to volunteer for a task, decide which attributes would be useful for the task, then ask the class to decide who would best carry it out. When you give the Big Picture for a lesson, list the attributes that will be necessary for success.

5   When you feel ready, spend another session giving a second or third label to each child. In subsequent lessons, when you notice a positive development, give an individual label to a child. Continue until every child has a desk covered with positive attributes. When the labels eventually become tatty, encourage your pupils to stick them inside homework folders or exercise books. These positive qualities are theirs for life so do not throw them out!

'Tread softly, for you tread on my dreams.' (W.B. Yeats)

A hundred desk labels

able	academic	active	adventurous	affectionate
agile	alert	amusing	animated	articulate
artistic	athletic	brave	bright	calm
capable	careful	caring	cautious	clever
comic	committed	compassionate	confident	conscientious
considerate	co-operative	courageous	courteous	creative
daring	determined	diligent	diplomatic	dynamic
eager	empathetic	energetic	enterprising	enthusiastic
expressive	forgiving	funny	generous	genial
gentle	gracious	hard-working	helpful	humorous
imaginative	independent	industrious	ingenious	intellectual
intelligent	inventive	keen	kind	lively
logical	loving	mathematical	methodical	meticulous
motivated	musical	nimble	original	outgoing
peaceful	persistent	persuasive	polite	precise
productive	quick	reflective	reliable	resilient
resolute	resourceful	respectful	scientific	sharp
single-minded	smart	sociable	sporty	steadfast
studious	tactful	talented	thinker	thorough
thoughtful	understanding	vibrant	warm	witty

Twenty cool desk labels

These labels can be used alongside the more serious ones above, or can be used for fun activities such as those that we suggest below. Children can also make up their own and allocate them to classmates or adults.

boffin	boss	brain box	brains	clever clogs
cool	dude	kickin'	my kinda' guy	my man
nobody's fool	scorchin'	sizzlin'	smartypants	sorted
steamin'	superbrain	supercool	the business	whizzkid

'Difficulties are opportunities to better things; they are stepping-stones to greater experience.' (Bryan Adams)

Games for desk labels

Here are six suggestions for team building and positive feedback activities that can be based upon desk labels.

1   Choose a desk label
Go through a selection of new desk label adjectives and describe their meanings, displaying them visually as you do so. Tell the children that they will all need to select the one that they think best describes them. Go through the labels again and ask the children to move into groups with the others who chose the same adjective as them. At the end of the activity, the groups can make a poster about their adjective, describing its meaning.

2   Share a desk label
Ask each child to choose one of his own adjectives and make a replica. He must then pass it to another child whom he thinks also shares that attribute, describing his reasons to the class as he does so. This activity should be organized so that every child receives a new label; for example, by working in groups or pairs.

3   Desk label 'Snap'
Ask children one by one to call out an attribute from their desk labels. Anyone who also has that adjective must quickly stand up and call 'Snap!'

4   Desk labels on the back
Display some new labels on the board and discuss their meanings. Then pin one of these adjectives to the back of each child. The children must then ask a partner or the group questions to find out which label they have been given.

5   Desk label 'Charades'
Ask children to mime the label. Once the class have guessed the adjective, it can be allocated to a child.

6   Desk label 'Oscar Ceremony'
Discuss with the class a selection of new desk labels. Then read through nominations and announce the winner for each label, who must come to the front and make an acceptance speech.

'There is nothing good or bad but thinking makes it so.' (William Shakespeare)

Twenty positive strategies

The **ADDS UP** model

A simple mnemonic provides the underlying principles for behaviour management in the ALPS classroom. The management of behaviour should be all the following: **A**ppropriate, **D**irected to specific outcomes, **D**ifferentiated, **S**ensitively handled and **UP**beat. We call this **ADDS UP**.

> **A**ppropriate
> **D**irected to specific outcomes
> **D**ifferentiated
> **S**ensitively handled
> **UP**beat

In the ALPS there should be an emphasis on modelling and reinforcing behaviour for learning. Children should not 'choose' to behave inappropriately when our positive discipline strategies are in place. Our aim is to manage behaviour with a purely positive approach. In the ALPS classroom good behaviour is actively reinforced.

The 20 strategies

Here are 20 complementary strategies for positive behaviour and for a positive and purposeful learning environment that support the ADDS UP method. They were first described in *The ALPS Approach*. We feel it is worth reminding ourselves of them here.

1 Describe the behaviours you do want, not the behaviours that you do not want!

2 Teach good sitting, good listening, good talking and good looking.

3 Use life mapping and the aspiration wall to help pupils remember the larger purpose and focus on the larger goals.

4 Put your own life map on the wall. Share your aspirations with the class and model the five dispositions for lifelong learning in your endeavours to achieve your personal goals.

5 Start every day and every lesson positively. Welcome each child at the door and use his name. Make the opening interactions with each child positive.

6 Use the 'about to' phrase. 'I'm so pleased that Janet is about to tidy her table' has a far more positive impact than 'Janet, I've asked you twice to tidy your table!'

'The ultimate measure of a man is not where he stands in moments of comfort and convenience, but where he stands at times of challenge and controversy.'
(Martin Luther King, Jr)

7 Set positive deadlines for desired behaviours. Use phrases such as: 'Oliver, when you have had a minute to think about this come back ...' or 'I know you are feeling cross Chelsea. Take a short break and in five minutes I'll come back and help you.'

8 Make your classroom a four-to-one classroom. Try to have four specific and positive units of feedback for one of every other type. Of course, the fifth comment should not be negative – it should merely be neutral.

9 Apply the four-to-one rule to your marking and your feedback to children about their work.

10 Give single instructions. Multiple questions have been correlated with underperformance of response. Questions that demand only simple recall of factual information are only going to achieve limited thinking on the part of your students.

11 Use only specific language. Avoid convoluted instructions such as 'If we haven't tidied up and put our coats on, then no one is going out to play.' Use clear language such as, 'Tidy up now, it's almost playtime,' followed by, 'Great! Put your coats on!' then, 'Let's all go out to play!'

12 Teach pupils to think in terms of desired outcomes: 'When you have successfully completed this piece of work, how would I know you have done well?' 'How would a visitor to the class know you had done well?'

13 Provide lots of opportunities for mental rehearsal of success. Encourage pupils to visualize themselves behaving in a positive way to others. Ask them to notice what is being said, who is saying it, how it is said, and how they feel about it.

14 Separate the person from the behaviours. The child will feel threatened by any sort of negative label attached to her. Attach labels to the behaviour only, not to the child.

15 Make it safe to say 'I do not understand'. Use fun techniques that are immediate and reflective, such as the traffic light, where green means 'I'm ready to go', amber means 'I'm uncertain' and red means 'I don't understand – yet.' Or ask children to score their understanding, where giving a score of five means 'I'm on a green light' whereas a score of zero means 'I need help!'

16 Practise behaviours. For example, practise making noise and being quiet.

17 Teach techniques for anger management. For example, teach children to 'wait for the bus' and 'fly in the private cloud'. Any immediate angry response is deferred as the child undertakes the visualization.

'The difference between what we do and what we are capable of doing would solve most of the world's problems.' (Gandhi)

◆ Timeline for behavioural flexibility. To help a child learn from an instance of bad behaviour, place him on an imaginary carpet. The carpet represents time. Encourage him to walk back into the past and forward into the future. Practise going back in time and putting things right. Practise the sorts of behaviour that you wish to encourage.

◆ Use names. Place the child's name at the beginning of the question. Give eye contact as you use names.

◆ Make your classroom a 'no put-down zone'. Write it above the door. In the no put-down zone any sort of put-down is banned.

How to see if your behaviour management 'ADDS UP'

It is easiest and most rewarding to do this activity with another teacher or adult. Being monitored by somebody else usually gives a clearer picture than self-monitoring. Ask your observer to use a checklist such as the sample below. She should write in the names of any children with whom you interact regarding their behaviour. If possible, she should follow some of her usual activities in the class while she observes, as the activity may alter the dynamics in your classroom, both for the children and for yourselves, particularly in a class where observation is not a normal everyday activity.

The first time you do this activity, you may wish to focus only on the management of undesirable behaviour, or maybe on the recognition of good behaviour. However, once you have done this a few times, it should be possible to monitor all management of behaviour within a lesson. The observer should put + or – in the second column to indicate whether the behaviour was positive or negative, and make a quick note next to the child's name to remind her of the incident for later discussion. This needs only to be one or two words, such as 'talking', or 'on task – praise'.

After the lesson, spend some time looking at the checklist and analysing the management of the behaviour in the class. Total the number of references that you made to good and to poor behaviours. Cross reference against a class list. Which children were 'managed' regularly, for either good or undesirable behaviour? Which were recognized less, or not at all? Where were the frequent interactions? Were they confined to one group, to one area, to one ability level, or to one gender? Which children were not mentioned by name at all? What uses did you make of non-verbal communication? With whom?

If it is not possible for you to use a second adult to observe your lesson, tick off the names of pupils yourself in retrospect, although be aware that you will not recall all incidents, or even have been aware of others.

ADDS UP observation sheet		
Name	+/- Behaviour	Notes

'The future belongs to those who believe in the beauty of their dreams.'
(Eleanor Roosevelt)

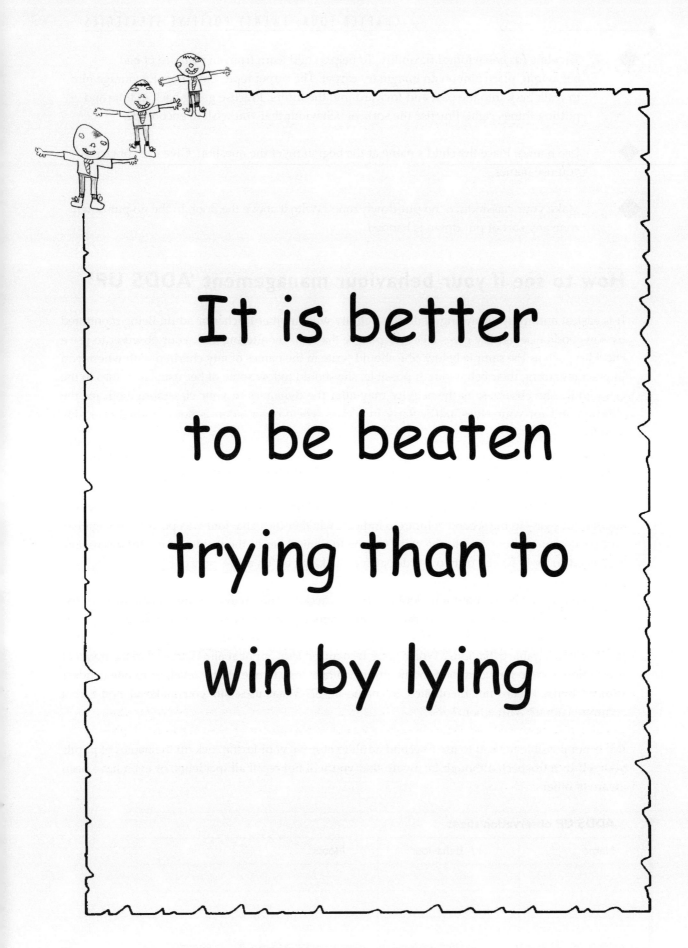

It is better to be beaten trying than to win by lying

Review of Part One

✔ What actions might you take in your classroom to address the essential physiological needs of:

Temperature	
Diet and nutrition	
Hydration	
Sleep	
Exercise	

✔ We discussed the importance of directly teaching the skills of attention. Which children in your school might benefit from specific teaching of good listening, good sitting, good asking or good looking? How might you teach these skills to classes, groups or individuals?

✔ Add to our list of strategies for securing quiet in the classroom. Ask each teacher to contribute at least one additional method to make a list for all staff.

✔ In the ALPS the teacher creates a base camp as an optimal learning environment. Work with a colleague to take five steps to build your base camp. Ask her opinion about the use of the space in your classroom. Make notes for each step:

Create a base for each student	
Create your own personal base	
Create a focus area around the board	
Clear out the clutter	
Organize the space that you have created	

✔ Assess the use of display space around the school. Take a walk around the building, either alone or with colleagues. Think about who uses each area. This is your audience. Do children need to see the same types of displays as parents and visitors? Use the checklist on the following page to see where displays could be used to accelerate learning. Make a note of what type of displays might be most effective in each area, using the ALPS criteria for display. Then draw up an action plan for ensuring that displays in your school meet ALPS criteria.

Cloakrooms	
Corridors	
Library(s)	
Hall(s)	
Cafeteria	
Office area	
Entrance hall	
Other: 1	
2	
3	
4	
5	
6	

✔ Read our suggestions of how to incorporate aspects of the ALPS approach into your lesson planning documents. How can you adapt your planning formats to ensure that the principles of ALPS are borne in mind as you plan your lessons?

✔ BASI(C)S stands for:

❖ **B**elonging
❖ **A**spirations
❖ **S**afety
❖ **I**dentity
❖ **C**hallenge
❖ **S**uccess

✔ Which of our strategies do you use to provide a BASI(C)S for your students? Which of our strategies could be useful in your classroom?

✔ For each child in your class, think of a negative phrase that she may use about herself. Write it in the first column. Then turn the negative into a positive!

Name	Negative comment	Turned into positive comment

Part Two

Into the foothills of learning

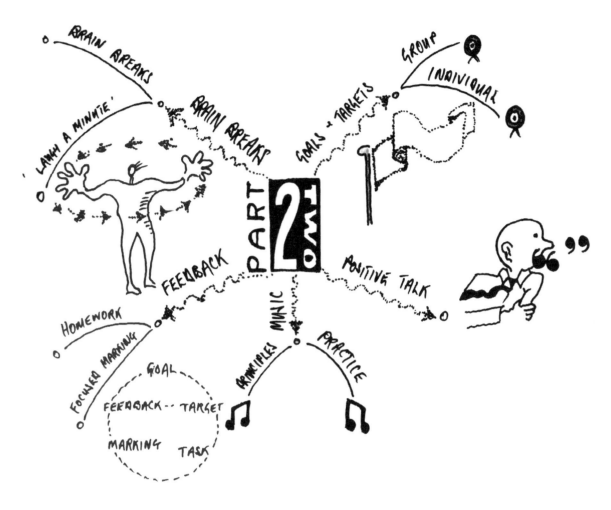

In Part Two you will:

*   find out about effective goal and target setting;
*   consider how to keep classroom talk positive and how to use the language of progression;
*   be given suggestions about formative assessment and uses of homework in the ALPS;
*   learn about the importance of brain breaks and be given many suggestions for activities;
*   find out about music and learning, and discover how and when to use music in your classroom.

Key vocabulary for Part Two:

Being PC in your marking	Formative assessment	Self-talk
Brain breaks	Language of progression	Target setting
Educative feedback	Laugh a minute	

'About me' questionnaire
for older children

Answer these questions about you and your future. Your teacher will use this information to help you decide what targets you need to set for your schoolwork this year.

1   My best piece of work this week was ....

2   My second best piece of work this week was ....

3   My favourite lesson this week was ....

4   My second favourite lesson this week was ....

5   The lesson I found hardest this week was ....

6   Apart from my class teacher my favourite teacher is ....

7   I prefer to work alone/with a partner/in a group/with an adult. ....

8   I work best when I am sitting with ....

9   At playtime I like to play with ....

10 At playtime the games I enjoy most are ....

11 I am better at English/maths ....

12 The subject that I find easiest in school is ....

13 The subject that I find hardest in school is ....

14 My favourite activity outside school is ....

15 When I leave this school I would like to go to ....

16 When I leave secondary school I think I will ....

17 When I grow up I would like to be: 1 ....
                                           2 ....
                                           3 ....

18 My reasons for wanting to do this are: 1 ....
                                               2 ....
                                               3 ....

19 The things that will help me to do this are: 1 ....
                                                   2 ....
                                                   3 ....

20 **To achieve my ambitions I will need to improve most in** ....

Goals and targets that work

We endorse the view that development and learning is shaped as much by feedback as by input or stimulus. We also believe that the best feedback is in or near the real experience, authentic, frequent, removed from threat or sanction, involving and part of a learning cycle. One of the best ways to move towards quality educative feedback is to teach the skills of target setting. A good way to start is in a neutral context; for example, in areas to do with behaviours or involvement in lessons rather than academic attainment. Starting early, when the learners are young, also helps. The more pupils can understand the mechanics of setting themselves and working towards realizable targets, the better:

* Involve them in discussing targets and how to achieve them.

* Use targets to discuss how improvements can be made.

* Make the targets visible.

* Put individual, group and class targets on posters alongside exemplar work and make them visible.

In work done in the United States reviewing 7,827 studies in education, Hattle found that accurate and detailed feedback to students could increase their level of understanding by 37 percentile points. From a neurological perspective 'constructive reflection is', according to Frydenberg and Lewis, writing in the *British Journal of Educational Psychology* in 1999, 'important in that it allows the brain's frontal lobe region a chance to filter and draw associations with prior learning'. To get you started we list five steps.

Five STEPS to National Curriculum target setting

1 Take a class list and write the subject areas across the top. Break this down further into sections that make sense to you. This may be by statements of attainment, or you may choose to use other classifications. Leave plenty of space down one side for notes. These will be more important than your figures.

2 If you have been given target figures by your headteacher, such as a percentage of children who must reach Level 2 or 4 in core subjects, forget this until you have completed the first stage of target setting. Do not begin with the figures, or you will lose the focus. The focus is the children.

3 Work your way down the class list, one child at a time. Visualize each child in class, think of how he interacts, how he concentrates, his strengths, his self-image. Now in your mind give him the perfect attitude to learning. Bless him with 100 per cent attendance, immaculate behaviour and excellent concentration skills. When you set a target level for that child, set the level that you think he would have the ability to attain if he were to have every obstacle removed from his path.

4 In the blank column down one side make a note of any factors that might hinder that child in achieving the level that you feel he is capable of achieving. These might be poor attendance, low self-esteem, poor listening skills, or a lack of concentration. If an obstacle such as poor reading skills has affected your target for him, go back to step 3 and imagine what he could achieve if his reading skills were accelerated. Re-set his targets accordingly.

5 Now turn your goals into an action plan – plan how you are going to remove those obstacles or, if you cannot remove them, how you will compensate for them. If you need to see a parent, plan to do it. Be honest and up-front. Tell the parent that their child has the ability, show them your figures and plan with them how to remove obstacles. For example, if the child does not complete homework, use the homework questionnaire on page 215, or if his reading is poor, plan an intensive programme to improve it.

'Whether you think you can, or whether you think you can't – you're probably right.'
(Henry Ford)

'About me' questionnaire
for younger children

Your teacher or another adult will help you to answer these questions. They will then help you to decide on some good targets for improving your work.

1   My best piece of work this week was ....

2   My favourite lesson is ....

3   Apart from my class teacher my favourite teacher is ....

4   I work best when I am sitting with ....

5   At playtime I like to play with ....

6   I am better at English/maths ....

7   My favourite reading book is ....

8   The subject that I find easiest in school is ....

9   The subject that I find hardest in school is ....

10 My favourite activity outside school is ....

Setting targets

For the whole class

An essential activity for setting targets with the whole class is the life mapping activity. Throughout the year, the class map on the aspirational wall should grow and develop as new targets evolve and old ones are achieved. At the start of lessons, some ways to reinforce whole class targets might include:

The life mapping activity is described on page 61

- ♣ setting class targets when giving the Big Picture;
- ♣ displaying a poster of a class target for the day or week;
- ♣ photocopying the class targets and sending them home for parents to share;
- ♣ putting copies of the class targets on each desk;
- ♣ suspending copies of target postcards on thread above desks but at eye level;
- ♣ asking children to write the class targets at the top of their page;
- ♣ making a checklist of class targets for the week for children to refer to when they finish a task;
- ♣ sending a list of class targets – followed by a progress report – to the headteacher;
- ♣ sharing class targets with a parallel class;
- ♣ speaking of class targets to adults when they visit the classroom and giving updates on progress.

For groups

Setting academic goals for groups can be a time-effective way of target setting, particularly when grouping by ability for a subject or activity. Effective ways of setting these targets and reinforcing them through the session might include:

- ♠ asking the group to set its own targets after you have given the Big Picture;
- ♠ asking one spokesperson from each group to tell the class what target their group has set;
- ♠ writing the targets on a tent card and placing it in the centre of the desk;
- ♠ giving a list of suggested targets on the board and allowing each group to select from the list;
- ♠ listing comments from previous group-work sessions as a basis for a target-setting discussion;
- ♠ asking groups to give a score periodically to represent how close they are to meeting their targets;
- ♠ allowing time at the end of the session for feedback about meeting targets;
- ♠ encouraging groups at the end of the session to begin to set targets for the next lesson.

'A single conversation across the table with a wise man is worth a month's study of books.' (Chinese proverb)

For individuals

When you made your National Curriculum targets for each member of the class, you were setting long-term goals, probably for the duration of one academic year. Each child therefore has an individual target level, probably for each area of the core curriculum. Class and group targets will help you to move towards fulfilling your National Curriculum targets, but you will also need to set individual short-term targets on a regular basis.

In order to write the first set of targets, you may wish to scan through the exercise books of each child and assess his main weaknesses. Alternatively, you could set the first targets when marking one specific piece of work, or you could meet with each child individually and agree targets together. It is a matter of personal preference whether you write the targets on the card yourself, or you ask the children to write them.

Five STEPS to individual target setting

1   Either make a set of target cards from our selection on pages 216–7, or design one of your own and make enough for each child. Use one card for each child per subject area, or for a type of activity. Large cards covering every subject will become meaningless due to a lack of focus. Narrow your focus and choose one area to pilot the cards, such as story-writing. When you mark a batch of stories, take the target cards home with you.

2   As you mark, focus on each individual child and identify two or three specific points for improvement. Write them on the card. Targets must be specific and measurable, such as 'Form letter m correctly' or 'Use four words instead of "said"'. Keep the number of targets on each card minimal, as too many targets will prove to be overwhelming.

3   At the next story-writing session, give the children their previous piece of work along with the target cards. Explain what the targets mean to any child who is unsure. Once every child understands their own individual targets, begin the lesson, ensuring that target cards are clearly visible on desks. At regular intervals during the lesson refer to targets and make affirmations such as 'Everybody in this class is looking at their cards and we are all meeting our targets.'

4   When you collect in the work, collect in the target cards. When you mark the stories, refer to the target cards and measure how far each individual has met their targets. It is vitally important that you give feedback. With younger children this is usually necessary on a one-to-one basis, and you may well give feedback as you mark during the session. With older children you may choose to give the feedback at a later date. The important thing is that you give feedback that is directly related to the targets.

5   Once a target has been achieved, communicate, praise, celebrate, and replace it with a new one!

'The only good luck many great men ever had was being born with the ability and determination to overcome bad luck.' (Channing Pollock)

Ten ways to recognize a Target Terminator

A Target Terminator is a child who has achieved all the targets on a target card. Here are ten ways to celebrate with a Target Terminator.

1   Display his target card on a Target Terminator display board.

2   Allow him to wear the Target Terminator hat for the afternoon.

3   Tie a balloon to his desk or chair for the day.

4   Give him a Target Terminator badge for the day that allows him special privileges.

5   Devise a Target Terminator song or chant that the class sing while pointing to him.

6   Make a Target Terminator Box from which he selects a forfeit, joke or treat.

7   Line up all the week's Target Terminators on Friday afternoon and give them three cheers.

8   Use a special piece of music to play as the Target Terminator bows to the class.

9   Applaud the week's Target Terminators in assembly.

10 Allow the Target Terminators to lead out of assembly first to a special piece of music.

Ten ways to share targets with parents

1   Send photocopies of the class targets home each half-term.

2   Post a copy of the class targets on the door for parents to see.

3   Stick copies of class, group or individual targets inside homework diaries or folders.

4   Send target cards home when first compiled for parents to sign and make comments.

5   Attach target cards to homework assignments.

6   Photocopy target cards and send them home for children's use during homework.

7   Encourage children to show their parents the Target Terminator display, along with their new target cards.

8   Attach new target cards to Target Terminator certificates.

9   Discuss target cards with parents at consultation evenings.

10 Ask parents to fill in their own target cards for their child for the term or the year.

'Success is going from failure to failure without losing enthusiasm.' (Winston Churchill)

Ten activities to help your class to set good targets

1   Once a week, set a piece of work for the class that they can complete independently. During this time, meet with each child to review his target cards and set new goals.

2   Organize children in friendship pairs. For each child choose a piece of work that relates to a particular target card. Ask each child to tell his partner how he thinks he has met one or all of his targets. If his partner agrees, they can then draw up a new target for each other.

3   Pair each child with an older child from another class. Ask the older child to 'mark' the work of the younger child and help him to draw up a new target.

4   Send Target Terminator cards home and ask parents to suggest new targets.

5   Invite Target Terminators to the front of the class to read out their terminated targets. Ask the class to suggest new targets for them.

6   Create a special target setting area where children can go when they need to review work and set new targets. Stock it with target cards, pens and pencils. Display good targets around the area and allow children time to go there to reflect and draft new targets.

7   Keep checklists of children's targets that can be used for others at a later date.

8   In ability groups, ask each child to read one of his targets aloud. Each child can then select one new target from those read by the others to add to his target card.

9   Write a selection of targets on pieces of card with enough for everyone and some to spare. Give some to each group and allow each child to read them, discuss them and select one.

10 Create a display board or a menu of 'Good targets' from which children can select new targets.

Target prompt sheet

Six good questions for children to ask themselves as they work:

1   Can I remember what my targets are?

2   Did I look at my target card before I started work?

3   Have I looked at my target card during the lesson?

4   Am I remembering my targets as I work?

5   Am I meeting my targets right now?

6   Do I need to ask an adult if I am meeting my targets?

'Two roads diverge in a wood, and I took the one less travelled by, and that has made all the difference.' (Robert Frost, writer)

2 Positive classroom talk

Self-talk: how to help children stay positive

Research has shown that the positive support of the class, teachers and parents 'correlates significantly ... to child and adolescent self-esteem' (Harter, CUP, 1996). In a study of children progressing from Year 6 to Year 7, Harter found that the significant factor in whether children gained or lost the intrinsic motivation for learning was whether or not they *felt that they were intelligent*. It is therefore essential to keep talk in the classroom positive.

Ten good questions to ask if you are stuck

1 What is another way that I could try this?
2 How would a teacher do this?
3 How could I show my younger brother or sister how to do this?
4 Where could I look in the classroom for ideas of how to solve this?
5 Who has done this before?
6 Who could I ask to show me how they did this?
7 Who could help me to solve this problem?
8 What books might help me to do this?
9 What activity could I do first before I return to this?
10 What would happen if I just had a go and see what happens?

Self-talk: 12 ways to help children to be positive

1 Use the phrase 'not yet' to replace 'not'.
2 Set the example that everyone is challenged sometimes.
3 Welcome the fact that children get 'stuck' and explore how 'stuckness' feels.
4 Create lots of opportunities for activities that do not have a right or a wrong answer.
5 Use a method for checking understanding that makes it safe to say 'I don't understand yet'.
6 Take the focus away from how many answers the child knows, but focus on what the child does when he does not know the answers.
7 Value the questions that children ask, as well as their answers.
8 Allow for processing time when you ask questions.
9 Ask questions such as, 'How many ways can we solve this problem?' rather than, 'Who can tell me, hands up?'
10 Use affirmations continually, stating the positive about all children in all situations.
11 Teach the language of problem solving, such as 'I can do this ... I'll try a different way and then it will work'.
12 Encourage children to develop positive self-talk – change 'low or no can-do' talk to 'I or high can-do' talk!

'Life is either a daring adventure or nothing.' (Helen Keller, deaf dumb and blind from birth)

Don't be a fool learning is cool

Changing 'low or no-can do' talk to 'I or high can-do' talk	
Low or no-can do talk	**I or high can-do talk**
No	Not yet
Never	When I'm ready to
I can't	I can
I'm no good at	I'm getting better at
It's not cool to be keen	I'm cool and I'm keen!
No one in my family can	I'll be the first in my family who can
I do not want to be different	I do not need to be the same
No one likes me	Sharon's my friend
I got a low score	I'll make sure I get better next time
I'm stuck!	I'll move on and come back to it
I can't do this	What will it be like when I can?

Using the language of progression

The DfEE report in late 2000 stated that nearly 40 per cent of pupils make a loss or no progress in English, maths and science in the year following transfer from primary school. Progression and performance at transfer is a big issue for all schools and UK schools in particular. A number of strategies are outside, and some within, the gift of ALPS teachers. There is real value in exploring the possibilities of:

- ✪ extended induction programmes for secondary school;
- ✪ staff accompanying pupils to secondary school on early transition in May/June;
- ✪ special transition modules in English, maths and science that overlap between Years 6 and 7 and can start from May of Year 6;
- ✪ a more extensive programme of teacher exchange between secondary and primary;

'Don't be afraid to go out on a limb. That's where the fruit is.'

- better use of data and earlier transfer of data;
- summer schools in literacy, numeracy and 'learnacy';
- mentors from secondary school and from further or higher education;
- transition mentors for children at risk;
- shared seminars with Year 7 and their teachers with professionals invited to talk about their professions; for example, nurses, doctors, vets and engineers;
- shared after-school clubs; for example, animal lovers' club, engineers' club, computer club, inventors' club, board games club.

Setting ambitious targets is also part of the current agenda for education. So too is the subsequent practice of talking about those targets in a persuasive manner. Talking up the language of achievement goes beyond rhetoric. It influences performance. Specific language of progression interventions can be added to the sorts of strategies described above.

Five practical ideas for using the language of progression in class

1 Look at the theme of transition in terms of transitions in our lives. Organize an assembly or class discussion on this topic.

2 As you work in class, sell the benefits of successfully completing activities not the features of the activity.

3 Use phrases such as 'when you have completed ... you will be able to ... and this will then mean you can ...'

4 Timeline major activities, including extended pieces of work, before starting them, and walk and talk through the timeline.

5 Use terms like GCSE, GNVQ, NVQ, A and A/S level, and degree in class. Identify where the local further and higher education institutions are and invite in students to talk about what they do there.

Improving your questioning strategies

Metacognition (thinking about thinking) can be modelled and taught in any lesson and is a skill that is genuinely life transforming. It begins with the quality of questioning used by the class teacher. Some basic principles include avoiding 'pouncing' unless of course what you seek is a spluttered and ill-considered response, utilizing wait or 'processing' time and encouraging pre-processing. A child needs to hear your question, assimilate it and relate it to others that he has heard before, formulate a response and surface the response in language. All this takes time. The true value of a question is to develop learning rather than test for knowing. It is not just how many answers pupils know, it is how they behave when they do not that counts. Helping the pupils generate their own questions is an important modelling role for you as a classroom teacher. Here are some ideas to help.

'If you want to stand out, don't be different, be outstanding.' (Meredith West)

Twenty-one ways to improve your questioning strategies

1   Allow processing time. The younger the learner, the more time they may need to assimilate the question.

2   Allow time for replies. Try allowing each child one minute to speak when making a response.

3   Do not rely on questions that reward simple recall of information.

4   Provide processing cues, such as 'In a minute I am going to ask you about x.'

5   Give parameters to help the child to shape the response.

6   Ask children to repeat the question to you to allow time for processing.

7   Embed questions at the outset of a learning experience, such as 'What would it be like if we had answers to the following ...?'

8   Encourage outcomes thinking by asking questions, such as 'What will the finished piece of work be like?'

9   Change the balance of teacher to pupil talk from 80 per cent teacher talk towards 20 per cent teacher talk.

10 Use open questions that offer the possibility of a variety of responses and solicit opinion.

11 Ask follow-up questions that take the thinking to a higher level.

12 Use numbers to put challenge within a task by asking 'Can you give me three examples of ...?'

13 Preface your questions with an individual's name.

14 Ask pupils to explain their thinking when they give an answer by asking 'What made you think that?'

15 Provide extending questions, such as 'What other alternatives did you consider?'

16 Reflect back by stating, 'So, if I'm right, what you are saying is ...'

17 Ask children to summarize and speculate.

18 Play devil's advocate by giving the opposite point of view, or an outrageous alternative.

19 Encourage thinking about thinking through your use of questions.

20 Provide opportunities for pupils to explain the processes they chose, as well as describe the outcome.

21 Resist the temptation to answer your own questions!

Imagination

is more

important than

knowledge

Albert Einstein

Providing educative feedback

Focused marking

In addition to verbal feedback, a considerable amount of feedback is given to children through the marking of their work. Marking is most effective when it supports the target-setting process and is an integral part of the cycle which looks like this:

(goal)
target
task
marking and feedback
revised target.

Marking work takes up many working hours for the average teacher and is a common source of stress and frustration. The ALPS method enables you to be more effective with your marking, but *without* taking more time.

The ALPS five steps to focused marking will help you to make good use of the time you spend marking and to ensure that your feedback has maximum effect on your pupils' learning.

Five STEPS to focused marking

1 **Establish some 'General Rules'**
Create rules for every piece of written work that your class will complete during the year. Spend time teaching the rules and then display them on a board in the classroom. You may need a few practice sessions to rehearse for success, but make it clear that these rules are to be applied consistently and without exception. If a child does not follow the rules, you will not read his work until he has corrected it.

2 **Establish specific 'Task Rules'**
Once you have taught your general work rules, you can begin to develop rules for specific types of work. At the beginning of the year you will need to devote a considerable amount of space to display these rules clearly and in view of all children. For each type of work, draw up a list of essential requirements. Make your rules specific and be ambitious. Remove the mystery by analysing what constitutes good quality work and teaching the skills directly.

'They always say that time changes things, but you actually have to change them yourself.'
(Andy Warhol)

3 Share your 'Lesson Targets'

Set out your lesson target at the beginning of each lesson. Do this as you give the Big Picture. You need to be direct and clear about your expectations. Write up your lesson target clearly to aid the visual learners. Refer to it frequently and make positive affirmations throughout the session to ensure that all students remember it. When you mark workbooks, have your task and lesson target in front of you. Do not be distracted from measuring achievement against targets.

4 Set each student 'Individual Targets'

If you have already developed the use of target cards, you will find systems that make your feedback individual. A basic principle must be that you have the target card in front of you as you mark work. You are now measuring against four sets of criteria:

✦ General Rules
✦ Task Rules
✦ Lesson Targets
✦ Individual Targets.

5 Create feedback codes

Now that you have focused on what you are correcting, you need to speed up the process. The answer lies in developing short codes that link to your system of RAP. It is essential that your children understand quickly and easily what your codes mean. Develop these systems so that your students can become responsible for their own learning and target setting.

Marking codes

It is essential that marking codes are used consistently and explained to the class. Here are some suggestions for marking codes, although you may wish to devise your own. A list of the codes can be displayed as a poster in the classroom, or individual copies can be kept as checklists for children to use when marked work is handed out. Alternatively, individual copies can be attached to desks or glued inside exercise books.

Code	Meaning
T1 ?	Check your target card – you have not met Target 1
T1 ✔	Good – you have met Target 1
New T	Here is a new target to replace the one that you have achieved
Set new T	Set yourself a new target to replace the one that you have achieved, then show it to me
T1 ✔ R	Good – you have met Target 1 and can claim your reward
Sp	Check this spelling and make a correction
D	Look in the dictionary to find a more interesting word
Th	Look in a thesaurus to find a more interesting word
R	Read your work to yourself and decide if you have met your targets
R to P	Read your work to a partner and see if he thinks that you have met your targets
TC:	Target challenge: (then write challenge)
TT	You're a Target Terminator – congratulations – you have achieved all your targets!

'To the man who only has a hammer, everything he encounters begins to look like a nail.'
(Abraham H. Maslow, psychologist)

The marking stamp

A marking stamp can help to speed up and focus marking when used in conjunction with clear target setting. A rubber stamp of a table such as the one below can be stamped in ink at the end of each piece of work then filled in by the teacher. Alternatively, the table could be photocopied and used to give focused feedback regarding each target on the child's target card.

	Comment
Target 1	
Target 2	
Target 3	
Target 4	
Target 5	
Target Challenge	

Twelve ways to display your targets and rules

1 Photocopy each set of work rules and glue them in the front of relevant workbooks.

2 Create a Rules Display Board where rules for every subject are displayed.

3 Pin up each set of work rules when you give the Big Picture.

4 Display work rules for each lesson on an OHP.

5 Peg a large copy of the set of lesson on a 'washing line' at the front of the class for each lesson.

6 Make checklists for each set of rules and ask children to tick that they have followed each rule before giving in work for marking.

7 Place tent cards on desks with group or individual targets.

8 Paperclip individual target cards inside workbooks.

9 Fix plastic wallets to desks in which to insert target cards.

10 Keep containers on desks containing colour-coded target cards that children remove and place in front of them for each individual lesson.

11 Hang class and group targets on large pieces of card from the ceiling, using strings and brightly coloured pegs.

12 Display class and group targets on OHPs during each relevant lesson.

'Life is 10 per cent what you make it and 90 per cent how you take it.' (Irving Berlin)

Seven samples of positive feedback

1 A thoughtful piece of writing. Good use of speech marks – just make them a little smaller. You describe Anthony as 'nice'? TC: think of six different words for 'nice'.

2 What a funny story! The cat was naughty to follow Tim to school. How did he get home? TC: learn to spell 'school' for three Team Points.

3 Why do you think Henry VIII took Hampton Court from Thomas Wolsey? Can you remember why he sacked him? TC: Pretend that you are Thomas Wolsey in 1529. Write a paragraph about how you felt about the king's actions that year.

4 A clear description of the Mayflower. I like your ideas about how relieved they felt to escape persecution in England, but how do you think the pilgrims felt as so many of them died that first winter? TC: write an account of the disease and deaths of almost half the settlement from the point of view of one of the pilgrims.

5 Your group made some careful measurement of the movement of the car. Be careful to use the same unit of measurement each time – don't switch between two different units of measurement in an experiment as it makes it difficult to compare the results. TC: predict what would happen if you added a weight to the car. You will be asked to test this in next week's lesson!

6 Good rhymes in this poem! Ask Mrs M. to help you with the full stops and commas.

7 A thoughtful investigation – discuss as a group if you could have organized the work better and finished sooner? TC: repeat this investigation with six columns of numbers instead of four. Organize your work so that you meet the challenge in the time allowed!

Grades and what to do with them

Sharing information about the curriculum with pupils and giving grades to provide clear targets and feedback about progress can be a positive tool if managed in conjunction with effective RAP. While you might choose to work without giving grades, it is essential to children's self-esteem that they understand the levels given in SATs and National Curriculum assessments.

Before any child is assessed, he has the right to understand what the assessment involves, what the grades represent and how he is currently performing. Some children may never attain national target levels by the end of each year, but every child can attain their own individual target level and be a high achiever. The key to using grades to motivate is to be PC! In the ALPS, the letters PC stand for:

P ositive and C reative

Be Positive in your target setting
Be Creative in your use of grades.

'It is not the position, but the disposition.' (J.E. Dinger)

Seven good ideas for feedback without marking

1   Gather all the target cards from the class. Organize them in a highly visible way into families of targets, talking through your thinking and inviting suggestions as you go. Take each family of targets in turn and discuss the learning that is necessary to meet the target. Then review any 'rules' – for example, 'in spelling 'i' before 'e' except after 'c' – that emerge.

2   Gather all the target cards from the class. Organize them in a highly visible way into families of targets, talking through your thinking and inviting suggestions as you go. Then take each family of targets in turn and allocate them to tables to work on ways of meeting those targets. Or, distribute one type of target from each family group to each table so that they have a variety of targets to work on together.

3   Organize a target fair where children visit each other and hear first what the target or targets have been, then three things the person has done to meet the targets and finally look at the work.

4   Organise a timed target carousel, where children move between tables, and for a designated time are introduced to the targets from that table.

5   Have a target 'theme of the day' or 'theme of the week'. where a target is nominated or chosen and the teacher goes through the target and how best to achieve it. At the end of the week the four targets from Target theme of the day can be reviewed together.

6   Create A3 laminated posters with selected National Curriculum attainment levels described in pupil-speak on one side. Provide suggestions for achieving them on other laminated posters. Get children to match them up, explain them to each other in pairs. Then share matched posters between tables and get pupils to introduce them to each other.

7   Use continuity lines or circles to provide opportunities to verbalize feedback. For example 'on a scale of 1–10, with 1 being by the wall and 10 being by the window, find a position that best represents how well you think you have done on your targets this week'.

'The greatest discovery of my generation is that human beings can alter their lives by altering their attitudes of mind.' (William James, psychologist)

Grading your pupils will tell them what they are currently achieving. Sharing grades will help them to aspire to higher attainment. Setting target grades will help them to measure their own progress, while focused marking will give them signposts to show them how to improve. Effective RAP will create the positive atmosphere necessary for success.

The ALPS principles to grading

Grades must:

☺ make the child feel academically competent

☺ be used in line with effective goal and target setting

☺ give clear feedback

☺ give indicators on how to improve

☺ be shared between child, teacher and parent

☺ be based on clear criteria

☺ motivate towards further improvement.

Eight examples of how to use grades as a powerful tool

1 Subdivide each level of the National Curriculum into the categories Low and High, or into three categories such as Foundation, Intermediate, Higher and Advanced. Grade key pieces of work according to your categories, so that children can then see a measurement of progression that spans less than one year, rather than a two-year step that is quite meaningless to a small child.

2 Display children's names on pieces of laminated card stuck temporarily with blu-tac, arranged according to the level that they are currently achieving in a subject. The challenge is to 'race' to the next level in that subject. Every child should be expected to move his name up from one level to the next as he improves. Once each child scores at a higher level, he should move his name up to the next list, to the recognition of a round of applause from his classmates.

3 As a variation, group the children and have 'Team Races' to the next level. Organize the teams yourself or allow the children to choose their own teams. It makes no difference if the children are on different levels because the race is to improve by one level.

4 Encourage children to challenge one another. Create a display board entitled 'I bet I could ...' to hang on the wall. Here children can set their own challenges and targets for any task or area of the curriculum.

5 Set scores out of ten or 20 for specific activities as targets, or give colour-coded levels for test results or assessments. Allow children to attempt the harder levels as they improve. Put the decision to move up a level in the hands of the child rather than the teacher.

6 Create a 'Roll of Honour' for children as they move up a level, for example on the reading scheme. Colour-code with bronze, pewter, silver and gold, and display children's names as they move up a level. In this way, a beginner reader can reach the Golden Roll of Honour before a more fluent reader! Replace the question 'What reading book are you on?' with 'Which Roll of Honour are you on?'

7 Create whole school systems of recognition for grades. For example, ask all the 100 per cent students of the week to stand up in assembly on Mondays to the applause of the whole school, or allow the 100 per cent students to lead out of assembly first to the sound of some celebratory music.

8 Send home a slip of paper with test and task results each week for children to share their achievements with their parents.

'You play the hand you're dealt. I think the game's worthwhile.' (Christopher Reeve)

Five ways to use grades to motivate

1 When children make an improvement, put a poster on the wall to celebrate their success.

2 Include grades in your Target Challenges by explaining what level the child would achieve if she met the challenge.

3 Set whole class targets such as for every child to attain an A grade in a science task. Differentiate the work appropriately, set clear criteria for each group for what constitutes an A grade, then celebrate once everybody has achieved it.

4 Give details of what would constitute an A or B grade, or a curriculum level, when giving the Big Picture. When you review the lesson with the class, give children your assessment of their achievement measured against these criteria.

5 When you review a lesson, ask children to assess themselves for grades or levels, measuring against the criteria that you set at the start of the lesson.

Five ways to give feedback without giving grades

1 Have one session a week where you meet each child individually to discuss a piece of work while the class does a task that does not require adult interaction.

2 Create some 'feedback cards' that you complete once a week with comments on each child's progress and improvement.

3 Keep a feedback journal for each child where he makes a comment on his week's work, followed by your comment.

4 Set target challenges where the child earns target points as he meets the challenge and keeps a score at the back of an exercise book.

5 Give a whacky award for achievement of a target or the earning of a certain number of target points.

'Optimism is the cheerful frame of mind that enables a teakettle to sing, though in hot water up to its nose.'

Nine suggestions of ways to share the curriculum with children and parents

1 Highlight the areas of the National Curriculum that you will be covering and display an enlarged copy on the classroom wall. Discuss it with the class and refer to it when you give the Big Picture.

2 Refer to the curriculum when you make your To Do lists with the class and show them what areas and levels of work you aim to cover each week.

3 Photocopy the curriculum and glue it inside the covers of children's exercise books. Refer to it as you start each lesson and in review sessions. As each area is covered, ask children to colour the relevant area, or tick boxes to show that the work has been done.

4 Glue copies of the curriculum inside homework books and encourage children to share the information with parents as they do each task.

5 When you set tasks, ask children to look at the curriculum and work out what areas the task will be working towards achieving.

6 Simplify and précis the areas of the National Curriculum that you will be covering each half-term and display it on parents' boards or send copies home.

7 Write the curriculum area and level you are working towards at the top of worksheets and homework assignments.

8 Create mnemonics to represent areas of the curriculum that are to be covered. For example, in one school the name MR GREEN was used as a mnemonic for the science curriculum.

9 Cross-reference children's targets on their target cards to the National Curriculum. Ask them to work out what levels they think they are working towards as they move to achieving their targets.

Homework in the ALPS

Homework should not be done as ritual, but should complement, extend and enhance good teaching in the classroom.

Policies and attitudes towards homework vary, but there are some underlying principles that cannot be ignored. First, within each school consistency of approach is essential. One of the most common complaints of parents is when they have an older child who receives less demanding homework than a younger. Schools need to ensure that they provide continuity for children as they progress from year to year. Lack of a consistent approach and expectation can potentially do more damage than too much, or too little, homework in one class or another. Below are some questions that will help you to write a homework policy, revise an old policy or clarify points from your existing policy.

☞ What is the purpose of homework in our school?

☞ How do we plan for homework?

☞ How do we teach children how to approach homework tasks?

'Between the optimist and the pessimist, the difference is droll. The optimist sees the doughnut; the pessimist the hole!' (Mclandburgh Wilson)

☞ How do we ensure that children understand homework tasks?

☞ How do we communicate to children our reasons for setting homework?

☞ How much homework is set for each year group?

☞ What is the maximum amount of time that a child should spend on a homework task?

☞ How do we motivate children to complete homework?

☞ How do we give recognition to children who complete tasks?

☞ How do we give recognition to children who do additional tasks voluntarily at home?

☞ How do we teach study and research skills?

☞ How do we provide for children whose home environments are not conducive to completing homework?

☞ How do we monitor the completion of homework tasks?

☞ How do we monitor the quality of homework tasks?

☞ How do we monitor the level of independence of each child in completing tasks?

☞ How do we communicate to parents about appropriate methods and attitudes for helping their children with homework?

☞ What action do we take if a child does not complete homework?

☞ How do we communicate our homework policy to children?

☞ How do we communicate our homework policy to parents?

☞ How do we monitor consistency in following the homework policy across age groups?

☞ How do children perceive homework? Does this vary from class to class?

☞ What do children in our school feel about our homework policy?

If your school has a policy of setting homework, it needs to be planned when you draw up your lesson plan. To set a task that is not planned in connection with the learning that is taking place in the classroom is to waste the potential that homework has in helping your class to accelerate up the mountain. There are a few basic principles to consider when setting homework. Each homework task must have a clearly defined purpose, such as to revise, to research, to practise skills, or to challenge thinking. If homework is set merely to fill time, it should not be set at all. Once you have decided that the homework is appropriate and worthwhile, you need to consider how your pupils respond to each task.

See page 215 for the homework questionnaire

The homework questionnaire, first used in *The ALPS Approach*, has been devised to pinpoint four skills that will help children with the skill of completing homework: section one focuses on organization of materials; section two on time management; section three on listening to explanations; and section four on handling distractions. It is important that the children understand that this is not a test and that everyone will score more highly in some areas than others. With young children, the questionnaire can be adapted and read to them. They can use hand signals to indicate how true each statement is to them, or just simple yes, no or sometimes. An adult can record their responses and work out strengths and weaknesses.

'It is all one to me if a man comes from Sing Sing Prison or Harvard. We hire a man, not his history.' (Henry Ford)

Getting stuck
is not a
problem,
staying stuck
is – practise
getting unstuck

Once the children have completed their questionnaires, they should be given the target card for the section for which they had the highest score. This is their main area of weakness. The target cards can be used in a number of ways. Parental involvement is very powerful. The entire process can be shared with parents, with children completing the questionnaire with their parents at home. This will probably ensure that the responses are honest! Parents often speak of the stress that homework can cause within the family, and this is a positive way to work in partnership to help children to become independent learners.

Fifty good homeworks!

1   At home, improve your memory by testing how many mixed up letters and numbers you can remember. Try to remember at least seven. Notice what helps you remember.

2   At home, improve your memory for spelling by writing difficult spellings on bits of card. Look at the spelling on the card and then turn the card over. Try to remember what you saw there. Do this three times so you can get it right before you write out what you remember.

3   At home, improve your memory for spelling by writing difficult spellings on bits of card. This time, look at the card and say the letters of the word to yourself as you look at the card. Now turn it over. Try to remember what you saw there and what you said to yourself. Say the spelling aloud as you remember the look of the word. Do this three times so you can get it right before you write out what you remember.

4   At home, improve your memory for spelling by writing difficult spellings on bits of card. This time, look at the card and say the letters of the word to yourself as you look at the card and practise making the shapes of each letter in the air in front of you. Now turn it over. Try to remember what you saw there and what you said to yourself and the shapes you made. Say the spelling aloud as you remember the look of the word and do the shapes. Do this three times so you can get it right before you write out what you remember.

5   List on a piece of card three different things. Turn the card over and try to say what the three different things were. Now add another thing and do the same again. Keep trying until you get one wrong. How many did you get? Five is OK, seven is good, nine is excellent and 11 is Supergenius!

6   Draw an unusual shape on the card and turn it over. Now go through the alphabet in your head, say each letter and draw with your finger in the air. This is supposed to distract you! Now on a separate card and from memory try and draw the unusual shape. How similar are they? Why do you think there might be differences? Bring your shapes to school.

7   Interview a neighbour or friend and find out what they think about …

8   Take a topic and do a GBI. G stands for good things, B stands for bad things and I stands for interesting things. List them in different columns.

9   Find a photograph of yourself from home and place it in the middle of a sheet of paper. By drawing around your picture turn it into an advertisement for a beauty product, or a wanted poster, or a headline from the front page of a newspaper or a poster for a film.

10 Try to think of as many friends or relatives whose first name begins with a consonant. List five of them. Try to think of as many friends or relatives whose first name begins with a vowel. List five of them.

'Ability is sexless.' (Christabel Pankhurst)

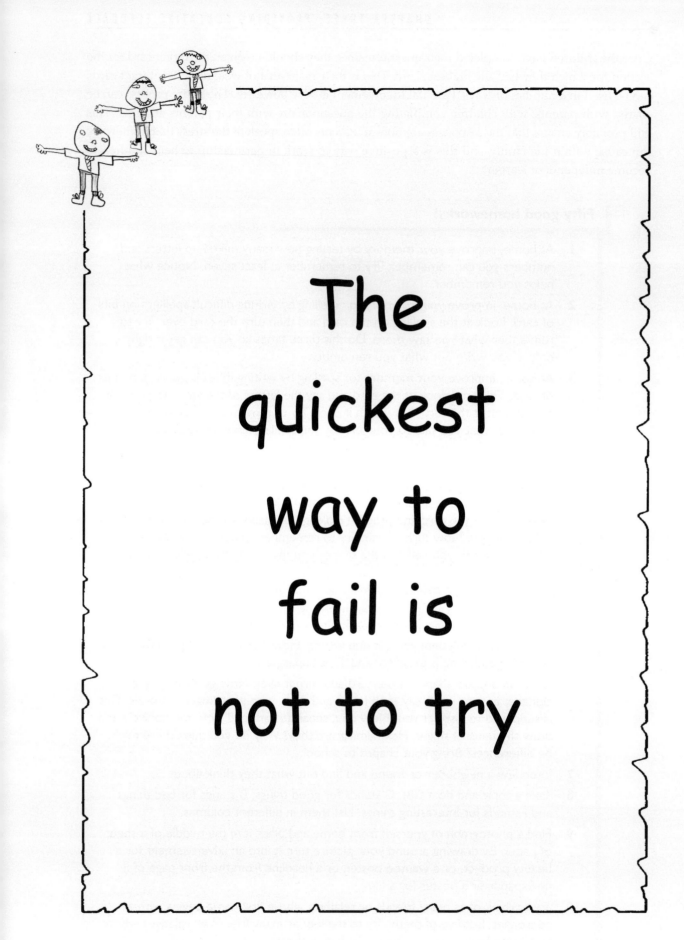

The
quickest
way to
fail is
not to try

11 Try to think of as many friends or relatives whose first name ends with a consonant. List five of them. Try to think of as many friends or relatives whose first name ends with a vowel. List five of them.

12 Find three different photographs from home and write one paragraph for each to explain what is happening.

13 Find three different photographs from home and write and explain as many connections between them as you can think of.

14 Think of the first paragraph of your life story, tell someone else at home what it will say, then write it out …

15 The film of your life story is about to come out, devise the title sequence …

16 Make a memory map with the title 'All about Me'.

17 A 'CV' is a description of all the things about you that someone needs to know. It is used when you apply for a job. Think of a job you might like and write out on one side of paper all the things you think your 'employer' ought to know about you.

18 Find listing of all the television programmes on this evening. Select one channel and count how many programmes there are between 5.00 pm and midnight. Which is the longest and how long does it last? Which is the shortest?

19 For your channel classify the programmes and list them under different headings. Use these headings to help you: children's, news and information, light entertainment, drama, soap opera, film, sport. Why are the programmes so different?

20 List all the shops you might pass on your journey to or from school, now add the names of any that you have visited in the last week, now add any that you know advertise on the television. How many have you got? Why do they not all advertise on the television? List three reasons.

21 Is advertising good or bad. List three good things and three bad things.

22 Watch three different television advertisements that you like. Say why you like them. How do the advertisers try and make you buy their product?

23 Watch the television news and make notes on one thing to tell the class about.

24 Listen to the radio news and write notes on two things to tell the class about.

25 Read the first two pages of a national paper and make a note of the main headlines.

26 Select an article from a national paper and prepare a report to make to your group.

27 Find as many advertisements as you can in a national newspaper and count them. Do the same for a local newspaper by 'estimating'. How does the number of adverts in a national newspaper compare with a local newspaper? Try to explain the difference.

28 List five things that a daily newspaper for school children should contain. List five things that a daily newspaper for your class should contain.

29 On paper, design the home page for your personal website. Remember to include any links you will have and also to describe what a visitor will find 'inside'.

30 On Sunday night find a quiet time to set yourself three positive goals for the week. Then practise mentally rehearsing the goals. See what it will be like when you get your goals. Try to remember your goals each day by practising rehearsing them in your head. Do not tell anyone what the goals were. Ask yourself at the end of the week if you got your goals. If not this time, what will you do differently next time?

'When one must, one can.' (Yiddish proverb)

31 Challenge yourself to do good sitting or good listening or good asking at home! How long can you do it for?

32 From the list of class affirmations your teacher uses, choose one for yourself and repeat it in your head. Choose one you really like and will remember. Write it down somewhere at home.

33 Practise the 'Private Cinema' that your teacher talks about in your head just before you go to sleep at night. See yourself being really good at reading, writing and asking at school. Concentrate on making a really positive film about yourself and then go back and see the 'repeats' on different nights!

34 Imagine you can float on your own private cloud. Shut your eyes and describe the view to yourself as you float above your house. Notice the size and shape of things and how different it looks. Now see yourself coming out of your house on your way to school, follow your journey. Now try and describe it aloud. Can you draw what you saw as a map?

35 Now float above the school playground at break time. Shut your eyes and describe what you see.

36 Bring your favourite book or magazine to school and tell your group why you like it.

37 Bring an item to school from home or from a trip or holiday and tell the class the two most important things about it.

38 Practise your brain-break exercises at home and then try them out on someone else in the family.

39 Devise a new brain-break activity that involves hands only.

40 Devise a new brain-break activity that involves feet only.

41 Devise a new brain-break activity that involves hands and feet.

42 Devise a new brain-break activity for your eyes.

43 Practise your new brain-break activities to music so you can demonstrate to the rest of the class.

44 Devise a new brain-break activity to help younger children learn their letters or their numbers.

45 Bring in an object from home and tell the class the history of that object.

46 Find a small object from home that you see everyday and devise the most amazing story about this object and its history.

47 Write a paragraph as if you were … living in …

48 Think of something that you can remember that happened to you a long time ago. Choose something you remember well. Now choose your favourite time in history. Now write about what happened to you as if it had happened in history.

49 List all the really good things that you can remember have happened to you. Then list all the things that you can remember that have made you sad. Divide your paper so that there is an even space for every year old you are. Now mark your 'highs and lows of life' on the chart against your age.

50 Look in a thesaurus for a new desk label adjective for yourself and for your partner.

'God does not ask about our ability, but our availability.'

Five homework motivators

At some stage, you may wish to use some extrinsic rewards and motivational tactics to kick-start any reluctant homeworkers! Here are five suggestions:

1   Make a class target to all complete tasks for one week. Write the target large on the wall. Refer to it frequently. Affirm that you will all achieve the target. Agree a reward for the end of the week when everyone has done so. Provide homework club for the week or a catch-up club on Thursday to help those who may find it difficult to complete tasks. At the end of the week, celebrate!

2   Make one child in each class a 'Homework Star' each week. Get the Homework Stars to stand up in assembly, give a certificate and applaud them loudly.

3   Create a 'Three Cheers for Homework!' board. Get children who have completed all their tasks to pin their name up. Give second opportunities and create time for those who have not done so. It is your aim to ensure that every child is successful. Affirm this over and over. Decorate the board with ribbons and balloons. Give 'Three Cheers!' certificates and thank parents for their help. Homework can be stressful for them too!

4   Send home certificates showing the number of assignments given and the number completed. Categorize them gold, silver and bronze. Your aim is for everyone to ultimately achieve a gold.

5   When children bring in homework, get them to bring it to the front one by one, to be applauded by the class for having completed it. Play some uplifting music such as 'We are the Champions!' to create an atmosphere of excitement and pride.

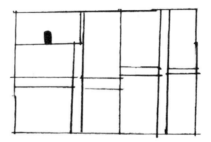

Homework with Mum

'They are able because they think they are able.' (Virgil)

Monitoring homework assignments

Here are six methods that we have seen teachers use to monitor the completion of homework tasks in ALPS classrooms:

1   Create a large grid with each child's name down one side and enough boxes for each task for the week, half-term or term. Display it at child height above the 'in-tray' for homework. As each child places his assignment in the tray, he ticks the next box by his name, or sticks up a coloured sticker. To avoid confusion over columns, blu-tac a piece of card over the adjacent column.

2   As you call each name on the register, ask the children to come to the front and place their homework in the 'in-tray'. If they do not have it, they must fill in an explanation sheet instead and place that in the tray.

3   Make homework collection a time of celebration. Play some uplifting music and call the children to the front table by table to the singing and clapping of their classmates.

4   Give five-minute warnings before collecting homework so that children are organized and do not waste class time through having to search for papers or books. Collect homework after a brain break or a timetable change, so that children have time to organize themselves without disturbing others.

5   When setting a number of activities, for example during school holidays, provide a checklist such as the one below, so that children and parents can record the completion of tasks.

6   Use a chart to check on day-to-day homework tasks. Make the charts into booklets, stick them on card, print them off weekly, or design your own.

Parental feedback form for homework activities					
Child's name:			Class:		
Homework checklist					
Task	Date	Time taken	Comments		Initials

'The world cares very little about what a man or woman knows; it is what a man or woman is able to do that counts.' (Booker T. Washington)

Brain breaks

Have a break? Have a brain break?

Research published in the UK in January 2001 entitled *Fit for Success* suggested that boys in the age range 9–11 who regularly exercised – at least three times each week – performed better in academic work than their peers who took little or no exercise. In the US similar research claimed that 'children engaged in daily physical education show superior motor fitness, academic performance and attitude towards school compared to their counterparts who do not participate in daily physical education'. Teachers in UK schools point out to us that increasingly children are being given fewer and fewer opportunities for structured play and active involvement in regular sport. They state that many children have lost the knack of playing the playground games that may have been familiar two generations ago. Many of these same teachers are experimenting with more physical movement in class as part of their teaching and learning repertoire. In some cases they do so with spectacular results.

At Headfield Church of England Junior School in Dewsbury, England, brain breaks are used as an integral part of some classes. Children were given weekly record charts to log the time spent on brain-break exercises at home as well as identify how many cups of water they were drinking. The children in Year 4 were taking part in a controlled experiment with their teacher, Alweena Zairi, as part of a research thesis on alternative learning led by Vicky Grossman.

Alweena's Year 4 class of 30 children had their reading ages taken in Year 3 and then again in Year 4. NFER tests were used. Three of the children had no reading score in Year 3, and only four children had reading ages above their chronological age. At the end of Year 4 all children had reading scores and 12 had scores above their chronological age. Among the improvements were improvements of 13, 15, 16, 17, 18, 18, 20, 21, 33, 31, 25 and 39 months, with the average improvement being 12.5 months. Alweena is convinced that using brain breaks and providing opportunities for drinking water contributed in significant ways to the improvement. Alweena is by nature a modest person but we were able to discover that she occasionally helps others use the ideas. Here is an excerpt from a thank you letter she received after introducing the brain-break ideas to a Year 6 teacher:

Following your visit I have used brain gym and magic spelling with my classes not just in English but in maths and science. The difference it has made is spectacular ... In English, children such as Q, R and A were able to achieve level 4 spelling. Others (I, K, I and H) showed a remarkable improvement. Some children are limited by their poor English and because it is not spoken at home. They were struggling with even the reception list words. Now they have progressed through the Y1 and Y2 lists successfully. R in particular is a changed person. This once elective mute pupil now puts his hand up and correctly answers questions in front of the whole set!

In maths I used the brain gym ideas to calm and focus the children ... it helped eliminate careless mistakes. The scores in SATs were the best ever:

'We all have ability. The difference is how we use it.' (Stevie Wonder)

The 'Give It A Go Club' meets here on weekdays

In 1999, Set 1 scored 13 @ Level 5, 12 @ Level 4
In 2000 Set 1 scored 6 @ Level 6, 20 @ Level 5

In science I adapted magic spelling for revision purposes. I made graphic posters summarizing key facts and used them as flash cards, both for the facts and as triggers to further information. As a result the SATs were outstanding:

In 1999, Set 1 scored 22/32 @ Level 5, 10/32 @ Level 4
In 2000 Set 1 scored 31/32 @ Level 5, 1/32 missing by just 6 marks!

Thank you so much for your help and expertise ...

Use brain breaks to provide reprieve from physical stress, enhance fine and large motor movement, improve co-ordination and laterality and link to learning. You can also use brain breaks to begin morning and afternoon sessions, to learn shapes of numbers and letters, to improve graphicacy and to displace unhelpful preoccupations.

Seventy examples of brain-break activities

1 Practise yawning! Stretch your mouth as wide as you can. Stick your chin out and move it from side to side.
2 Practise rolling your head in circles: slowly one way, then slowly the other way.
3 Practise rolling your eyes in circles: slowly one way, then slowly the other way.
4 Close your eyelids and try it again.
5 Hold your ears and slowly roll your ear lobes between finger and thumb.
6 Hold your ears with your opposite hand and slowly roll your ear lobes between finger and thumb.
7 Make a steeple with your fingers in front of your face, now lift each pair of fingers together starting with your index fingers. Keep your lips and teeth together.
8 Make a steeple with your fingers in front of your face, now lift each pair of fingers together starting with your index fingers. Count quietly aloud as you do so.
9 With your forefinger and thumb of each hand pinched together, extend your hands out in front of your face and trace large circles in the same direction. Keep your lips and teeth together.
10 With your forefinger and thumb of each hand pinched together, extend your hands out in front of your face and trace large circles in the opposite direction. Keep your lips and teeth together.
11 Stand with a partner shoulder to shoulder, now move apart so that you can touch the tips of your forefingers. Now try to trace a circle together.
12 Stand with a partner shoulder to shoulder, now move apart so that you can touch the tips of your forefingers. Now try to trace different shapes together. Agree on what shape and its size beforehand.

'A jug fills drop by drop.' (Buddha)

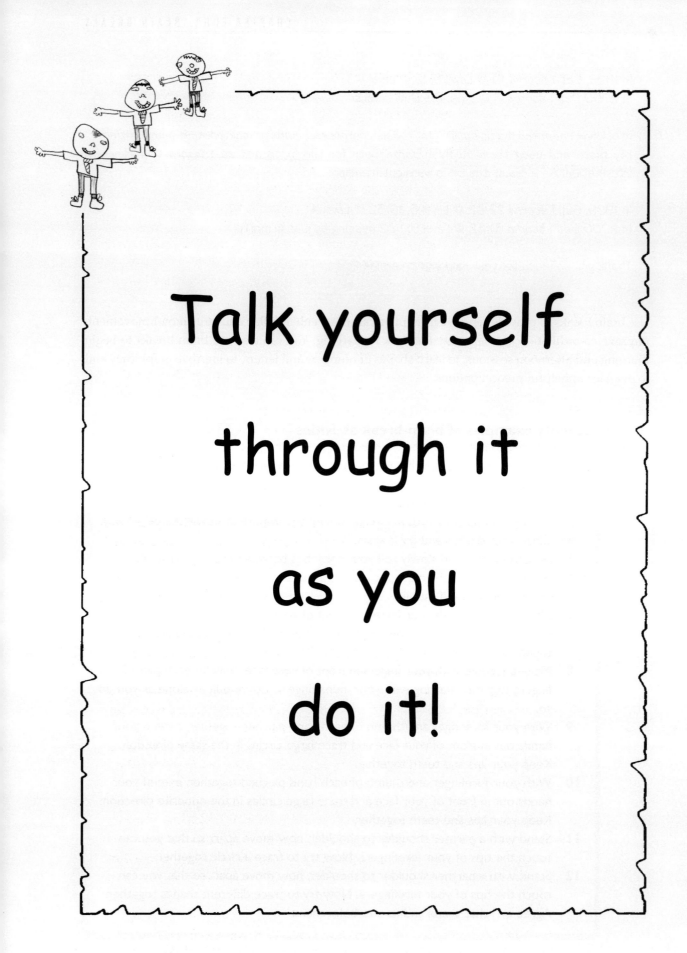

Talk yourself

through it

as you

do it!

13   Practise shrugging your shoulders slowly forwards, then slowly backwards.

14   With your elbows at shoulder height, practise making big circles, then small circles, forwards and backwards.

15   Practise good breathing – deep and slow. Count in and count out. Do not hold your breath, just breathe deeply.

16   Practise good breathing for ten breaths – deep and slow. Count in and count out. Do not hold your breath, just breath deeply.

17   Practise placing your feet flat on the floor, now gently rock onto your heels, now back onto your toes.

18   Sitting in your seat with your hands holding the seat, extend your feet forwards and rotate your feet together one way then the other.

19   Sitting in your seat with your hands holding the seat, extend your feet forwards and rotate your feet in opposite directions.

20   Stand up tall and in a space to yourself. Bend gently from the waist and stretch your fingers towards your toes.

21   Stand up tall and in a space to yourself. Place one foot out in front and flat on the floor, slide the other foot back with just your toes touching. Bend gently at the knee and stretch carefully.

22   Swap over and concentrate on stretching the other way.

23   Write the keywords from the lesson in the air with one hand.

24   Write the keywords from the lesson in the air with two hands held together.

25   Trace circles in the air with two hands held together. Follow your hand movements with your eyes only. Keep your head still. Keep your lips and teeth together.

26   Trace the number 8 in the air with two hands held together. Follow your hand movements with your eyes only. Keep your head still. Keep your lips and teeth together.

27   Trace the number 8 on its side in the air with two hands held together. Follow your hand movements with your eyes only. Keep your head still. Keep your lips and teeth together.

28   Face a partner so you cannot touch each other and draw their outline in the air with two hands held together. Follow your hand movements with your eyes only. Keep your head still. Keep your lips and teeth together.

29   With a partner sit either side of a desk. Your partner should place both hands flat on the desk. With your finger and thumb 'draw' round the shape of their hands. Do it three times forwards and backwards, then swap.

30   With a partner sit either side of a desk. Your partner should place both hands flat on the desk and so should you. Take turns to lift different fingers without taking any other fingers off the desk. The partner has five seconds to lift exactly the same finger from the same hand.

31   Do finger aerobics! With a partner sit alongside each other or either side of a desk. Your partner should place both hands flat on the desk and so should you. Take turns to lift different fingers without taking any other fingers off the desk. Do it together and in sequence. Start with simple lifts with each finger in turn, then do taps, then go for bends, then big stretches!

32   With a partner sit either side of a desk. Place your elbows on the desk against your partner's. Your partner places his hands either side of yours with open palms. You have to push your hands out without moving your elbows.

'You are never a loser until you quit trying.' (Mike Ditka)

33 Swap with your partner and now try again.

34 With a partner sit on chairs facing each other with your knees and toes touching. Hold hands over the middle. Slowly try these actions: raising a flag, swatting a fly, serving at a tennis match, driving a bus with a large steering wheel, boxing, picking up a very delicate flower. Hold hands all the time. Stay seated.

35 Place your right hand above your head and then slowly take it down your back as far as it will comfortably go. Now with your left hand hold your right elbow gently.

36 Swap hands and try again.

37 Try tickling yourself! Does it work? Try different places!

38 With your right thumb and forefinger pinch your nose, and with your left thumb and forefinger hold your right ear. Now swap and swap again.

39 Touch your forefingers together out from the front of your face. Touch the tips of the outstretched fingers together. Now rotate in a circle but in opposite directions.

40 Try the same thing with your arms! Rotate them at the same time in wide circles from the shoulder but in opposite directions.

41 Write the keywords from the lesson in the air with your nose.

42 Write the keywords from the lesson in the air with your right ear.

43 Write the keywords from the lesson in the air with your left ear.

44 Try all the above with your eyes closed and saying the letters of the keyword to yourself as you go.

45 Write the keywords from the lesson on your partner's back and see if they can guess what you wrote.

46 Write out letters in the air and say their names and sounds.

47 Write the alphabet in the air as fast as you can, or do it all together while singing an alphabet song.

48 Stand on one leg while you write the alphabet in the air.

49 Stand opposite a partner and place your palms against your partner's palms, then make big sweeping shapes together in the air.

50 Stand opposite a partner and place your palms against your partner's palms, then make the letters of the alphabet together in the air.

51 Stand opposite a partner and place your palms against your partner's palms, then make the numbers 1–20 together in the air.

52 Swap sides and do it again. What happens?

53 Write your name in the air – write it big, write it small, backwards, forwards and with left hand and right hand, then with both.

54 Take it in turns to come to the board – fast – and write up one word each from the lesson, handing the chalk or pen to the next person before sitting down.

55 Conduct a timed piece of music as if you were the key character from history or the story – do it in the way that you imagine he or she would behave.

56 Mime a conversation with a partner, as if you were the character from history or the story.

57 Imagine that you are the character from the story and mime one of his or her activities. For example, if you are Cinderella, scrub the floor, or if you are the Fairy Godmother, wave your wand and make some spells.

'Many of life's failures are people who did not realise how close they were to success when they gave up.' (Thomas A. Edison)

58 Mime an everyday activity around school or in the house. For example, changing a light bulb, washing dishes, changing a nappy or choosing lunch. Do so only with the upper part of your body and standing still. Ask your partner to guess what it is.

59 Create a 60-second roleplay to demonstrate a key part of the lesson.

60 With a partner, make numbers with your bodies. Work your way from one to ten.

61 Make 2D shapes with your body – a square, circle, rectangle, octagon.

62 Make 3D shapes with a partner – a cube, sphere, cylinder.

63 Rotate your arms to represent angles, 90 degrees, 180 degrees, or turn a full circle for 360 degrees.

64 Rotate your arms to represent the time. Ask your partner to guess what time it is. Do not cheat!

65 Following your teacher's directions, jump back and forth to represent multiplication or division.

66 Ask the teacher to practise 'teacher says' with you. The teacher makes a movement and you copy it. If the teacher says 'do this', you do it. If the teacher says 'do that', you don't do it! Make sure you listen carefully.

67 On a partner's back do gentle chops with the back of your hand. Do them across your partner's back but do it gently.

68 On a partner's back do gentle squeezes with your fingers. Do it across your partner's back but do it gently.

69 Put your hands together and clap. Now move your hands in a circle as you clap. You have just given yourself a round of applause.

70 Put your hand on your back. Now give yourself a big pat and say 'well done'.

Useful apparatus for brain-break activities

* Large foam hands such as those you see at football matches
* Plastic blow-up bananas, cod, hammers, hats – again of the sort seen at football matches
* Glove puppets
* Koosh balls
* Bean bags
* Skipping ropes
* Beach ball
* Wobble board
* Skateboard

'Perseverance is not a long race; it is many short races one after another.' (Walter Elliott)

> **Ten indicators that your class needs a brain break**
>
> 1 You have to remind the class twice of the agreed noise level for the lesson.
> 2 Your delivery of RAP has become increasingly deliberate.
> 3 You have to scan the class constantly while speaking to groups or individuals.
> 4 You cannot continue with a task and have to patrol the classroom.
> 5 You have to redirect a child or group more than twice in two minutes.
> 6 The children queuing at your desk become restless.
> 7 You have to deal with children's disagreements.
> 8 Children are out of their seats unnecessarily.
> 9 A glance around the room reveals several children being off task.
> 10 You start to feel stressed!

Laugh a minute for a sense of belonging

Laughter and humour are essential elements of the ALPS classroom, where learning takes place without put-downs and students take risks and learn from mistakes. Brain breaks are used to relax, revitalize or refocus.

In *The ALPS Approach* we give some suggestions for fun brain-break activities. Here are ten more laugh a minute brain breaks.

1 Funny Faces

Practise with the class making three faces: really happy, really sad and really puzzled. You can add actions to this, such as thumbs up for happy, down for sad and pointing to your head for puzzled. The children stand up, while you stand at the front. Turn to face away from them and when you turn back, do so pulling one of these three faces. The children must all try to guess which face you will pull and must pull one to match. If they pull the same face as you, they score a point. Alternatively, this brain break can be done in pairs or groups, or a child can be chosen to stand at the front and lead. You can race to three correct guesses, or sit down when you have been incorrect twice, or simply just repeat a few times until everybody is laughing!

2 The Orchestra

Select a particularly rousing piece of classical music. Organize the class into groups and tell each group which instrument they are to mime playing, leaving them to 'warm-up' as you move on to the next group. Once every group in the orchestra has tuned their instrument, put on the music and conduct the orchestra as they play. Alternatively, choose children to conduct groups or the whole orchestra. You can add to the fun by conducting with walking sticks, board rubbers, streamers or children's ties! Ensure that your performance comes to a dramatic finale and that everybody applauds and takes a bow!

'Some men give up their designs when they have almost reached the goal; while others, on the contrary, obtain a victory by exerting, at the last moment, more vigorous efforts than ever before.' (Herodotus)

3   Balloon Research

This is an extremely successful once-only brain break for a group of older children, or a group of adults! Tell the class that you are going to demonstrate a vital scientific principle and do some research for the Guinness Book of Records. This is an extremely important experiment and could have very great consequences for world scientific knowledge. Really go to town, stressing the seriousness of this activity. Organize the class into several research groups and elect a leader of each group. You can even give each leader a badge. The more groups you have, the more fun you will all have when the experiment begins. Blow up several balloons, but do not tie them. Hand one balloon to the leader of each research group. Tell them to hold the balloons tightly until you have explained the task.

Finally, explain the task, which is to see whose balloon will make the loudest noises as they all let them go and watch them whizz around the classroom!

4   Mystery Prize

Blow up several balloons and inside put token prizes or a written message. Organize the children into small groups, and give each group a balloon. They are to place the balloon on the floor and sit together back-to-back on it until it bursts. They then take the prizes, or carry out the task or forfeit!

5   The Rolf Harris Challenge

Divide the class into two teams. Each team needs a large area on which to draw, such as a flip chart, half the whiteboard, or a large sheet of paper taped to the wall. By each team, put a selection of coloured marker pens. Give the children a challenge, such as:

☆   an elephant taking tea

☆   a rhino having a bubble bath

☆   a rabbit getting married

☆   a gorilla mowing the lawn.

Each team must draw a picture. Children take it in turns to go to the board, draw for about ten seconds, then touch hands with the next player, who goes to the board to take his turn. Use a funny instrument or hooter to make the signal to swap places and keep the pace fast. Each child should have long enough to draw a little, but the fun is from the feeling of speed. Work out a system for ensuring that turns are taken and tell the children that at any time you will blow the final hooter and the game will be over!

6   The Body Part Game

This is a simple game that leads to a lot of giggles and fun. Tell the children to imagine, for example, that their hands were their feet. They then have to demonstrate how they would do various tasks, such as:

✳   eat their dinner

✳   do their writing

✳   wash their hair

✳   cut their finger nails.

'It's a little like wrestling a gorilla. You don't quit when you're tired, you quit when the gorilla is tired.' (Robert Strauss)

There are endless possibilities for this game, such as imagining that their eyes were no longer on their faces, but on their knees; their ears on their feet; or their noses on their elbows. Give just a few moments for trying out each position, and then move on to keep the interest and the laughter buzzing!

7   The Silly Sound Game

For this brain-break activity you need a variety of instruments for making funny sound effects. Hooters, whistles, rattles and party poppers are better than proper musical instruments, especially if they are visual, in addition to making silly noises. If you do not have enough for every child, create a few funny verbal noises for those without an instrument and swap around so that everybody has a turn at making sound effects.

The children all need to be able to see a piece of text. This could be written on the board, on an overhead projector, on individual sheets, or in books. The more fun the text, the more laughter you will generate, although this activity can also be done with serious material as a part of a lesson. Assign each of your funny sound effects to a particular high frequency word, a name that you want everyone to remember, or to a punctuation mark. You can also add actions for groups or the whole class. For example:

.	one toot on whistle
,	hooter
!	party popper
?	everyone stand up and scratch their heads
and	rattle
"	clap clap

You can choose to display the code, to group the children, or to have every child make every sound effect. As long as everyone is involved as you read through the text together, you will generate a lot of laughter and fun.

8   Musical Accompaniment

Give out a selection of silly instruments such as blowers, hooters and drums to half the class. Ask the other half to stand together and form a choir. Suggest a well-known song for them to sing and tell the rest of the class to accompany them. They must watch you as they do so, as you will be conducting and telling each group of musicians when to hoot or bang. The more imaginative you are with the instruments, and the more dramatically you conduct your musicians, the more fun the class will have!

9   The Backwards Walk

Give some of the class baseball caps and tell them to put them on backwards. They are team leaders. Their job is to take their group for a backwards walk, holding one another's shoulders or waist. You can add a few little conga steps as they go!

10   Stand-up Comedians

Create a list of one-line jokes. You can start with the list opposite. The cornier the jokes, the better! Tell the class to stand up. Give one child the list and a silly hat. He then stands at the front of the class and quickly reads one joke aloud. He then goes back to his place, giving the list and hat to someone else, who quickly comes to the front, reads a joke, then returns to his place, giving the hat and list to someone else. Keep up the pace, help poorer readers to read or let them do a joke with a

'Oh man! There is no planet sun or star could hold you, if you but knew what you are.'
(Ralph Waldo Emerson)

friend. If necessary, organize the list to have better readers go first or last, and include some familiar, well-known jokes. It is important that this is quick and fun, so help out where necessary and keep the children moving fast. Take it in turns until everyone has had a turn and the whole class is in fits of giggles!

Twenty Jokes

1	What do you call a pig's curly tail?	A porkscrew
2	What is green and lumpy and flies through the air?	SuperPickle
3	What do cats eat on a hot day?	Mice cream
4	What do cats eat for breakfast?	Mice crispies
5	What did the ocean say to the other ocean?	Nothing, it just waved
6	What did the rabbit say to the other rabbit?	Nothing, rabbits can't talk
7	What has four wheels and flies?	A dustcart
8	How do you know an elephant has been in your fridge?	Footmarks in the butter
9	How do you know an elephant has been in the cupboard?	Footmarks in the jam
10	What do snowmen have for breakfast?	Snow flakes
11	Why do bees hum?	They don't know the tune
12	What is green, two feet tall and has wheels?	Grass – I lied about the wheels
13	Why can't you play cards in the jungle?	There are too many cheetahs
14	What is grey and has a tail and a trunk?	A mouse going on holiday
15	What is brown and has a tail and a trunk?	A mouse returning from holiday
16	What do you get if you cross a pig with a zebra?	Striped sausages
17	What is yellow and jumps from cake to cake?	Tarzipan
18	Where does a sheep go to get a haircut?	The baa-baa shop
19	What do you call a blind dinosaur?	Doyouthinkesauras
20	What do you call a blind dinosaur's dog?	Doyouthinkesauras Rex

'Personally I'm going to skip learning and go straight to knowing.' (Charlie Brown)

Put on your memory

See it
Personalize it
Exaggerate it
Connect it
Share it

Music in the classroom

Music has a number of applications in accelerating learning all of which are secondary to following the discipline of the Accelerated Learning Cycle. Too often music gets talked about as though it was the essence of the accelerated learning methods. It is not. In the context of accelerated learning it is a tool that can be used to enhance aspects of the learning experience.

In 1984 at the University of California, Irvine, Gordon Shaw and Frances Rauscher completed an experiment using a piece of music played to control groups before they undertook a mathematical activity that involved mental rehearsals of spatial and rotational symmetries. The control groups were 'primed' in various ways before undertaking the task. In some cases the priming involved music and, in particular, the Sonata for Two Pianos in D by Wolfgang Amadeus Mozart. The performance of this control group improved considerably and the 'Mozart Effect' was born. The subsequent misinterpretations have led to a situation where the effect of music on learning and on intelligence has become obscured by commercial imperatives. Boxed sets of pieces with titles like 'Baroque a Bye Baby' sum it up. Music on its own does not provide a short-cut to enhanced academic ability.

A very specific use is to demarcate time on task. To get you started and to remind us that it is not all intended to be serious here are two everyday school tasks with some appropriate pieces of pop music for each.

Task	Song	Artist(s)	Year
Moving classroom furniture	Move It	Cliff Richard	1958
	Move Mania	Sash	1998
	Movin on Up	M People	1994
	Pick up the Pieces	Average White Band	1975
Getting changed for PE lessons	Move that Body	Technotronic	1991
	Baggy Trousers	Madness	1980
	Born to Run	Bruce Springsteen	1980
	Change	Lightning Seeds	1995

'The way we choose to see the world determines what we find important in that world.'

Nine ways to use music in the classroom

1   Music with a measured and light quality for entering the classroom.

2   Music to accompany brain breaks.

3   Music to accompany a class review or connect activity.

4   Music for accompanying the development of memory maps.

5   Music for tidy-up activities.

6   Music for timed challenges.

7   Music for concert reviews at the end of the day or at the end of the week.

8   Music for relaxation and guided visualizations.

9   Music for ritualizing achievements such as target terminator awards.

Thirteen ways to use music to enhance learning

Here are some uses, some specific applications and some suggestions of musical pieces to use in your classroom.

This list of music was compiled with the help of Phillip Davis, teacher at Bannockburn Primary School, Plumstead. It also drew on suggestions made by Elizabeth Miles in her book *Tune Your Brain*.

1   Beginnings

Music has a powerful influence on mood and atmosphere. Choose from the following list for entry music on arrival in the classroom to create an appropriate atmosphere.

Sonata for Two Pianos in D	Wolfgang Amadeus Mozart
Jupiter Suite (*The Planets*)	Gustav Holst
Paganini for Two (*performers: Shaham and Sollscher*)	Nicolo Paganini
Paco De Lucia	(Flamenco music)
Parce mihi domine (*Officium*)	Jan Garbarek and the Hilliard ensemble
The Power of Goodbye (*Ray of Light*)	Madonna
The Universal (*The Great Escape*)	Blur
What Have You Done Today To Make You Feel Proud (*M People's Greatest Hits*)	M People

2   Demarcation of time on task

You can use music to set up a timed challenge. Set a challenge for the class such as, 'For the duration of this piece of music, I'd like you in pairs to think of as many words as you can about the topic we did last week. The music is the Theme Tune to *Mission Impossible*. It lasts three minutes and that's how long you have.' Or use a piece of music to provide a more relaxed timeframe for an activity.

Flight of the Bumble Bee	Nicholas Rimsky-Korsakof
Bolero	Maurice Ravel
The Best of Louis Jordan	Louis Jordan
Everyday is a Winding Road (*Sheryl Crow*)	Sheryl Crow

'Can you imagine what I would do if I could do all I can?'
(The artist formerly known as Prince)

Wannabe — Spice girls
Connected (*Connected*) — Stereo MCs
Theme tune from *Mission Impossible*
Theme tune from *Match of the Day*

3   Enhancing a mood

Music can be used to make a qualitative change in the atmosphere in the classroom. For example, when celebrations are taking place in the ALPS classroom, an appropriate piece of accompanying music anchors the experience, such as the rock band Queen's song 'We Are The Champions!'

The Hallelujah Chorus (*Messiah*)	George Freiderich Handel
No. 1 Hits – The Glenn Miller Band	The Glenn Miller Band
We Have All The Time In The World (*Greatest Hits*)	Louis Armstrong
Oh What a Beautiful Morning (*Oklahoma*)	Doris Day
The Hills are Alive (*The Sound of Music*)	Rodgers and Hammerstein
Greatest Hits	Gypsy Kings
20 Greatest Hits	Creedence Clearwater Revival
Holiday	Madonna
Tubthumping	Chumbawamba
Reach for the Stars	Steps
Stronger	Britney Spears

4   Energizers

When you wish to clean the classroom quickly, Rossini's *William Tell Overture* can help speed the class along. The pieces listed immediately below are definitely energizing!

March of the Toreadors (*Carmen*)	George Bizet
Movement 2, Suite No. 2 D (*Water Music*)	George Freidrich Handel
Rock and Roll (*Led Zeppelin IV*)	Led Zeppelin
Song 2 (*13*)	Blur
Roll With It	Oasis
Blowing Bubbles (*Sense*)	The Lightning Seeds
Alphabet Street (*The Hits 1*)	Prince
Nothing Really Matters (*Ray of Light*)	Madonna
Australia (*Everything Must Go*)	Manic Street Preachers
Hoodoo Voodoo (*Mermaid Avenue*)	Billy Bragg and Wilco Johnson
Let Me Entertain You	Robbie Williams

5   Relaxers

If you wish to relax after PE, or before the class begins on a piece of creative writing, try listening to music to relax and change the children's mood.

Symphony of Sorrowful Songs (Symphony No. 3)	Henryk Gorecki
Symphony No. 6	Ludwig Van Beethoven
Intermezzi Op. 118 No. 2 and Op. 117 No. 1	Johannes Brahms
Nocturnes	Frederic Chopin
Piano Music Volume 1	Eric Satie
The Goldberg Variations	Johann Sebastian Bach
Imagination	Gladys Knight and the Pips
Rapture (*Rapture*)	Anita Baker

'How far is far, how high is high? We'll never know until we try.' (Song from the California Special Olympics)

Watermark (*Watermark*)	Enya
The Visit	Loreena McKennitt
The Air That I Breathe	The Hollies

6   Music for guided visualizations

Music can be used to enhance the guided visualizations described in earlier chapters. The music provides the background for relaxation and helps children to focus on the visualization.

Air (Suite for Orchestra No. 3)	Johann Sebastian Bach
Symphonies No. 94, 100 and 101	Franz Joseph Haydn
Preludes to the Afternoon of the Faun	Pierre Boulez
Clarinet Quintet in A	Wolfgang Amadeus Mozart
Four Last Songs	Richard Strauss
The Four Seasons	Vivaldi
Celtic Treasure: The Legacy of Turlough O'Carolan	Celtic Treasure
The Celtic Harp: A Tribute to Edward Bunting	The Chieftains

7   As an aid to discussion

On a very practical level music can be used for background to provide an appropriate atmosphere for discussions in class. When you lower the volume of the music the level of noise in the class goes down accordingly. It is difficult to shout across the class and expect to be heard, but a student can, nevertheless, listen to other students nearby as they talk through an activity.

Aretha Gospel	Aretha Franklin
Totus Tuus (*Ikos*)	Gorecki
Space March (*Themology*)	John Barry
Scenes from a Café	Penguin Café Orchestra
Life is a Rollercoaster	Ronan Keating
Never had a Dream Come True	S Club 7

8   Evocation of a theme

A theme being explored in class can be enhanced by related music. Period music from the time of the Tudors could be used as a stimulus activity, or as an accompaniment to artwork, or used as part of review of content. Another good source is theme music from well-known films.

Love Scene (*Romeo and Juliet*)	Hector Berlioz
Fantasies, Airs and Dances	The Julian Bream Consort
Theme tune to *Braveheart*	
Anthology	Ennio Morricone
Out of Africa (*Themology*)	John Barry
Dark Side of the Moon	Pink Floyd
Big Yellow Taxi	Joni Mitchell
American Pie	Don MacLean/Madonna

9   Active concert

This is a specific application of music in relation to accelerated learning. The teacher reads information to the class while dramatic and emotionally engaging music is played. The best time to do this is after you have given the Big Picture and before detailed work begins. Your voice should

'Learn as though you would never be able to master it; hold it as though you would be in fear of losing it.' (Confucius)

'surf' the music, rising and falling appropriately while the students follow the information in written form. The music creates emotional associations and simultaneously connects left and right brain. Music by Brahms, Rachmaninoff, Beethoven, Tchaikovsky and Haydn is suitable, while some more contemporary pieces can be used to good effect.

Symphonies No. 1 and 2	Ludwig Van Beethoven
Symphonies No. 42, 45 and 46	Franz Joseph Haydn
Lifeboat (*Union Café*)	Penguin Café Orchestra
Sonnerie de Ste Genevieve du Mont de Paris	M. Marais
(*Tous les Matins du Monde*)	
Tocatta and Fugue in D Minor	Johann Sebastian Bach

10   Passive concert

This is another specific application of music in relation to accelerated learning and it is used following the active concert. The passive concert can take place as a review at the end of the lesson. The material presented can be the same as the active concert but the method of presenting it and the intended outcome differ. The students settle into a state of 'relaxed awareness' while listening to slower pieces of music such as some baroque pieces with less rigorously structured qualities. Students should listen to the music while you read naturally. The passive concert is a concluding activity intended to encode and sublimate the material into the brain.

Adagio in G Minor	Tomaso Albinoni
Symphony No. 38	Wolfgang Amadeus Mozart
The Art of the Fugue	Johann Sebastian Bach
Concerto for Two Harpsichords	Johann Sebastian Bach
The Four Seasons	Antonio Vivaldi
Vivaldi Guitar Concertos	Antonio Vivaldi
The Piano	Michael Nyman
The Wall	Pink Floyd

11   To enhance brain breaks

Music can appropriately accompany the physical activity of a brain break. Compilations of current pop pieces are good here, as are:

Rondo (Sonata Concertata Ms. 2 – *Paganini for Two*)	Nicolo Paganini
Rondo (Eine Kleine Nachtmusik)	Wolfgang Amadeus Mozart
That's the Way I Like It (*Best of KC and the Sunshine Band*)	KC and the Sunshine Band
The Immaculate Collection	Madonna
I Feel Good (*James Brown's Greatest Hits*)	James Brown
Take it Easy (*Eagles Greatest Hits*)	The Eagles
I'll Take You There (*Top of the Stax: Twenty Greatest Hits*)	The Staples Singers
Free Bird	Lynyrd Skynyrd
Kick	INXS
Wooly Bully	Sam the Sham and the Pharaohs
Macarena	Los Del Rio
Mambo No. 5	Lou Bega
The Only Way is Up	Yazz
La Bamba	Los Lobos
Let's Twist Again	Chubby Checker
Dancing Queen	Abba

'To give yourself the best possible chance of playing to your potential, you must prepare for every eventuality. That means practice.' (Seve Ballesteros, world champion golfer)

12   Endings

There are two possible applications for music for endings. First, for practical purposes like 'clean-ups' use upbeat and humorous pieces: 'No one can finish doing the class clean-up until the music stops.' Use the music to change the atmosphere, elevate the mood and get the jobs done more efficiently. Second, use music to provide a sense of closure. As you review the day or introduce the To Do list for the next day, ending music can help ritualize the moment. Use familiar pieces to embed this sense of completion.

Fourth Movement of Symphony No. 8	Gustav Mahler
Things Can Only Get Better (*M People's Greatest Hits*)	M People
Theme tune to the *Lion King*	
Beat It (*Thriller*)	Michael Jackson
Everybody Wants to Rule the World	Tears for Fears

13   Learning with music to enhance our ability to store and retrieve related information

Content is more readily recalled when learned to musical accompaniment. There are many familiar tunes that can be used for learning key facts to music, or you can compose tunes yourself. Once children are familiar with this activity, they can create their own rhymes to music to accelerate their learning. In order to exploit all aspects of VAK, a large poster or individual word sheets should be used and actions added to give a physical feel for the information. These activities then can be used as brain breaks or to fill 'dead time'.

Here are 20 tunes that can be used for this activity. Limit their application to your own classroom. Some of these tunes are subject to copyright legislation.

1   My Darlin' Clementine
2   The Grand Old Duke of York
3   My Old Man's A Dustman (Lonnie Donnegan)
4   Dem Bones, Dem Bones
5   Sur la pont D'Avignon
6   Frere Jacques
7   If You're Happy and You Know It Clap Your Hands
8   Michael Row the Boat Ashore
9   Somewhere over the Rainbow
10   Kumbaya my lord
11   Doh a Deer, a Female Deer
12   I'm Singin' in the Rain
13   Theme tune to Dambusters
14   Two Little Boys
15   One Man Went to Mow
16   Theme tune to Rawhide
17   Swing Low, Sweet Chariot
18   Ten Green Bottles
19   Oh You'll never get to Heaven
20   Theme tune to Eastenders, Neighbours or any other soap opera

'When I was young, I never wanted to leave the court until I got things exactly correct. My dream was to become a pro.' (Larry Bird, US basketball star)

Review of Part Two

✔ When you have taken the five STEPS to National Curriculum target setting, consider what major obstacles were in the path for the children in your class. Were there any that were common to more than one or two children? Note the obstacles and their frequency on a chart such as the one below. Discuss the results with your colleagues. Were there common themes, such as poor reading skills, poor attitudes to homework or lateness or attendance issues? Decide what you might do as a team to address these problems as a whole school.

Obstacle	Frequency tally

✔ Work with a colleague to set up a display area in your classroom for information about targets, such as to display rules, targets, set Target Challenges or recognize Target Terminators. Then work in her classroom to do the same.

✔ Keep a notebook on your desk for a week and make a note of any negative comments made in your classroom. Then reframe them as positives. Discuss the process with the class and show them how you did this. Try playing games where children have to turn negatives into positives, or give a forfeit for every negative spoken and an award for every positive!

✔ Plan five ways that you could actively promote the language of progression in your classroom. Team up with another colleague if it makes it easier.

Action plan for promoting the language of progression in my classroom
1
2
3
4
5

✔ Using either our suggestions or creating codes of your own, make a list of the marking codes that you could use with your class. Put the list on the wall and tell the children that it is a trial. Practise using them for a set time, then report back to colleagues. Decide on a school set of marking codes, graduating from simple for younger children to more complex for the older pupils.

✔ Consider the use of grades and scores in your classroom. Decide on two ways that you could use feedback to motivate your pupils. Try them out for a few weeks, then feedback to colleagues about the results.

✔ Consider our key questions for drawing up a homework policy. How does your homework policy measure against these questions? Give a score between 1 and 10 for each statement and discuss the results with colleagues.

1	We communicate our homework policy to children.	
2	We communicate our homework policy to parents.	
3	There is a consistent approach to the type and amount of homework given throughout the school.	
4	We ensure that children understand homework tasks.	
5	We teach children how to approach homework tasks.	
6	We work to motivate children to complete homework.	
7	We have systems for monitoring the completion of homework tasks.	
8	We have systems for monitoring the quality of homework tasks.	
9	We give recognition to children who complete tasks.	
10	We encourage children to do additional tasks voluntarily at home.	
11	We teach study and research skills.	
12	We provide for children whose homes are not conducive to completing homework.	
13	We communicate with parents about appropriate methods for helping with homework.	
14	We have a consistent policy for action if a child does not complete homework.	
15	We monitor consistency in following the homework policy across age groups.	

✔ Create a method for planning for brain breaks and recording the information on planning documents.

✔ Calculate approximately how many brain breaks your class took last week. If it was not sufficient, analyse why. Were you in too much of a hurry to deliver content? Do you find it difficult to remember to take breaks, or to think of activities when you realize that the class needs a break? Try making a 'Brain-Break Menu' display for the classroom wall – see our example below. Ask children for suggestions and allow them opportunities to choose brain breaks from the menu during lessons.

BRAIN-BREAK MENU	
Subject	Brain-Break Activity

✔ Consider the use of music in your school. Ask every teacher to create a 'wish list' of the resources that would help her to make better use of music in her classroom. Work as a team to add this to your School Development Plan.

✔ Trial one of our 13 ways to use music in the classroom. You may wish to trial a different use of music in your classroom – or you may prefer to work in pairs. Give feedback at a staff meeting to colleagues and learn from one another's experiences.

Part Three

The learning journey

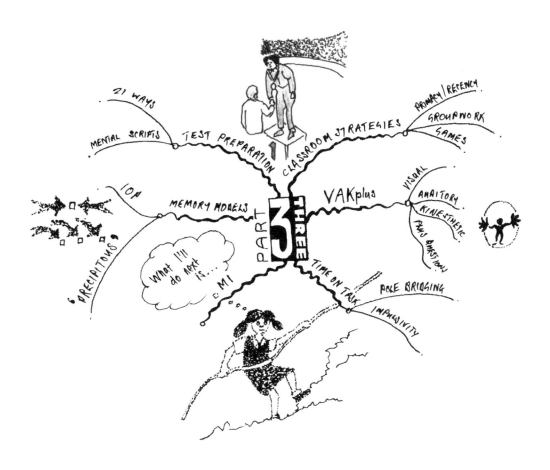

In Part Three you will:

* be given some ideas about how to maximize learning in your classroom by exploiting the primacy and recency effect and find out some of the best group-work strategies;
* learn how to use VAK – visual, auditory and kinesthetic learning in your classroom – and be given suggestions about how to plan for VAKPlus;
* consider how to structure the time spent on task, how to teach pole-bridging and how to help children learn to manage the moment of impulse;
* be given suggestions about how to teach for the different sorts of intelligences in your classroom;
* read about a model of memory and how to use it in your classroom;
* consider how to ensure that children are successful and confident in standardized testing and assessments.

Key vocabulary for Part Three:

Furniture teams	Positive starts	Reconstruction rather than recall
Managing impulsivity	Precipitous	Structured variety in group-work
Multiple intelligence	Primacy and recency	VAKplus
Pole-bridging		

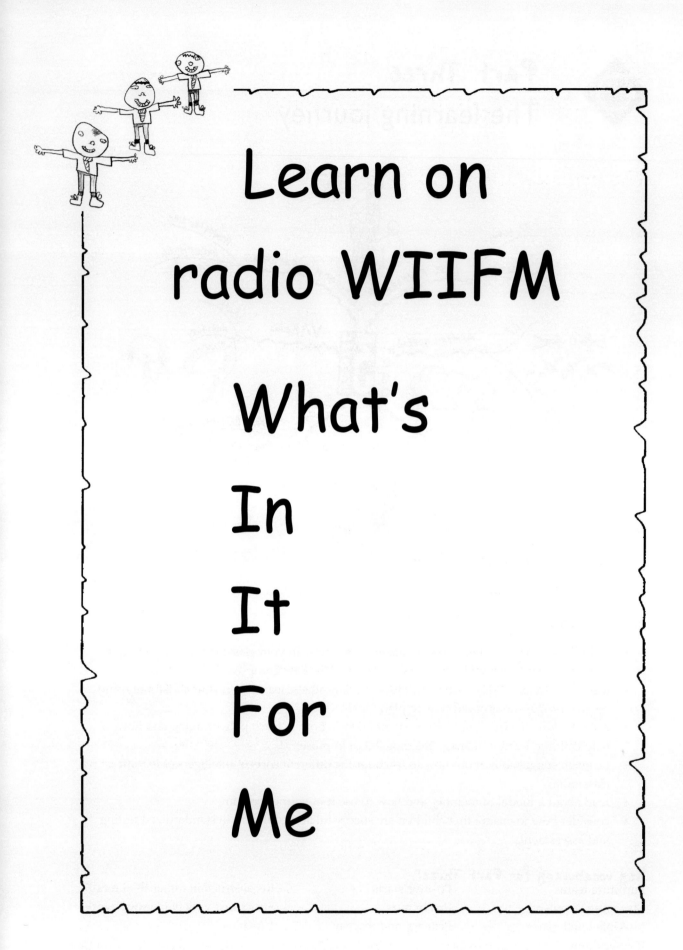

Learn on radio WIIFM

What's

In

It

For

Me

Using beginnings and endings

The primacy and recency effect

Research has shown that humans seem to assign significance to the beginning or the ending of an experience. Our curiosity tends to be engaged at the beginning of an experience and we derive satisfaction from the sense of its ending. Some memory researchers refer to this as the 'primacy and recency effect'. It is therefore essential that you clear space for the significant moments of primacy and recency and give value to beginnings and endings.

Five ways to maximize the primacy and recency effect on learning in your classroom

1 Begin lessons on time and positively.
2 Immediately direct children's thinking about what they are going to do and how.
3 Throughout the lesson provide lots of 'mini' beginnings and endings.
4 Ensure that key content is given during a beginning or an ending, or a 'mini' one during the lesson.
5 Stop each lesson early for a variety of short, participative review activities.

How to give the Big Picture

1 Say what you are going to do and how you are going to do it.
2 Make the processes that you have chosen to use explicit.
3 Display the information visually as you talk to help the visual learners.
4 Check for understanding at each stage.
5 Ensure that you identify both process and content.
6 Begin to embed open-ended questions to encourage pre-processing at a number of levels.
7 Identify and assign significance to the key vocabulary.
8 Use child-centred connecting activities to engage prior understanding.

How to start positively and stay there

To start positively involves engaging different modes of thinking, providing parameters for such thinking to occur and structuring interactions to maximize opportunities for such thinking to occur. A good way to get off to a good beginning is to *consolidate*, then *reflect* and then *speculate*. Consolidation involves agreement of what children already know and understand individually and

'Practice is the best master.' (Latin proverb)

as a class. Reflection involves testing some of this consolidated knowledge and understanding against fresh criteria. Speculation then involves taking the consolidated knowledge and understanding and applying it to new contexts.

Five ways to start lessons positively

1   Before children enter the room, display on the board or a poster a positive statement such as 'Last week we all learned about the boiling point of water. Today we are going to discover what happens if we add salt to the water. Superbrains will be hard at work in here!'

2   Make cue cards with the key points from the previous lesson. Invite children to the board to pin up a card and read the information. Have a round of applause as each card goes up to acknowledge the learning that has previously taken place.

3   Put cue cards on desks with key points from previous lessons. Ask each child to choose one and read it to his group to help everyone to recall prior learning.

4   Put a list of questions on the board from previous lessons. Ask children to stand up to answer the questions verbally with a partner, then to sit down once they have finished.

5   Give out 'Superbrain' badges to half the class and 'Quizmaster' badges to the others. Tell the Quizmasters to move around the room asking 'Superbrains' one question each. They can either make up their own questions or be given a list.

Games

In *The ALPS Approach* we give suggestions of games to play as consolidation, reflection and speculation activities. Here is a further selection of games based upon popular games where the protocols and rules are easily understood:

Blind date – One child sits behind a screen, with three on the other side. He asks the 'contestants' three questions – these can be made up by you or by the class. Each of the three contestants gives an answer to the three questions, then the first child chooses the contestant who gave the best answers. Alternatively, the class can vote to decide which of the three contestants should win. The successful contestant then takes the chair to ask three new contestants three more questions.

So you want to be a Millionaire – One child sits in the hot seat and the quiz leader asks her questions on what has been learned or has happened that week. Each question has four choices of answer but only one is correct. The questions get progressively difficult but so do the rewards. The rewards are either for the whole class or for the group whose candidate has been selected (at random). The candidate has three lives and can use them for one each of the following: ask the audience (class or group), ask a friend or get a 50–50 (two wrong answers are taken away). To get fair outcomes have each group or table rotate their nominated candidate who then competes in an open-ended quiz with questions that involve best guessing. Manage the nominations so that over the course of the year everyone gets a chance.

'I fear nothing, except not being the best.' (Jenson Button, Formula 1 Racing Driver)

Whose Line is it Anyway? – Children compete in home groups. The activity involves the teacher structuring role-plays, charades and little word games around things that have been learned recently. Props and silly rules are used to make the activities more imaginative and more humorous. Points are awarded for accuracy, for imagination and by audience response. Examples include: three from a group to tell the story of ...; one from a group to tell the story of ... until the teacher rings a bell when the next person carries on; using a traffic cone, a hoop and a chair as props explain how ...; at desks, groups take turns to do parts of speech – start with nouns – stand up for concrete nouns stay sitting for abstract.

Catch Phrase – The teacher chooses a key phrase from the learning that week. It could be 'the Romans came to the British Isles in 55BC'. However, none of the letters are included. The teacher simply writes dashes to represent letters on the board. Children are told the subject beforehand and every third go they are allowed a vowel. Rules of number, spelling rules, scientific principles can all be reviewed this way.

Call my bluff – Write a keyword on the board, either from a previous lesson or a new word that you are going to introduce later. Give three different definitions of the word and read them out in a convincing tone. Then ask children to vote on which they believe to be correct, or write down A, B or C. Once children are familiar with this game, they can begin to write their own definitions of words already learned, or ones that you wish them to learn. The preparation for this game can be done as a homework activity.

University Challenge – Divide the children into teams and give each team a name and a mascot. It is fun to rearrange the room so that teams sit in rows around the outside. Ask a series of questions, some to each individual team, some for the fastest finger on the buzzer – or hand in the air – and some to individual children. Keep the score on the board and maintain a fast pace. This can be an excellent end-of-week review activity.

Connect Four – Set up a 'Connect Four' game at the front of the room. Divide the class into two teams. Ask questions of alternate teams. The team cannot place its counter in the Connect Four grid until it gets a correct answer. Every wrong answer counts as a penalty point. At the end of the game see who won the Connect Four grid and who had least penalty points. If the same team won both, they are declared winners. If not, the game was a tie.

Hangman – Divide the class into groups. Give each group a big piece of paper and pencil. Ask a question, to which the groups must write the answer. If they get it correct, they draw the first part of their 'hangman'. Continue with a series of questions until a team has completed its hangman picture and is declared the winner.

'The skills needed by headteachers surpass those used by business leaders.'
(Hay McBer, Management Consultants)

The best group-work strategies

The ALPS method™ stresses the need for a variety in learning diet and experiences for children. A rigid adherence to whole class teaching or to grouping by ability for all tasks is not, in our view, best practice for either the holistic development of learning skills or the deeper understanding of content. Similarly, slavish adherence to group-work can be limiting. Structured variety is at the centre of the ALPS approach.

The ALPS rationale is that structured group-work can:

✖ provide quality opportunities for pupils to maximize directed and purposeful language exchange;

✖ give an authentic audience and a safe test area for the ideas of others;

✖ offer challenging structures in which learning can be engaged at a number of levels;

✖ extend the quantity and quality of pupil response;

✖ develop the skills of social interaction;

✖ develop the intelligent behaviours of managing impulsivity, empathy and flexibility of thought;

✖ provide a mechanism for differentiation.

Eight ways to organize groups

1. Home and Away. Home groups are friendship groups and the groups to which we return. Away groups are teacher designated and depend on the activity. Because they are a little more challenging we play 'away' for half of our fixtures over a season.
2. Mixed contribution groups. Deliberately assign different roles within the group. Roles could include timekeeper, writer, reporter, chairperson.
3. Mixed gender pairings. Ensure that groups include boys and girls. Try seating arrangements that are boy–girl–boy–girl.
4. Single gender pairings or groups. This should be a fairly infrequent arrangement, but use it to encourage children to be metacognitive – what differences do they notice when working in mixed or single gender groups?
5. Pre-chosen groups. Each group works on a different aspect of a whole class project then feeds back to the class. It is sometimes useful to group children according to current levels of attainment for this type of activity.
6. Individual – pair – share – present. Begin with individuals and give them something that they can achieve. They then share their achievement with someone else using descriptive language and responding to clarifying and reflective questions. They form into groups and then the groups feed back to the class. At each stage the challenge gets higher but every pupil has a contribution to make.
7. Carousel. Groups move around different activities.
8. Snowball. Progressive accumulation of information: 'Find one fact, now exchange it with someone else so you have two, now exchange your two with someone else so you have four.' Try doing this to the clock or to music.

'Creative input, benefiting society, applying knowledge, working with people.'
(Undergraduate ratings for teaching career)

Ten methods for choosing groups

1 Play group-work bingo. Write the names of pairs of children on cards and pull out two cards to make a foursome, or three to make a group of six. This ensures that each child has at least one friendship – their partner – in the group.

2 When children are comfortable with working in flexible groups, put every child's name individually in a hat and pull out names for each group.

3 Make a pack of coloured cards and deal them out to the class randomly. All children with the same colour card are in the same group. Again, before children are confident about working in random groups, deal out the cards to friendship pairs.

4 Make a pack of cards with numbers. Shuffle them and deal them out randomly. Then organize the numbers into groups – for example, numbers 1–5, 6–10 and so on.

5 For more structured groups, deal out cards according to a pre-plan. For example, dealing two sets of cards if you are going to set two separate differentiated tasks.

6 Appoint group leaders. List attributes that will be necessary for the task that is planned. Ask the group leaders to choose members of the class for their team according to those attributes and to explain their reasoning as they do so.

7 Make sets of cards with attributes such as 'thoughtful', 'imaginative', 'creative', 'logical'. Give an appropriate one to each child. Then ask the children to organize themselves into groups with one of each attribute in each group. It helps to colour-code the backs of the cards for the children to see if they have sorted themselves out appropriately.

8 Use a pairs or group wheel, as described in *The ALPS Approach*. Prepare children for the fact that the groups will change each lesson, but that it is predictable, as you will spin the wheel forwards one section each time.

9 Use a group chart. Allow each child to come to the front one by one and place their name on the chart in the group where they would like to work. Make rules before you begin – each group must have two boys and two girls, you are not allowed to choose the same group as your partner.

10 Describe the tasks you have planned. Allow children to go to the group where they feel they can make the greatest contribution.

'The educated person of the future is the person who realises they never stop learning.'

Five ways to teach the protocols for group-working

1   Work with the class to agree a set of 'Group-work Rules' and display them for all to see.
2   Make prompt sheets or tent cards with the rules and place them on desks at the start of every group session.
3   Roleplay situations where groups get into conflict and how to solve such difficulties.
4   Encourage groups to reflect on the processes that were involved as they worked when they give feedback, not just on the end result.
5   Display key vocabulary about group-work and use it regularly, such as 'co-operation', 'listening', 'turn-taking', 'negotiation', 'consensus', 'clarifying'.

Plan, Do, Review

Very young children can be taught the simple steps of 'Plan, Do, Review'. Each stage can be broken down by asking groups to consider these questions:

1   **Plan**
    ◆   What have you have been asked to do?
    ◆   What are some good ideas on how best to do it?
    ◆   Choose the best idea and say what you will do.
    ◆   How will you know you have done well?

2   **Do**
    ◆   What things need to be done?
    ◆   Who will do each of these things?
    ◆   How will you each know you are doing well?
    ◆   How will the group check that progress is being made?

3   **Review**
    ◆   When you have finished how will you know you have been successful?
    ◆   What will you do differently next time?
    ◆   Who did what to help the team?

'Two processes take place in a classroom – teaching and learning: sometimes they are connected!' (Max Coates)

2 VAKplus

The VAKplus tool can be an effective way of ensuring that you balance and broaden your teaching range. Teach children to see it, hear it, do it, and be curious about it!

There are an abundance of inventories and profiles for adults and learning preference. There are not so many for children and few for parents. The inventories that exist tend to be worthy but dull. To break the mould we introduce the VAK joke test followed by questionnaires for pupils, parents and teachers. Use both resources to explore what makes us different, the ways in which we are different and what it means for learning. Do so with a light touch.

The jokes and VAK

The jokes are listed below in the three categories, VAK. Those which require some sort of visual cueing, those which rely on recognizing patterns of sound and those where some sort of physical experience is being described. To make sense of any joke requires certain shared understandings. That is why these jokes use simple puns or obvious visual absurdities or unusual juxtaposition. Also, the jokes are written and need to be heard or read. For some there is nothing so funny as seeing a man fall off a bike. For others it is the story itself. For others practical jokes and physical gags are what is amusing. The skill of the reader or teller will influence how funny the shared experience becomes. But nevertheless, the activity is a good one for talking about and sharing difference. It can then cue you to talk about difference in learning preference.

Visual jokes

☺ There's a cake in the baker's window that says, 'cakes 66p, upside-down cakes 99p'!

☺ What did the 0 say to the 8? I like your belt!

☺ Why is 6 afraid of 7? Because 7 ate 9.

☺ Why have elephants got big ears? Because Noddy won't pay the ransom!

☺ What do you call a boomerang that doesn't come back? A stick!

☺ 'Doctor, doctor I keep thinking I'm a set of curtains!' 'Pull yourself together man!'

'Leadership is about being as well as doing.'

The VAK Joke Book

Which of these jokes do you find funniest? Because we are all very different, we all laugh at different things. If we laughed at the same things that would be funny wouldn't it? Or would it? I don't know. Sometimes you can find out about people by the things they laugh at.

Below there are 18 different jokes. Have your teacher or someone else read them to you. Then use the form to vote for the most funny.

1   Why do hens lay eggs? Obvious, if they dropped them they'd break!

2   There's a cake in the baker's window that says, 'cakes 66p, upside-down cakes 99p'!

3   How can you tell if there's an elephant under your bed? Your nose is touching the ceiling!

4   What do you get if you cross a grass field with a cow? A lawn-mooer.

5   'Tell me nurse, how's the boy doing that ate all the 5p pieces?' 'Still no change doctor!'

6   Two cockney owls were playing pool. One misses a shot and says to the other, 'that's two 'its mate. The other replies, 'two 'its to who?'

7   Why do birds fly south? It's just too far to walk!

8   How could the vampire's mum tell he had been smoking? Because of his coffin!

9   In a busy hotel the receptionist shouts out, 'telephone call for Mr Grobenmeisterhimbergmannsturnburnbagerant.' An old man comes to the desk and asks, 'what initial is that?'

10 What did the 0 say to the 8? I like your belt!

11 What do you get if you cross a chicken with a parrot? Fowl language!

12 What do you call a boomerang that doesn't come back? A stick!

13 Why is 6 afraid of 7? Because 7 ate 9.

14 Why have elephants got big ears? Because Noddy won't pay the ransom!

15 'Doctor, doctor I keep thinking I'm a set of curtains!' 'Pull yourself together man!'

16 Which side of a chicken has the most feathers? The outside!

17 What do you get if you cross a pool of water with a spy? James Pond.

18 How do you stop a dog from barking in the back garden? Put it in the front garden!

Auditory jokes

☺ What do you get if you cross a pool of water with a spy? James Pond.

☺ Two cockney owls were playing pool. One misses a shot and says to the other, 'that's two 'its mate. The other replies, 'two 'its to who?'

☺ How could the vampire's mum tell he had been smoking? Because of his coffin!

☺ In a busy hotel the receptionist shouts out, 'telephone call for Mr Grobenmeisterhimbergmannsturnburnbagerant.' An old man comes to the desk and asks, 'what initial is that?'

☺ What do you get if you cross a chicken with a parrot? Fowl language!

☺ What do you get if you cross a grass field with a cow? A lawn-mooer.

Kinesthetic or physical jokes

☺ 'Tell me nurse, how's the boy doing that ate all the 5p pieces?' 'Still no change doctor!'

☺ Why do hens lay eggs? Obvious, if they dropped them they'd break!

☺ How can you tell if there's an elephant under your bed? Your nose is touching the ceiling!

☺ Which side of a chicken has the most feathers? The outside!

☺ Why do birds fly south? It's just too far to walk!

☺ How do you stop a dog from barking in the back garden? Put it in the front garden!

The questionnaires that are provided on the following pages have their true value in helping us think further about learning.

Me and my partner working as a pair

'Good leaders don't let the urgent crowd out the important.'

VAK Joke Voting Form

Use the information below to mark your scores and add the totals. Decide out of 4 how funny the joke is – 4 is really funny, 3 is funny, 2 is OK and 1 is not funny. Ring your score for each joke then read across to see if it is a (V) or an (A) or a (K). Then put your score in the column and total at the bottom.

Joke No.	Joke	Score				V	A	K
1	Hens lay eggs (K)	1	2	3	4	_	_	_
2	Upside down cake (V)	1	2	3	4	_	_	_
3	Elephant under your bed (K)	1	2	3	4	_	_	_
4	Lawn-mooer (A)	1	2	3	4	_	_	_
5	The 5p pieces (K)	1	2	3	4	_	_	_
6	Two cockney owls (A)	1	2	3	4	_	_	_
7	Birds fly south (K)	1	2	3	4	_	_	_
8	Vampire's mum (A)	1	2	3	4	_	_	_
9	What initial is that (A)	1	2	3	4	_	_	_
10	Your belt (V)	1	2	3	4	_	_	_
11	Fowl language (A)	1	2	3	4	_	_	_
12	Boomerang (V)	1	2	3	4	_	_	_
13	7 ate 9 (V)	1	2	3	4	_	_	_
14	Noddy (V)	1	2	3	4	_	_	_
15	I'm a set of curtains (V)	1	2	3	4	_	_	_
16	Chicken feathers (K)	1	2	3	4	_	_	_
17	James Pond (A)	1	2	3	4	_	_	_
18	Dog barking (K)	1	2	3	4	_	_	_
				Total		☐	☐	☐

VAK learning preference questionnaire for children

Below are 15 statements about ways of learning. Look at each of the statements and decide how much it is like you. Score each statement from 0 to 5. If it is really like you, score it 5. If it is not like you at all, score it 0. Use the numbers in between as well. Circle your score then add all the scores according to the key at the bottom

		Not like me				Really like me	
		0	1	2	3	4	5
1	I listen to music when I do my homework	0	1	2	3	4	5
2	I like it when we make things in class	0	1	2	3	4	5
3	To spell correctly I write it first	0	1	2	3	4	5
4	I remember how the pages of my textbook look	0	1	2	3	4	5
5	I can remember the titles to my favourite TV shows	0	1	2	3	4	5
6	Art is my favourite lesson	0	1	2	3	4	5
7	At break I like to run about a lot	0	1	2	3	4	5
8	I like the pictures in books the best	0	1	2	3	4	5
9	I can remember the words to songs	0	1	2	3	4	5
10	When I spell I see the word as I spell it	0	1	2	3	4	5
11	I know the theme tunes to my favourite TV shows	0	1	2	3	4	5
12	Singing is my favourite lesson	0	1	2	3	4	5
13	I'd rather play sport than watch it	0	1	2	3	4	5
14	PE is my favourite lesson	0	1	2	3	4	5
15	When I spell I say the word in my head	0	1	2	3	4	5

Marking Your Questions

Visual		score
Question	4	_____
Question	5	_____
Question	6	_____
Question	8	_____
Question	10	_____
Total		

Kinesthetic		score
Question	2	_____
Question	3	_____
Question	7	_____
Question	13	_____
Question	1	_____
Total		

Auditory		score
Question	1	_____
Question	9	_____
Question	11	_____
Question	12	_____
Question	15	_____
Total		

What your score means

There are three different totals. One each for visual, auditory and kinesthetic. Each total represents how you think you prefer to learn. So does the order the totals come in.

If you had a high total for visual, this means that you learn by the look of things and you can remember by keeping pictures in your head. If you had a high total for auditory, this means that you learn by the sound of things and you can remember by keeping voices and sounds in your head. If you had a high total for kinesthetic, this means that you learn by doing it for yourself and you can remember by actions.

It is good to practise our learning. You practise by being even better at what you enjoy but also by trying to learn in other ways too.

Good ways for high visual scorers to learn
- Try to remember the look of the words and pictures on the page: close your eyes and test what you see.
- Practise spellings by seeing the correct word before you try to say or write it.
- Notice the shapes of words and how some go up and down, and how some are short and fat, and others are long and skinny.
- Test yourself until you get good at remembering the look of a spelling or a learning poster or a diagram – cover up parts of it and try to remember the look of what's underneath.
- Make yourself a poster with all the things you need to remember on it.
- Practise memory mapping by taking the important words and organizing them on a page.
- Symbols are visual shortcuts for helping us make connections. Put symbols in your workbook such as a little brain for 'remember this' or an exclamation mark for 'you got this wrong last time!' or a picture of a little girl's face with a sum on her forehead for this is the most important sentence, it's a 'sum-mary!'

Good ways for high auditory scorers to learn
- Try to remember the sound of the words on the page: close your eyes and say to yourself what you have read. Practise the important sentences and difficult words by repeating them to yourself.
- Practise spellings by saying the correct word before you try to write it. Does it sound right?
- Notice how different letters can make different sounds in different words. Pick the funniest sounding or most difficult words and just say them for fun. Try them in different voices!
- Test yourself until you get good at remembering a spelling or a learning poster or a diagram – cover up parts of it and try to say to yourself what's underneath.
- Make yourself a poster with all the things you need to remember on it and then talk to yourself or someone else about what's on the poster. Cover it and try it again.
- In pairs test each other by: putting what the teacher said in your own words, explaining the meaning of unusual words and using them in a sentence.
- Talking yourself through an activity aloud is good for learning and remembering. So is making a rap or a song or a jingle.

Good ways for high kinesthetic scorers to learn
- Practise spellings by writing with your finger in the air or on the desk; say it aloud as you write it.
- Have lots of spare paper on which you can practise things in rough until you feel it's right and then copy it over.
- Test yourself until you get good at remembering the look of a spelling or a learning poster or a diagram – cover up parts of it with a sheet of paper and, without looking, trace with your finger the look of the information underneath.
- As you learn things at home, get up and move around. Use learning posters in your bedroom and then take them down and put them in order. Mix them up and put them back in order.
- Practise gestures that represent different things. For example, punctuation mark gestures – exclamation marks, speech marks, colon, comma, full stop. As you read and see these punctuation marks make the gestures with both hands!
- Practise memory mapping by taking the important words and organizing them on a page then moving your finger around the words and explain how they are connected.
- When studying at home, set yourself study time targets using a clock or watch. Don't make the targets too long and have a physical break when you have worked for the target time. Have lots of space so you can spread out all your work and workbooks around.

VAK learning preference questionnaire for parents

Below are 18 statements about ways of learning. Look at each of the statements and decide how much it is like you. Score each statement from 0 to 5. If it is really like you, score it 5. If it is not like you at all, score it 0. Use the numbers in between as well. Circle your score then add all the scores according to the key at the bottom

		Not like me				Really like me	
		0	1	2	3	4	5
1	I like to listen to music when I work	0	1	2	3	4	5
2	I enjoy being busy doing things	0	1	2	3	4	5
3	I read the instructions when I'm assembling furniture	0	1	2	3	4	5
4	I have a hobby which is practical	0	1	2	3	4	5
5	I can put a face to name	0	1	2	3	4	5
6	I can remember the look of every photo in the house	0	1	2	3	4	5
7	I prefer going for a walk to watching TV or reading	0	1	2	3	4	5
8	When giving directions I look for landmarks	0	1	2	3	4	5
9	I remember the look of my primary classroom	0	1	2	3	4	5
10	I prefer reading to watching TV or going for a walk	0	1	2	3	4	5
11	I can remember my primary teacher's voice	0	1	2	3	4	5
12	When giving directions I describe the route	0	1	2	3	4	5
13	I prefer watching TV to reading or going for a walk	0	1	2	3	4	5
14	I look at the diagrams when I'm assembling furniture	0	1	2	3	4	5
15	I remember what it felt like to be at primary school	0	1	2	3	4	5
16	I can put a name to a face	0	1	2	3	4	5
17	I use trial and error when I'm assembling furniture	0	1	2	3	4	5
18	When giving directions I draw a map	0	1	2	3	4	5

Marking Your Questions

Visual		score		Kinesthetic		score
Question	5	_____		Question	2	_____
Question	6	_____		Question	4	_____
Question	8	_____		Question	7	_____
Question	9	_____		Question	15	_____
Question	13	_____		Question	17	_____
Question	14	_____		Question	18	_____
Total		☐		**Total**		☐

Auditory		score
Question	1	_____
Question	3	_____
Question	10	_____
Question	11	_____
Question	12	_____
Question	16	_____
Total		☐

VAK learning preference questionnaire for teachers

Below are 24 statements about ways of learning. Look at each of the statements and decide how much it is like you. Score each statement from 0 to 5. If it is really like you, score it 5. If it is not like you at all, score it 0. Use the numbers in between as well. Circle your score then add all the scores according to the key at the bottom

		Not like me				Really like me	
		0	1	2	3	4	5
1	When I listen to music I see pictures	0	1	2	3	4	5
2	Listening to music quickly changes my mood	0	1	2	3	4	5
3	To spell a difficult word correctly I see it first	0	1	2	3	4	5
4	My classroom feels good	0	1	2	3	4	5
5	My best teaching involves being practical	0	1	2	3	4	5
6	To spell a difficult word correctly I write it first	0	1	2	3	4	5
7	My classroom looks good	0	1	2	3	4	5
8	I recognize children by their clothes and appearance	0	1	2	3	4	5
9	When giving directions I describe the route	0	1	2	3	4	5
10	Listening to music distracts me	0	1	2	3	4	5
11	To spell a difficult word correctly I say it first	0	1	2	3	4	5
12	I recognize children by how they act in class	0	1	2	3	4	5
13	If I'm on a course I look at the handouts first	0	1	2	3	4	5
14	With a new computer I'd quickly get started	0	1	2	3	4	5
15	With a new computer I'd read the manual	0	1	2	3	4	5
16	When giving directions I draw a map	0	1	2	3	4	5
17	My best teaching includes lots of discussion	0	1	2	3	4	5
18	If I'm on a course I choose where I'm sitting first	0	1	2	3	4	5
19	With a new computer I'd look at the diagrams	0	1	2	3	4	5
20	My classroom sounds good	0	1	2	3	4	5
21	When giving directions I look for landmarks	0	1	2	3	4	5
22	I recognize children by the sound of their voice	0	1	2	3	4	5
23	If I'm on a course I talk to my neighbour first	0	1	2	3	4	5
24	My best teaching utilizes lots of visual aids	0	1	2	3	4	5

Marking Your Questions

Visual		score		*Kinesthetic*		score
Question	1	_____		Question	2	_____
Question	3	_____		Question	4	_____
Question	7	_____		Question	5	_____
Question	8	_____		Question	6	_____
Question	13	_____		Question	12	_____
Question	19	_____		Question	14	_____
Question	21	_____		Question	16	_____
Question	24	_____		Question	18	_____
Total		☐		**Total**		☐

Auditory		score
Question	9	_____
Question	10	_____
Question	11	_____
Question	15	_____
Question	17	_____
Question	20	_____
Question	22	_____
Question	23	_____
Total		☐

3 Structuring time on task

The optimal time on task

A one-hour lesson could be broken into four sessions of 15 minutes, or three of 20 minutes, or even five of 12 minutes. With the literacy or numeracy hours, or indeed any other lesson, it is necessary to chunk it down, giving attention to the transition between activities, ensuring that the Big Picture is given and providing opportunities for physical reprieve. To just move from one activity to the next without refocusing, connecting the learning and giving the Big Picture, is to immediately set limits on learning.

The ALPS model for optimizing time on task involves chunking in a structured way, with the 'chunks' linked by activities that accelerate learning. It looks like this (see poster on page 66):

> **Connect – preview – focus on task – diffuse – focus on task – diffuse – focus on task – diffuse – review.**

Our model for optimizing time on task derives from research into the human ability to give sustained attention. Structure the lesson down, using the crude formula of 'the younger the learner the shorter the task' and then string the chunks together with meaningful learning interventions called 'diffusions'.

To connect. Provide quick activities that share understandings and make connections with the child's world. Make links with what the class has learned before. Tease out what they already know about the topic. In pairs, and in small groups, get them to generate lots of questions.

To preview. Provide the Big Picture. This means say and show what you will do and how it will be done. Take time over the how. This is learning to learn at work. Say what the class is about to do and how – use open-ended questions and record some or all of these on or by the board. Assign significance to the key vocabulary, which ought to be on posters around the room, or on laminates on each desk or, at the very least, written somewhere it can be seen.

To focus. Try for – and reinforce – focused, vigilant and external attention, but limit its duration. Do this by challenging youngsters to attend to the task you have set up in particular ways. Tell them about human attention. Encourage the self-discipline of focusing for a limited time on the task and in a way that excludes other competing stimuli. Describe the diffusion that will come when they have been successful in managing their attention.

To diffuse. After focused, vigilant and external attention comes a space for diffusion. Diffusions enhance the learning by structured re-engagement with the task. Examples include paired reflection or speculation with a requirement to use certain keywords on what has happened or will happen and why. Pole-bridging, as we undertake the activity, is a form of diffusion. Setting up coaching protocols can discipline purposeful language exchange. Brain-break activities such as those we described on page 133 can also be useful diffusions.

'Noah was the leader – he had the vision and the foresight – the captain was the manager – he ran the ship.'

To focus again. Out of the diffusion and back to the task. The diffusion has allowed the child to explain his thinking. It has given space for reflection. It has changed the way the task is attended to. It has helped get under the activity to expose understanding. Going back to the task ought now to be possible, but with fresh eyes.

To review. Allow time for reflection and recall. Start individually, then in pairs, then whole class. Reinforce key points visually. Go back to the questions and keywords written or positioned on the board at the outset. Answer the questions again. Rehearse the use of the keywords.

Five useful and quick diffusion activities

1   Have a physical break with a stretch that connects in some way to the content. For example, we are reading a book and pause at an exciting moment and ask the class to stand and pose as the principal character, or mime what the character should do next, without leaving the spot.

2   Ask children to take turns to describe three things they have learned to a partner.

3   'Take a minute – person A turn to person B and explain what I've just said in your own words. Ready, go.'

4   'In pairs, taking no more than a minute, list as many keywords that I have used as you can. Ready, go.'

5   Here are your three keyword starters on the board. Person A, use each keyword in a sentence and then explain what each means. You have a minute. Person B, you are next. Person A. Ready, go.'

Pole-bridging to increase intelligent response

Pole-bridging is a deliberate attempt to connect-up internally the child's own understanding using the vocabulary that relates to the real experience, within the experience. Pole-bridging requires the child to be self-aware, paying attention to detail while simultaneously verbalizing understanding. It encourages observation of detail, classification, reflection and speculation. All powerful tools for developing an intelligent response. When a child does this at a very early age, he is laying down discrete neural pathways: connecting language sites with other 'poles' within the brain.

WHAT I'M DOING NOW IS...

'A leaderful school has a wide understanding of the challenges children face.'
(Heather du Quesnay, Director NCSL)

Five ways to encourage children to pole-bridge

1   When you work with children or demonstrate a technique to the class, model the process by pole-bridging yourself.

2   Use novel methods of pole-bridging to help promote it as the norm. For example, chain it together with a line of pupils around the room talking through an experience such as 'all we learned last week starting Monday at 9 o'clock!'

3   Draw attention to the vocabulary related to an experience. Write this vocabulary on the board when you give the Big Picture. Insist children use it in their paired and group-work.

4   Provide key vocabulary during a lesson on laminated cue cards around the room above eye level. For younger children, use flashcards with picture cues.

5   In paired activity work, ask a child to be a radio commentator with an imaginary microphone as someone else goes through an activity. Swap.

Managing the moment of impulse

In the ALPS, children are encouraged to set goals and targets, follow through on plans, practise outcomes thinking and act with forethought and after deliberation. Managing the moment of impulse – the ability to delay immediate gratification – is a desirable lifelong learning attribute and is modelled and taught explicitly in the ALPS classroom.

Twenty ways to teach children to manage impulsivity

1   Describe personal lesson targets aloud before and during a task.

2   Make continual positive affirmations about each child's ability to act with control and forethought.

3   Encourage pole-bridging during a task.

4   Use music to create the mood for reflective thinking.

5   Demonstrate activities, drawing attention to how you are managing any desire to act impulsively – be explicit about how to manage one's mood.

6   Give time-outs for individuals, groups or the whole class to allow for reflection and planning.

7   Create a time-out space for children who need space to think – make this a positive place to be!

8   Teach and model reflective and predictive thinking during the process of pole-bridging.

9   Practise outcomes thinking before embarking on a task.

10   Allow time for mental rehearsal before the lesson, such as the 'Private Cinema' activity (see *The ALPS Approach* for details).

11   Set children prediction exercises before a task.

'If you have a dream, you can make it happen.' (Ellen McArthur, round the world yachtswoman)

12 Allow time for speculation activities in pairs or small groups.

13 Share your memory map of the lesson plan with the class.

14 Use music for timed activities and do not allow any action before the music starts!

15 Give warnings of what is to come, such as 'in five minutes we are going to stop and sit on the mat'.

16 Use sounds to indicate stages of the lesson, such as chime bars or bells to indicate that a review session is soon to begin.

17 Teach children to look at you and follow your slow breathing pattern before they begin a task.

18 If the mood of the class – or of an individual – is becoming impulsive, stop and practise slow breathing.

19 Teach children relaxation techniques with eyes closed and practise these at moments where impulsive behaviour is likely to occur.

20 Discuss the emotions that lead to impulsive behaviour and roleplay how to control those emotions; for example, in circle time.

'When teachers stop growing, so do their students.' (Roland Barth)

Demonstrating understanding

VAK gives a basic model for structuring classroom activities that maximize the learning potential of each unique individual. Howard Gardner's multiple intelligence theory gives a more expansive guiding framework. While it is possible to plan for the multiple intelligences, Howard Gardner himself warns against trivializing the use of the intelligences. His wish is that the multiple intelligences be used for more effective pedagogy and assessment. The educational power of multiple intelligences is 'exhibited when they are drawn on to help students master consequential disciplinary materials'.

Every individual has a unique profile of strengths and weaknesses. It would be ridiculous to suggest that anyone is entirely a 'musical' or 'mathematical' learner. The job of the ALPS teacher is to present lessons in varying formats so that each child can draw from the aspect that best suits him as a learner. Any topic of learning can be accessed and understood in different ways. It is like using seven or eight different doors into the same house. Each door is a different access point. Each door better suited to different children. So access could be via a story, a logical step-by-step theory, modelling, artwork, a mathematical diagram, a series of visual images, a dramatic realization involving dialogue and movement, or a series of debates and discussions.

How to identify the children in your class according to Howard Gardner's multiple intelligences

Interpersonal – The Conversationalist

- After school can be found at your desk waiting to tell you her life story.
- Waylays OFSTED inspectors in the corridor to tell them her life story.
- Is never asked a question by OFSTED inspectors, who instead seek out The Acrobat to ask for his interpretation of the lesson.
- Is always the first to volunteer to come to the front in assembly and is usually the cause of it overrunning.
- Can tell you – and does tell you – the reasons behind most disagreements in the classroom.
- Sorts out, better than you, most disagreements in the classroom.

Intrapersonal – The Thinker

- **?** Rarely puts up her hand in class as she is too busy thinking about the question that you may ask later to answer the one that you ask now.
- **?** Gives answers to questions, when pushed, that pose further questions and confuse her peers.
- **?** Makes profound statements that you are not sure you understand.
- **?** Scores poorly in SATs tests as she assumes that nobody could be asking her for basic facts.

'A good past is positively dangerous it makes us content with the present and unprepared for the future.'

? Scores poorly in SATs tests as she spends half an hour answering a question at length for one mark and does not complete half the test.

? Floors OFSTED inspectors by responding 'Of course, don't you?' when they ask if she understands the lesson.

Linguistic – The Orator

❝ Always volunteers to read aloud in class. Is upset if not chosen.

❝ Turns up for every audition for every school production and is usually given a leading role.

❝ Is frequently found at the front in assembly, whether or not he has been invited.

❝ Lets everyone know when things go wrong in his work, with dramatic gestures and sighs.

❝ Uses long words that the other children do not understand and often sends you reaching for your dictionary.

❝ After school, can usually be found in the book corner or library, or smuggling books out in his rucksack.

Mathematical and logical – The Engineer

⚖ Measures his desk labels with a ruler and uses a protractor to ensure that they are stuck on straight.

⚖ Makes perfect corners when he folds paper for 'Look, cover, write, check' and gets upset if his partner's corners do not meet exactly.

⚖ Spends hours with the Lego® at wet playtime and builds intricate models that he refuses to break up.

⚖ Is frequently to be found at the computer showing other children how to exit a programme, whether or not they want his help.

⚖ At other times, can be found under the computer reconnecting wires and trying to make it work faster.

⚖ After school, can be found putting toys in orderly places and lining up books in precise rows by alphabetical order.

Visual and spatial – The Artist

✎ Decorates the borders of her homework in intricate detail, taking longer over the decoration than the actual task.

✎ Rearranges post-it notes on the class memory map to make it look more aesthetically pleasing.

✎ Brings regular notes from her mother complaining about paint on her clothes.

✎ Draws swirly lines and always illustrates her work, whether or not you ask her to. Her exercise books are full of diagrams and minimal amounts of writing.

✎ Dots her letter 'i' with a huge circle, no matter how many times you tell her not to.

✎ Brings you pictures that she has drawn on scrap pieces of paper on a daily basis to pin up on your noticeboard. Uses your entire stock of drawing paper in one wet playtime.

'Every teacher a learner, every learner a teacher.'

Kinesthetic – The Acrobat

- Is rarely in his seat. Last time you looked, he was under the sink where he insists he last saw his pencil.
- Chews his pencils, if he has not already broken them.
- Has pockets full of marbles, Pogs, Pokémon cards, or items for the latest playground craze. They rarely stay in his pockets during lessons, so you have a desk full of his possessions.
- Participates so enthusiastically – and noisily – in brain-break activities.
- Reaches the top of the large apparatus in the gym before you have given instructions about safety when climbing.
- Captains the football team, wins the cross-country championship and talks continually about Manchester United.

Musical – The Musician

- Attends every type of extra-curricular music lesson.
- Is rarely in the classroom for any form of test or assessment, as he is always at a music lesson.
- Hums while writing, despite the irritation of other children on his table.
- Conducts the music in assembly with his fingers, even when the headteacher is glaring at him.
- Competes with The Orator at every audition for every school production and is usually given a leading role.
- Makes up songs and raps in the playground and stays behind after school to sing them to you, along with extravagant dramatic gestures and a girl-group of dancers.

Naturalist – The David Bellamy

- Arrives at school with matchboxes filled with worms and bugs, which he leaves on your desk.
- Is fascinated with the wormery, stick insects and ant farm, and frequently leaves the lid off.
- Tells you about his lizard, rattlesnake, pet rat and tarantulas at home, and offers to bring them in for 'Show and Tell'.
- Has umpteen books on dinosaurs and tells you every type, characteristic and name – regularly.
- Always volunteers to take the guinea pig home for the holidays, whether or not his mother agrees.
- Stays behind after school every Friday to clean out the rabbit hutches.

'Our experience with hundreds of organisations over 30 years has led to the conclusion that organisations and nations don't change – only individuals change.' (Michael, Fullan)

Six ways to develop each of the multiple intelligences in your classroom

Interpersonal

1 Use circle time or some other mechanism for developing social co-operation.
2 Vary groupings.
3 Share protocols about groupings and about the variety of learning methods used.
4 Teach children how to play with others.
5 Agree class rules.
6 Set and work towards group goals.

Intrapersonal

1 Allow lots of processing time for reflective thinking.
2 Be patient and answer all the open-ended and philosophical questions.
3 Find out about philosophy for children and begin to use it as an adjunct to literacy hour.
4 Explore feelings and motivations as part of circle time.
5 Use life mapping and the aspirational wall.
6 Use desk labels.

Linguistic

1 Minimize your talk and maximize children's talk.
2 Maximize purposeful, structured on-task language exchange.
3 Encourage pole-bridging.
4 Use keyword and themed vocabulary techniques.
5 Use writing frames.
6 Explore different uses of language for different purposes and audiences and via different media.

Mathematical and logical

1 Draw attention to the protocols and routines that you use in the classroom and explain why you use them.
2 Do lots of number work across different disciplines and make numbers exciting.
3 Explore the connections between maths and everyday life.
4 Teach categorization, classifying, prioritizing and prediction skills.
5 Provide problem-solving templates for use in different disciplines.
6 Promote interest in logic; for example, by starting a puzzle club.

'Mordja Amari Bradja (Those who lose their dreaming are lost).' (Aboriginal proverb)

Visual and spatial

1   Use learning posters and memory maps around the room and make regular reference to them.
2   Change the visual display regularly.
3   Complement written and oral work with visual realization techniques such as mapping, flow-charts, annotated graphs and poster displays.
4   Bring in props and artefacts and integrate their use into lessons.
5   Set homework assignments such as making posters and diagrams.
6   Use yourself and your movements as a visual and spatial prop to enhance learning, to exaggerate for effect and to make extravagant gestures.

Kinesthetic

1   Structure practical activities into each day.
2   Rehearse learning through movement, roleplay, simulation and practical activities.
3   Practise skills that require physical dexterity such as handwriting, through brain-break activities.
4   Build in frequent physical breaks to your class work.
5   Set challenges and targets in PE sessions for improvement of physical skills.
6   Teach and practise playground games.

Musical

1   Use music to demarcate time on task, for beginnings and endings, authentication of a theme, to change mood and to energize or relax.
2   Use music to recall content.
3   Use patterns of sound to learn to discriminate changes in pitch and improve awareness of variety and modulation of sounds.
4   Encourage individual interest in the various ways of making and enjoying music.
5   Create opportunities for free music-making sessions and for children to share their personal musical tastes.
6   Create regular opportunities to experience music as a whole class participative activity.

Naturalist

1   Find time to visit local environmental sites.
2   Be responsible, with your class, for the upkeep of a designated area in or around the school.
3   Explore the impact of man on the environment alongside thinking about cause and effect.
4   Conduct species counts and observations.
5   Keep class pets and teach about their care.
6   Model responsibility for both natural and man-made environments in and around the school.

'Life is like a dogsled team – if you ain't the lead dog the scenery never changes.'
(Lewis Grizzard)

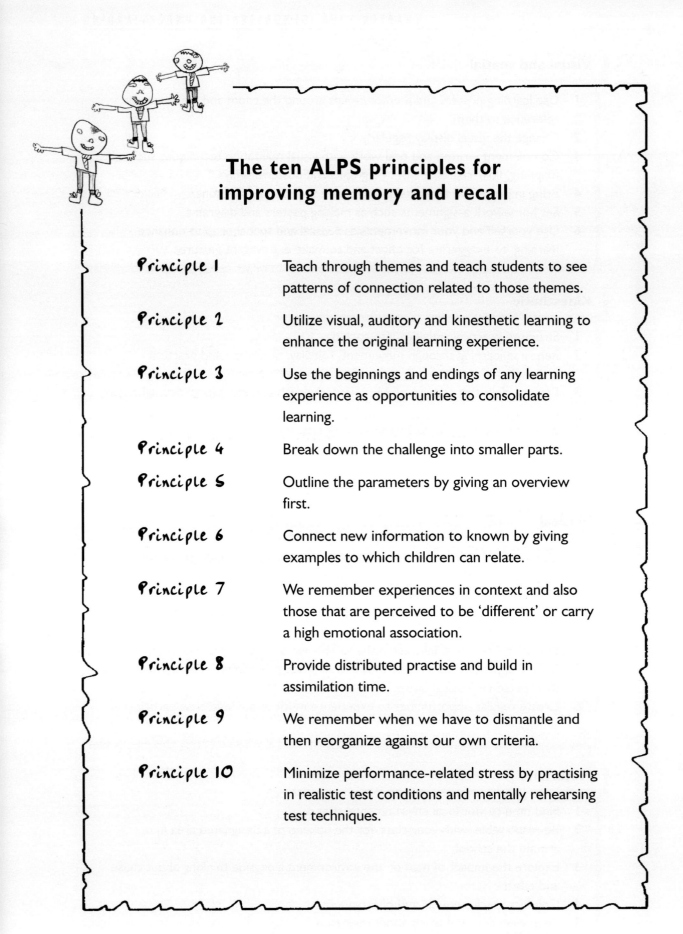

The ten ALPS principles for improving memory and recall

Principle 1   Teach through themes and teach students to see patterns of connection related to those themes.

Principle 2   Utilize visual, auditory and kinesthetic learning to enhance the original learning experience.

Principle 3   Use the beginnings and endings of any learning experience as opportunities to consolidate learning.

Principle 4   Break down the challenge into smaller parts.

Principle 5   Outline the parameters by giving an overview first.

Principle 6   Connect new information to known by giving examples to which children can relate.

Principle 7   We remember experiences in context and also those that are perceived to be 'different' or carry a high emotional association.

Principle 8   Provide distributed practise and build in assimilation time.

Principle 9   We remember when we have to dismantle and then reorganize against our own criteria.

Principle 10   Minimize performance-related stress by practising in realistic test conditions and mentally rehearsing test techniques.

Using review for recall

It is undoubtedly true that to succeed in the present UK testing system a child needs to be able use his memory effectively. It may also be true that in many, maybe most, cases developing memory skills is left to chance. What a travesty. Not only is work on memory fun and easy to do, but it can also be layered easily in to everyday classroom teaching and is brilliant for independent practise at home.

In the human brain there is no single site for memory. Memory is more to do with reconstruction than recall. So, with more pathways available to revisit experiences the more likely we are to be able to do so successfully.

Twenty ways to help children to remember

1   Use mnemonics for remembering key information.
2   Use posters for key information.
3   Use colours to represent key aspects of concepts – such as blue for oxygen and green for carbon dioxide.
4   Encourage children to draw diagrams of key points during lessons or in review times.
5   Set homework activities that reinforce what has been studied in class.
6   Send posters and cue cards home for children to show to parents.
7   Use cue cards for games and activities.
8   Revisit learning through brain breaks in later lessons.
9   Draw children's attention to previous learning when giving the Big Picture.
10 Display large memory maps until information is absorbed.
11 Use desk tops to display key information.
12 Make tent cards with diagrams, rhymes or mnemonics for key facts.
13 Ask children to suggest strategies that they could use to remember the lesson.
14 Use music, rhyme and rhythm to reinforce learning.
15 Review lessons regularly.
16 Create brain breaks that can be used in subsequent lessons for review.
17 Use strategies such as 'each one, teach one' so that every child has a turn at teaching someone else.
18 Encourage children to draw parallels to other lessons or notice anything quirky that will help them to remember facts.
19 Ask questions that draw on previous experiences when learning something new. Allow processing time.
20 Continually build up memory maps that link concepts and visually display learning.

'Creativity in management is the defeat of habits of mind through originality.'

No-one can do everything but everyone can do something

The **PRECIPITOUS** way to practise and develop memory techniques

P personalize it | Make learning personal to the children.
It is easier for a child to remember if he makes a strong personal connection with the information. Say things like, 'How will you explain this to your mum or dad when you get home tonight?' Check next day that children have done it.

R relate it | Relate it to other things.
Encourage thematic and connective thinking by the use of topic webs, spider diagrams and memory maps. Encourage 'compare and contrast' activities, and promote awareness of similarity and difference through lots of examples. Use metaphors.

E exaggerate it | Exaggerate it so that it is unusual.
Experiencing or rehearsing learning in ways that are unusual helps children to recall facts. Deliberately practise spellings or keywords in loud or soft voices, use dramatic gestures and unusual props.

C chunk it | Chunk it down – rehearse it in smaller units.
Break things up and rehearse a little at a time. Encourage children to break things into parts by teaching them how to make 'family trees' of information using keywords. Whole units of work can be remembered this way.

I imagine it | Imagine you are using the skill or information.
Ask children to imagine aspects of lessons. For example, ask them to describe a journey from the source of a river to the sea, or imagine that they are walking around different geometrical shapes. What do they see?

P package it | Package it up into recognizable units.
Practise learning things in little packages, then sequence the packages and give them names. Mix up the packaged information, then restore it to the original order. Add numbers to provide parameters: 'Three things you need to know about ...', 'List the five steps involved in ...'.

I imitate it | Use VAKplus to imitate.
Teach through seeing, hearing and doing.

T talk about it | Tell the story.
Talking through an experience and then attempting to explain it to an imaginary audience will help children to remember all the details. Teach children to pole-bridge.

O organise it | Organize your thinking in a different dimension.
Ask children to learn and review their learning by writing information in order or by using a flow chart, a series of prompt postcards or by making a poster.

U use it | Use what you have learned.
Think of ways in which the information can be used. By thinking of applications for knowledge and generating lots of questions you will make it easier for children to remember.

S share it | Share it, test it and teach it to someone else.
Provide lots or structured opportunities to test understanding as a powerful aid to recall. Use strategies such as 'each one, teach one', preparing a lesson plan for teaching a group of peers, or explaining a memory map to the class and answering key questions.

'Success comes before work only in the dictionary.'

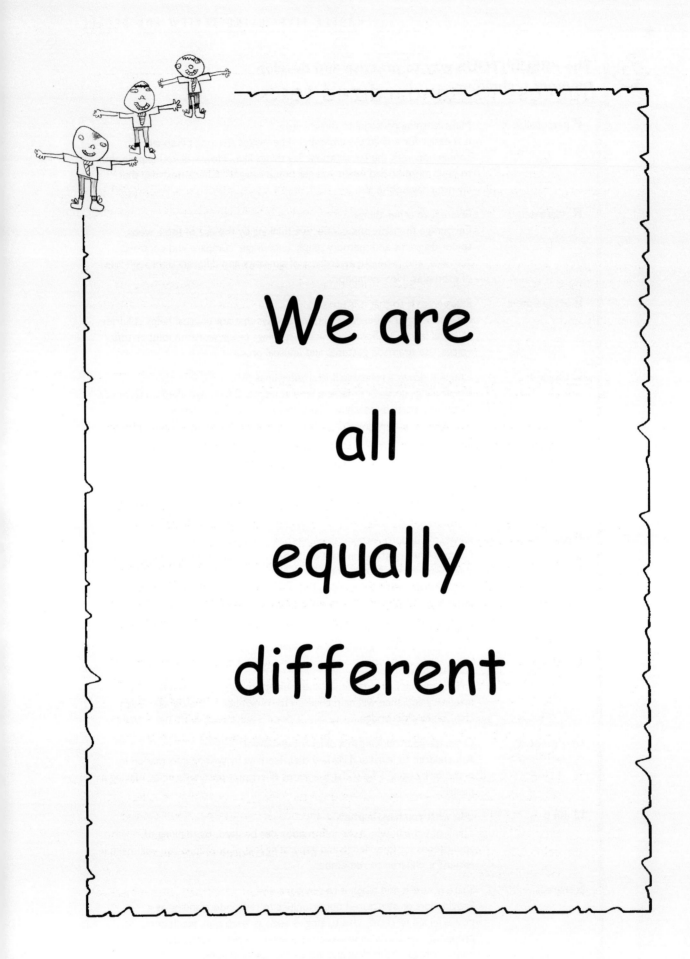

We are all equally different

Success in standardized tests

Leaving aside the question of whether schools should be formally testing young children at all, there are clearly ways in which tests and testing can be used positively to give teachers and children useful information, to motivate and to rehearse performance improvement under challenging conditions. Any testing regime should test understanding and not purely test nerve.

There are physiological responses to anxiety that often impact performance. In these cases, one is merely testing the child's ability to be tested, rather than making a useful assessment that can lead to effective target setting and teaching. ALPS teachers test and assess children's levels of attainment continually and work directly to prepare children for statutory assessments.

Five STEPS for preparing children for SATs

1   Share information! At the beginning of the year meet with parents and children to give an overview of what the assessments entail, what the levels represent and what preparation the class will undergo. If possible, also meet with individual parents to make a personal plan for their child.

2   Life map! When making life maps, plan specifically how to prepare for SATs. Set class, group and individual targets. With older children, be explicit about the curriculum that is to be covered and what the levels represent.

3   Adapt normal tasks! Throughout the year, take every opportunity to practise through adapting normal classroom tasks. For example, in creative writing sessions, practise using the paper that will be used in the SATs assessments, and when you make worksheets, indicate by the side of each question how many marks are allocated for a correct answer.

4   Practise early! Have regular practise sessions throughout the year, not just in the last few weeks. Make the layout of SATs papers familiar to children early on – this relieves stress and anxiety. Work SATs practise into your normal routine. Teach and practise relaxation techniques. Talk positively about SATs on a daily basis, telling children what fun they will have and how they will rise to the challenge.

5   Have a practise week. Nearer the time, practise the timetable for the SATs week. Use the equipment that will be used for SATs, go out to play at different times, take timed tests in test conditions and practise in the place where the tests will be taken. Use this opportunity for confidence building, for fun and for celebrations! Affirm how confident and mature the children will be and celebrate their success.

'It is a funny thing about life: if you refuse to accept anything but the very best, you very often get it.' (Somerset Maughan)

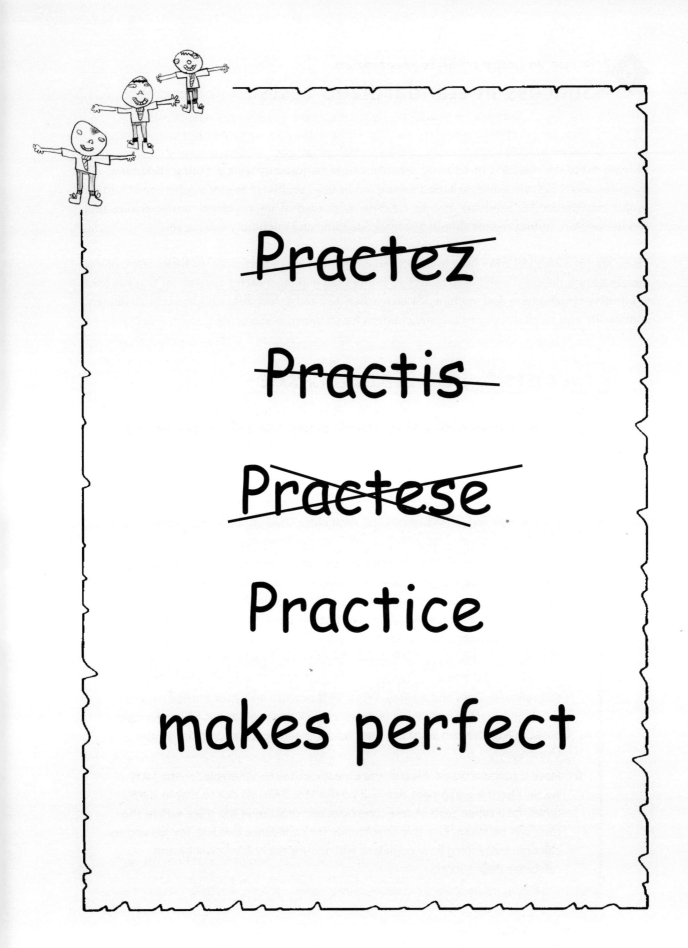

~~Practez~~

~~Practis~~

~~Practese~~

Practice

makes perfect

A sample policy on SATs preparation

At Handley Primary School we believe that assessment, record keeping and target setting should form an ongoing cycle to ensure the effective delivery of the curriculum in the classroom. Each assessment should inform the teacher about the levels of skills and concepts of the children in her class, should be recorded for future reference and should lead to focused target setting. Data from tests should be analysed in order to assess the quality of teaching and learning, then used for further target setting with an aim of making continued improvement. This is as true for weekly spelling tests as it is for Key Stage 1 and 2 SATs.

We recognize the pressure that SATs can place upon children, parents and staff, and aim to minimize the stress of these assessments. Our aim is to use the assessments to inform our practice and to share that information with parents. We see parents as the primary educators and influencers of their children and foster strong partnerships wherever possible. For this reason, we work to be explicit about the curriculum and the levels that we expect children to achieve. If children and their parents understand what the assessments entail and what each level represents, we believe that performance improves and stress is minimized.

We believe that children perform better when in a familiar and relaxed environment, and therefore invest time and energy in SATs preparation. Some of the many strategies that teachers use to create a positive attitude towards SATs assessments might include:

* Target setting linked directly to National Curriculum.
* Sharing targets with parents at the beginning of Years 2 and 6.
* Active teaching of relaxation techniques.
* The use of affirmations and positive visualization techniques.
* Regular practise of SAT-style papers; for example, on teacher-made worksheets.
* More informal class-based tests, rather than fewer, with results leading to further target setting.
* SAT-style assessments in all year groups to create a sense of familiarity.
* The use of positive displays celebrating success in practice tests.
* Regular discussion about testing and assessments in classrooms.
* After-school and lunchtime clubs for the improvement of related skills.
* Homework assignments that practise SATs skills and test knowledge.

Regular testing and practising of exam technique ensures that children approach SATs in the way we would wish them to approach any other activity in school: with confidence and enthusiasm. We see this preparation as an essential part of our role in preparing our pupils with the life-skills that will help them through secondary school and beyond. We take pride in the success of our pupils in SATs each year. Our criteria for success includes the level of calmness and confidence with which children are judged to have approached the tests and not just the National Curriculum levels attained. However, we believe that these criteria are interconnected, as confident children are assessed on their skills and knowledge, rather than on their ability to perform in test situations. This is our aim: to achieve high standards not just through effective delivery of the curriculum, but also through producing students who have the confidence, self-esteem and skills to perform well in test situations.

'Just go out there and do what you've got to do.' (Martina Navratilova)

183

Twenty-one ways to prepare children for statutory assessments

1   Set long-term goals for SATs when life mapping. Decide what work is necessary throughout the year to prepare children for the assessments.

2   Link target setting to National Curriculum levels so that children understand the levels that they are working towards.

3   Be explicit about grades and levels, and display the curriculum plans so that children and parents become familiar with them.

4   Use continual affirmations that everyone is working to their targets and is a successful student.

5   Talk through the feelings of students about tests – well before the tests and with practical ideas about how to combat nerves. Repeat the same tests after giving feedback so that children practise skills without the challenge of new content and experience 'getting it right'.

6   Rehearse the tests frequently in the environment where children will take the real test. Ideally this should be a familiar and friendly place – like in base camp! If this is not possible, attempt to make the place you have to take tests feel friendly by practising there.

7   Have a rehearsal day or week where you get as authentic a practice of the test as possible: practise using different timings, different times for playtime, different structure to the day.

8   Use familiar 'entering music' for the time before formally beginning tests.

9   Teach relaxation and visualization techniques and practise these before each test begins.

10   When you practise, do so with the adults who will be present on the day. Keep the number of adults as low as possible.

11   Use the visual display posters as part of your learning strategy but reassure students that they will not need to see the posters to remember the facts. Cover the posters regularly and test informally.

12   Teach children to look through all tests at the beginning to see how much they have to do.

13   If your tests allow for some children to be read questions by an adult, do not put them in the same room as those reading to themselves. The other children will begin going back over their papers to check that they read the question properly and get distracted.

14   Practise tests using the sort of paper you will use on the day. Teach children to know how much they can write in the time allowed.

15   Practise using the correct equipment and explain how children will find sharp pencils or erasers.

16   Teach students to note how many points are allotted for questions so that they do not waste time expanding an answer for only one point.

17   Where appropriate, tell children to make a memory map plan – in an essay for example – and work from the plan.

18   Practise how you will remind children of the amount of time left in a test.

19   If an audio cassette is used in the statutory tests, make mock cassettes with a wide variety of different readers. Use people with different accents, both male and female, use 'posh' voices and stern voices – remember that these differences have an impact on children and prepare them for every eventuality.

20   Teach children to move on if they are unsure, and to mark the page and return later.

21   Use familiar celebration music when tests are over.

'Those who act receive the prizes.' (Aristotle)

Mental rehearsal of success

The following strategies work by helping the pupil practise positive approaches to learning in their head. First, we practise relaxation, then mental rehearsal of exam technique, then some short visualisations. The teacher guides the pupils through them on the first few occasions and then uses the scripts less and less.

For the anchoring activity, which is common to all three scripts, you may need to give some examples and prompt the children's responses. The idea is to locate a very positive experience that evokes in the child a feeling of satisfaction. Revisiting the experience can do the same thing again. We repeat the process and create an association or 'anchor' by using a small physical gesture made by the child just at the point when she remembers how good it 'felt' to be successful. A typical example might be to have the child 'press' her tummy button.

Some teachers may be nervous of using mental rehearsal techniques. Their purpose is to help children experience relaxation. Some never do so and may never genuinely do so. Many have lives that mitigate against this occurring other than through an intervention. The other purpose is to give them alternative and perhaps more positive mental images to relate to. Many children's mental rehearsal of exams and test are those of failure, dislocation and even humiliation. People who report a lot of anxieties about tests tend not to do well on the tests. This is not inevitable. Children have successes in their lives to which they can anchor positive mental images and associations. The scripts, which should be rehearsed beforehand, are part of your repertoire for helping them do so.

Where the text says (Pause) this means you pause in your reading. Relax as you read. Read slowly and deliberately without obvious change in emotion.

Me at my desk listening to my teacher

'He who is not courageous enough to take risks will accomplish nothing in life.'
(Muhammad Ali)

Relaxation scripts

'Before we start I'd like you to think of something that you have done recently that you were really good at and enjoyed being good at. It could be in school, or at home or when you were playing with friends. Slowly close your eyes. Try to remember what you did to make you feel so good. Did you enjoy doing really well? Did it make you feel nice? Can you remember just how nice you felt? When you remember it really well and you remember just how nice it was, push your magic button.

Being relaxed is really good for learning and for doing your best at anything. Being relaxed is when you are not worried about anything, you are calm and in control. To learn to relax we start by doing good sitting and good listening. Today we are doing good sitting on (describe) and we have our eyes closed. We are keeping our hands nice and still to practise being relaxed and now we will begin. With our eyes closed and taking nice long slow breaths. Breathe through your nose. Keep your mouth closed. Continue to breathe slowly and relax your head. Relax your head by keeping it nice and still and moving your eyebrows ever so gently. Now relax you mouth. Take nice deep breaths through your nose and let your mouth open just a little. Keep your head still and listen to your breathing going nice and deep and slow. Now we are going to relax our head even more. We do this by gently moving it from side to side, slowly, slowly. And now forwards and now backwards. And from side to side again. Now keeping perfectly still. Listen to your breathing ever so slow and quiet. Now we will relax our shoulders. Ever so gently wriggle them backwards and forwards. Notice how slow you can do it. And now we are feeling ever so relaxed. Feel you chest going slowly up and down as you breathe in … and then … out. Sit comfortably on the chair. Feel your feet flat on the floor. Take nice, deep, slow breaths and sit perfectly still. Now you are properly relaxed we can …'

Mental rehearsal for success

Before we start I'd like you to think of something that you have done recently that you were really good at and enjoyed being good at. It could be in school, or at home or when you were playing with friends. Slowly close your eyes. Try to remember what you did to make you feel so good. Did you enjoy doing really well? Did it make you feel nice? Can you remember just how nice you felt? When you remember it really well and you remember just how nice it was, push your magic button.

Now we are going to relax and practise our success technique. Take nice, deep, slow breaths and with your eyes watch yourself coming into the hall to do your test. You know where your desk is and you walk slowly to it. You are confident because you have practised your success technique. Now see yourself as you sit down at your desk and relax. Take some more nice deep slow breaths. Watch as you look at the desk and lay out all the things you need for your test: (list items). Now see yourself looking around and noticing how calm everyone is and how relaxed you feel. Now see yourself with the question paper in front of you. It is familiar. It is like the ones you practised on in class. It is (list features).

Either A
See yourself picking it up and looking at the front cover where it says (list). Watch as you open it and scan the questions before you start. You are reading to the end. Now you are about to start your first answer.

Or B
See yourself picking it up and looking at the front cover where it says (list). Watch as you open it and read all the questions carefully. You are reading to the end. Now you are organizing your answer paper and are about to start your first answer.

Or C
See yourself picking it up and looking at the front cover where it says (list). Watch as you open it and read all the questions carefully. You are reading to the end and deciding how much time for each question. Now you are organizing your answer paper and are about to start your first answer.

Watch carefully as you keep your eyes closed and continue to take nice, deep, slow breaths. As you successfully go through the questions you are being really clever and doing well. Notice how you are reading the question carefully and writing some keywords on your spare paper before you start. Every answer is really good because it is in proper sentences and paragraphs.

Visualization scripts

Good learner

Before we start I'd like you to think of something that you have done recently that you were really good at and enjoyed being good at. It could be in school, or at home or when you were playing with friends. Slowly close your eyes. Try to remember what you did to make you feel so good. Did you enjoy doing really well? Did it make you feel nice? Can you remember just how nice you felt? When you remember it really well and you remember just how good nice it was, push your magic button.

Now we are going to relax and practise being a good learner. Take nice, deep, slow breaths and with your eyes watch yourself coming into class. You know where your desk is and you walk slowly to it. You are a good learner. See yourself sitting down at the desk and ready to learn lots of new and interesting things. The things you learn will help you be confident and clever. Continue to breathe deeply and relax as you notice how good you are at asking questions. (Pause) When you ask a question you are good at thinking about it first, then knowing what you want to say then putting your hand up to catch your teacher's attention. You can wait for an answer. When you get an answer you like to think about it. In your head you ask yourself lots of questions when you learn. You are a good learner and good learners ask themselves lots of questions. (Pause) With your eyes still closed, breathe slowly and deeply and think of all the times when you got questions right and all the times when you practised until you had become really good at something. Good learners show patience and stick at it till they get it right. You are a good learner. Remember how good it feels to go home at the end of class knowing that you know lots and lots more things. The things you have learned make you even more confident and clever.

Stay a little longer noticing how good it feels to have become even better at learning. Notice how it feels to be confident and clever. Take deep breaths as you do so … and when you are ready, allow your eyes to open slowly, stretch out, move your shoulders back and turn to your partner and say, 'I am a really good learner!'

Good speller

Before we start I'd like you to think of something that you have done recently that you were really good at and enjoyed being good at. It could be in school, or at home or when you were playing with friends. Slowly close your eyes. Try to remember what you did to make you feel so good. Did you enjoy doing really well? Did it make you feel nice? Can you remember just how nice you felt? When you remember it really well and you remember just how good nice it was, push your magic button.

Now we are going to relax and practise our spelling. Take nice, deep, slow breaths and look at the word on the card in front of you. Look at all the letters of the word. Now close your eyes and see the word again. See all the letters. Open your eyes and see the same letters. Now as you slowly close your eyes again, see the word and all the letters and this time see the word move up and then move left. (Pause) As you continue to relax and breathe gently see the word and all the letters up and to the left, now with your eyes closed take your finger and trace over the word. Now trace over it again and say the letters to yourself. Do it again but this time make the word look bigger. Trace the letters and say them. (Pause) Now, as you get really good at spelling, see the word and spell it backwards, say each letter as you go. (Pause) When you are ready, choose another word and this time try it yourself.

Stay a little longer noticing how good it feels to have become a really good speller. Notice how it feels to be able to spell your words. Take deep breaths as you do so … and when you are ready, allow your eyes to open slowly, stretch out, move your shoulders back and turn to your partner and say, 'I am a really good speller!'

Review of Part Three

✔ When you write your next lesson plan, make a note of what content you will deliver at the beginning and end of the lesson to maximize learning through the primacy and recency effect. Plan for some mini-breaks where you will repeat the most important information. After the lesson, look at your plan and assess how well you timed the delivery of the key content.

✔ Try out some of our ten ways for organizing groups. List other ways that you use in your classroom. Share your methods with colleagues, and draw up a school list of suggestions for group organization that can be circulated or put in your staff handbook.

✔ Using the list below, select a lesson for an assessment of your effective use of VAK. Either ask a colleague to observe you, or give yourself a score between 1 and 10 for each of the statements. Then draw up an action plan for how to achieve a VAK balance through delivery of the next lesson.

Key vocabulary is visually reinforced through visual aids
Key vocabulary is kinesthetically reinforced through actions
Key vocabulary is aurally reinforced by the teacher and children
Key concepts are described verbally
Key concepts are demonstrated visually with diagrams, pictures or apparatus
Key concepts are experienced kinesthetically through practical activity or role-play
Regular brain breaks are used for movement and for reinforcement of learning
Music is used to evoke mood or to add significance to the delivery of part of the lesson
Memory maps are used to summarize learning and make connections
Posters are displayed to remind of concepts and connect the learning to other lessons

✔ Look at our model for structuring time on task on page 167. When you write your next lesson plans, prepare especially for diffusion tasks. These may be brain-break activities. Our suggestions for diffusions on page 168 may be a useful reference, as might our list of brain-break activities on page 133.

✔ Reread our light-hearted description of children and the multiple intelligences on pages 171–3 and think about the individuals in your class. Use the chart over to analyse each individual's strengths across the multiple intelligences. List the children's names in the first column. Then taking each child in turn, write 1 in the column that you would judge to be his greatest strength, 2 for the second greatest, and 3 for the third. When you have completed the list you will have a rough profile of what you consider to be the multiple intelligence range in your classroom.

Name	Linguistic	Mathematical/Logical	Inter personal	Intra personal	Visual/ spatial	Musical	Bodily/ kinesthetic	Naturalist

✔ Use the checklist below to measure how far you prepare children for statutory assessments. You may wish to do this as individuals, teams, or as a whole staff. You can then decide which activities could be introduced in your school.

Technique	Regularly	Sometimes	Never
Setting goals through life mapping			
Setting clear National Curriculum targets for individuals			
Sharing National Curriculum targets with parents			
Sharing National Curriculum targets with children			
Using test data to target set for improvement			
Making children aware of the curriculum			
Making parents aware of the curriculum			
Using visual posters and aids to reinforce learning			
Testing on the content of posters informally in class			
Making informal testing part of the everyday experience			
Practising realistic tests throughout the year			
Rehearsing in real-life test conditions			
Teaching skills such as noticing how many marks per question			
Using guided visualizations			
Discussing feelings about tests with children			
Using affirmations that everyone is successful in tests			
Teaching relaxation techniques			
Using music to enhance mood and atmosphere before tests			
Repeating tests after giving feedback about how to improve			
Celebrating success in tests			

Work on the computer

Dell

Do Maths

Fraction
$\frac{1}{4}$ $\frac{1}{2}$ $\frac{1}{3}$

Do English

Verbs

Do Art

Play the keyboard

Power

Doing P·E

When I learn I like to . . .

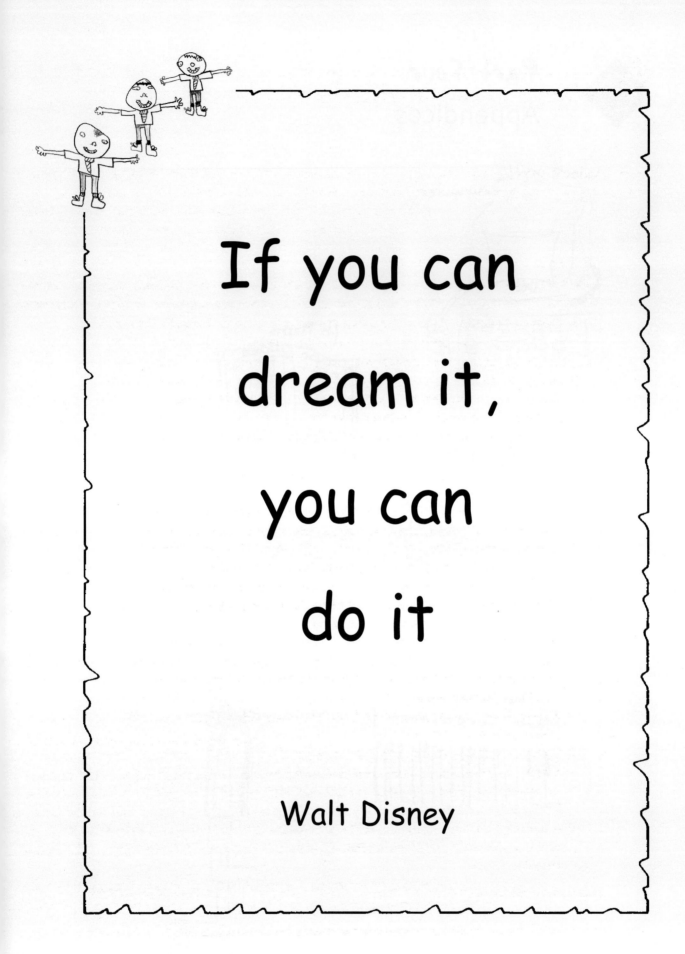

If you can dream it, you can do it

Walt Disney

Where to begin with the ALPS method™

Although some aspects of Accelerated Learning may be new to you, you will probably recognize some aspects of the ALPS method™ as systems that you already use in your classroom.

Ten ways that schools may choose to begin their journey into the ALPS

1 Each teacher selects one activity from this resource book or *The ALPS Approach* that appeals to her. She trials it in her classroom and gives a report back to the whole staff at the next staff meeting.

2 Each year group selects an area for development and works on it for a set time. They report to one another informally, then to a later staff meeting.

3 Each teacher or group of teachers agrees to produce the resources for an aspect of ALPS for the whole school; for example, target cards, desk labels, affirmation posters or Big Picture sheets.

4 An audio cassette on a subject such as relaxation techniques or mind mapping is circulated among the staff. Teachers listen to the cassette on their way to or from school, or at home, and then begin to use the techniques in their classrooms.

5 A whole school approach to RAP – recognition, affirmation and praise – is agreed. Ways that children's achievements are recognized are listed and, if necessary, increased. Whole school celebration times are developed. Ways of informing parents of their children's achievements are increased.

6 Marking codes are agreed in order to create a whole school approach to marking work. A poster of the school's marking codes is displayed in every classroom.

7 Each teacher develops an agreed number of recognition systems for her classroom. A minimum number of systems per class is agreed; for example; five weekly Superbrain awards, a daily Target Terminator celebration, or a weekly class celebration of achievement.

8 Each teacher agrees to display class, group and individual targets clearly so that a visitor would immediately understand the aims within the classroom.

9 An agreement is made about the purpose of display and a policy drawn up to facilitate visual learning in all areas of the school.

10 A tour of the school is taken by the whole staff to decide subjectively where the environment could be developed to facilitate greater learning. An action plan is then drawn up.

Forty small-scale action research projects that primary schools have trialled over one term

1 Providing breakfast clubs for parents and children with food and drinks before the formal start to school.

2 Looking at classroom layout and how it influences pupil language exchange.

3 Applying a whole school protocol to beginnings and endings of lessons with an emphasis on preview and review.

4 Redesigning a scheme of work to accommodate VAK.

5 Redesigning the school pupil planner and homework diaries to enhance their contribution to KS2 learning.

6 Using music and movement to improve recall of parts of a sentence, sentence construction and grammatical terms.

7 Using roleplay and drama to improve creative writing in Year 6.

8 Using the VAK strategy for mental maths.

9 Using kinesthetic learning approaches to timelines in history.

10 Working with a professional landscape architect to redesign the playground on accelerated learning principles.

11 Trialling the use of writing frames and problem-solving templates at KS2.

12 Intervention strategies for at-risk children in term five of schooling with particular reference to enhancing self-concept.

13 Teaching pole-bridging to Year 5 and evaluating their recall of mathematical processes.

14 Evaluating ways of introducing VAK to target setting with children.

15 Increasing the use of speculation and prediction activities in science at KS1.

16 Introducing a mentoring programme called 'Study Buddies' to improve reading in Year 1. Study Buddies drawn from pupils in Years 5 and 6.

17 Using kinesthetic approaches to teaching the functions of the human body and evaluating recall of the functions with another class as a control group.

18 A whole school approach with a progressive rewards system to positive affirmation of success and to esteeming children.

19 A whole school approach to brain breaks with suggested activities by year group described and listed in staff handbook.

20 Teaching good looking, good sitting, good sharing, good listening and good asking in reception class.

21 Using class, desk and individual memory maps to improve understanding of *A Midsummer's Night's Dream* with a high ability Year 6 English group.

22 Teaching the use of vowels and their sounds by using foam letters and puppets.

23 Teaching relaxation and mental rehearsal techniques prior to SATs tests.

24 Using themed assemblies around motivation, learning and achievement.

25 Testing recall of science through the use of classroom learning posters and memory maps.

26 Using Gardner's multiple intelligence model to redesign the school reward scheme. Gold, Silver and Bronze recognitions for achievements across the different intelligences.

27 Designing and delivering a 12 x 2-hour module for parents on 'how to talk to and read with your child'.

28 Introducing a VAK approach to spelling across the school and measuring using base-line data.

29 Using the five Rs learning questionnaire to initiate a Year 6 Learning to Learn programme.

30 Introducing and using a negotiated target-setting approach and evaluating it after one term. Starting in numeracy and literacy with targets copied onto A5 card, laminated and attached to pupils' desks, copied and sent home for signature.

31 Using different learning themes of the week and promoting those themes via the staff briefing paper and peripheral posters in the staffroom and around the school.

32 Testing recall of peripheral affirmation posters – who notices them and what do they notice.

33 Investigating how accelerated learning principles can be embodied into the pedagogy of a city farm.

34 Using the 'My Attitudes to Learning' questionnaire to examine changes in pupils' perceptions over time.

35 To redesign the ICT facility to accommodate accelerated learning principles and, in particular, to make it a positive and supportive learning environment for under fives.

36 Utilizing oral strategies for target setting and outcomes thinking prior to written work.

37 Examining the role of paired-shares and the pupil as coach in ICT.

38 Designing a six-week module on the five Rs for Year 6 pupils as part of PSHE and/or citizenship.

39 Renegotiating the school teaching and learning policy to accommodate the accelerated learning methods.

40 Planning a 'Use it or Lose it!' week with children to include guest speakers, learnathons, talent shows, memory techniques, problem-solving challenges.

Your engagement chart

This chart is to help you think about your attention and energy levels. Read the key that tells you all about attention. Then on the chart below write the letter that you think best suited you above each hour. You will probably need to use different letters to complete the chart. Next read the key that tells you all about your energy levels. Then on the chart mark a cross for the energy level that best suited you above each hour.

Was your attention?

Focused	means you are thinking of nothing else	(write F)
Wandering	means you are thinking of lots of different things	(write W)
Inside	means you are thinking your own thoughts	(write I)
Outside	means you are thinking about something happening in class	(write O)
Alert	means you are really curious	(write A)
Relaxed	means you are not thinking about much at all	(write R)

Was your energy?

Bursting

Full

Middling

Low

Flat

8 a.m.   9 a.m.   10 a.m.   11 a.m.   12 noon   1 p.m.   2 p.m.   3 p.m.   4 p.m.   5 p.m.   6 p.m.   7 p.m.

The 'how good am I at learning?' questionnaire

To do this questionnaire read each statement one at a time. Think about what it says. Think whether it is true about you or not. If it is really true, score 5. If it is completely untrue, score 1. If it is sort of true, score 4. If it is not very true, score 2. If you really can't decide, then score 3.

Once you have filled in all your scores, use the form to add up your totals. Then your teacher will explain to you what they mean!

		Not like me			Very like me	
		1	2	3	4	5
1	I rarely fall out with others in the class	1	2	3	4	5
2	I prefer to know why I am doing something before I begin	1	2	3	4	5
3	If I get lost I retrace my steps and try a different way	1	2	3	4	5
4	I don't make the same mistake twice	1	2	3	4	5
5	I stick at something till I get it right	1	2	3	4	5
6	I always think about what I got wrong and then try to improve	1	2	3	4	5
7	I sometimes change my mind after I've thought about it longer	1	2	3	4	5
8	If I think about it carefully, I can usually work it out	1	2	3	4	5
9	I always look over my work before I hand it in	1	2	3	4	5
10	If I get stuck, I move on and come back to it later	1	2	3	4	5
11	Sometimes I wait a bit and the answer comes	1	2	3	4	5
12	If I do wrong, I own up straight away	1	2	3	4	5
13	I work problems through step by step	1	2	3	4	5
14	I like to ask questions	1	2	3	4	5
15	I prefer to think about something for a while before I begin	1	2	3	4	5
16	I can look for the answers on my own	1	2	3	4	5
17	I set myself targets	1	2	3	4	5
18	I would help someone else in class	1	2	3	4	5
19	I will change my mind if something persuades me I'm wrong	1	2	3	4	5
20	I am good at working to deadlines	1	2	3	4	5
21	When I am beaten I forget about it and make sure I do better next time	1	2	3	4	5
22	I like to plan ahead	1	2	3	4	5
23	I will give up a treat to do something more important	1	2	3	4	5
24	I would never cheat	1	2	3	4	5
25	I don't give up	1	2	3	4	5

The 'how good am I at learning?' questionnaire total sheet

Add the scores

Add the scores

Statement		Scores
Statement	5	_____
Statement	17	_____
Statement	21	_____
Statement	23	_____
Statement	25	_____

Total for Resilience

Statement		Scores
Statement	2	_____
Statement	8	_____
Statement	13	_____
Statement	19	_____
Statement	22	_____

Total for Reasoning

Statement		Scores
Statement	1	_____
Statement	12	_____
Statement	18	_____
Statement	20	_____
Statement	24	_____

Total for Responsibility

Statement		Scores
Statement	4	_____
Statement	6	_____
Statement	9	_____
Statement	11	_____
Statement	15	_____

Total for Reflectivity –Reflexivity

Statement		Scores
Statement	3	_____
Statement	7	_____
Statement	10	_____
Statement	14	_____
Statement	16	_____

Total for Resourcefulness

What the scores mean: teacher explanation and script

These are scores that you have given yourself. This does not mean that this is how you are. It means that this is how you think you are.

Resilience

Resilience means you don't give up easily. The person who is resilient is also good at setting targets in their mind and giving themselves little rewards when they beat their targets. For example, you might say 'I'll finish this homework and then I'll watch television'. Or you might say 'I'll throw this ball against the wall and catch it 10 out of 10 and when I do it I'll have another sweet'. Another word for resilience is 'persistence'.

21–25

If you scored 21–25, you see yourself as someone who sticks at it until you get it right. This is very good for learning because not all problems are easy and straightforward. You will often be successful in lots of other things in life. You can talk to yourself positively and say things like 'I'm going to do this no matter what' or 'I'll get it right eventually'. You are good at setting targets and enjoy succeeding with the targets. You can easily imagine yourself being good at something.

16–20

If you scored 16–20, you see yourself as someone who works hard at getting things right. You are someone who is honest about being good at some things but maybe not so good at others. Knowing your strengths and weaknesses in learning is good because it helps you make changes for the better. Not all problems are easy and straightforward and working at them is important. You will be successful in lots of other things in life. You will be able to talk to yourself positively and say things like 'I'm going to give this my best' or 'I'll get it right eventually'. You are good at setting targets and enjoy succeeding with the targets when you think they are important. You can imagine yourself being good at something.

11–15

If you scored 11–15, you see yourself as someone who can work hard at getting things right when you feel like it. You sometimes get bored and give up even though you know you should stick at it. Knowing your strengths and weaknesses in learning is good because it helps you make changes for the better. Not all problems are easy and straightforward and working at them is important. You will be successful in some things in life but only those that quickly catch your interest. You can talk to yourself positively sometimes. You would say things like 'I'll give it a try' or 'I'll see if I like it'. You are reluctant to set yourself targets or start to do something if you think it is beyond you. When you imagine yourself trying to do something that is hard you feel anxious.

6–10

If you scored 6–10 you see yourself as someone who is easily bored. You find it hard to get going and motivate yourself on anything except what you feel like doing. You give up quickly when your interest goes, even though you don't feel good about this. Knowing your strengths and weaknesses in learning is good because it helps you make changes for the better. Avoid comparisons with others. Not all problems are easy and straightforward and working at them is important. To be successful you may need to become better at setting targets for yourself and giving yourself rewards when you achieve them. Practise talking to yourself positively. Make yourself say things like 'I'll give it a try' or 'I'll give it my best whatever'. Remember when you did something you were pleased with and did it really well and try to imagine yourself doing it over and over. When you are able to do this you have captured the feeling of success.

0–5

If you scored 0–5 you see yourself as being easily bored. Perhaps you compare yourself badly with other people. You find it hard to get going and motivate yourself on anything except what you like best. You give up quickly when your interest goes, even though you don't feel good about this. You should get a teacher to help you set targets. Make sure you finish one target successfully before going on to the next. Set yourself challenges. Because you give up on some learning tasks quickly doesn't mean you will always do this. Avoid comparisons with others. Practise talking positively to yourself. Make yourself say things like 'I'll give it a try' or 'I'll give it my best whatever'. Think of a time when you did something really well. Run your memory of this in your head like a film. If you can do this lots of times, you will begin to feel like a winner again!

> ### Teacher strategies for Resilience
>
> - ✪ Target-setting
> - ✪ Positive self-narrative
> - ✪ Self-rewarding
> - ✪ Visualization
> - ✪ Transfer talk

Responsibility

Responsibility means you know about right and wrong. It also means you know what you should and what you should not do in class to help your own learning. Finally, responsibility means that you do things that help the others in the class learn.

21–25

If you scored 21–25, you see yourself as someone who knows what they have to do and tries hard. You are aware of right and wrong and try to avoid getting into trouble. If you are asked to do something, you would do it. You can get work handed in on time and don't see homework as a chore. If someone in the class needed help, you would give help straight away. You are very honest. You enjoy the challenge of learning and you like being a member of a big team like the class. You are quick to volunteer.

16–20

If you scored 16–20, you see yourself as someone who knows what they have to do and can try hard. You know what is right and wrong. You try to avoid getting into trouble and avoid distractions. If you are asked to do something, you would usually do it. You can get work handed in on time. You do homework and try your best. If a friend in the class needed help, you would give help straight away. You enjoy learning new things and you like being a member of a big team like the class. You sometimes volunteer.

11–15

If you scored 11–15, you see yourself as someone who knows what they have to do and would usually try. You know what is right and wrong. Occasionally you get into trouble. Sometimes you get 'caught up' in distractions. If you are asked to do something, you would do it unless something better came along. You could get work handed in on time if you wanted. You usually do homework.

If someone you knew well in the class needed help, you would give help straight away. You enjoy learning most new things. You prefer to sit with your friends most of the time. You don't usually volunteer.

6–10

If you scored 6–10, you see yourself as someone who knows what they should do in class and mostly do it. You know what is right and wrong, but sometimes others get you in trouble. Some things you do annoy other people and stop them learning. You quite enjoy distractions. If you are asked to do something, you would usually do it unless something better came along. You don't usually get work handed in on time unless forced. You try to avoid homework. If someone in the class needed help, someone else would be better doing it. You don't enjoy learning most of the time. You prefer to sit with your friends. You rarely volunteer.

0–5

If you scored 0–5 you see yourself as someone who is on their own in the class. Some of the rules are pointless anyway. You know about right and wrong, but sometimes trouble is more fun. You do things that annoy other people and stop them learning. You enjoy distractions. If you are asked to do something, you would start it until something better came along. You don't get work handed in on time unless forced. You avoid homework. If someone in the class needed help, someone else would be better doing it. You don't enjoy learning much. You prefer to sit on your own. You don't volunteer.

Teacher strategies for Responsibility

☆ Groupings
☆ Time management
☆ Modelling what is desired
☆ Shared responsibilities

Resourcefulness

Resourcefulness means you know what to do when you get stuck. The person who is resourceful knows where to go for help and asks good questions. If you are resourceful, you would be quick to think of alternatives. You might try doing something in a different way. You would be prepared to change your mind if the evidence convinced you to do so.

21–25

If you scored 21–25, you see yourself as someone who is very curious and likes to try different ways of doing things. You are not afraid to get it wrong first time because you know there are other ways to get the right answer. When you get stuck you say to yourself 'what other ways could I do this?' In the class you ask lots of questions. You are not always the first to finish because you are thinking of alternatives. The questions you ask are not always the obvious ones. You enjoy visiting the library and searching for information. You enjoy looking up things on the internet and are good at finding your way around on it. You like to invent unusual things. If you were on your own in a strange place, you would enjoy finding out about it.

16–20

If you scored 16–20, you see yourself as someone who is curious and sometimes enjoys trying new things out. You usually like to get it right first time even though you know there might be other answers. When you get stuck you say to yourself 'could I do this another way?' In the class you ask questions. You are among the first to finish even though you are thinking of alternatives. The questions you ask are good ones. You sometimes enjoy searching for information. You enjoy looking up things on the internet and have favourites. You like to design unusual things. If you were on your own in a strange place, you would try to find someone to help you.

11–15

If you scored 11–15, you see yourself as someone who sometimes enjoys trying new things out. You try to get it right first time even though you know there might be other answers. When you get stuck you say to yourself 'should I have done this another way?' In the class you sometimes ask questions. You sometimes finish early and then look for something else to occupy you. You ask some good questions. You enjoy searching for information when you are asked to. You can look things up on the internet. You like to design things. If you were on your own in a strange place, you would be a little scared and try to find help immediately.

6–10

If you scored 6–10, you see yourself as someone who prefers familiar things. You prefer to be told what to do and try to get the right answer. When you get stuck you say to yourself 'what did I do wrong?' In the class you rarely ask questions, unless you need help. If you finish early, you wait for something else to occupy you. You ask questions. Searching for information on your own makes you nervous. You need help to look things up on the internet. You like to copy things. If you were on your own in a strange place, you would be very scared and not know what to do.

0–5

If you scored 0–5 you see yourself as someone who sticks with familiar things. It's best to be told what to do and then you try to get the right answer. When you get stuck you say to yourself 'I need help'. In the class you avoid asking questions. If you finish early, you wait to be told what to do next. You ask some questions. You don't like to look things up on your own. You need help to look things up on the internet. You enjoy copying things. If you were on your own in a strange place, you would be very scared and not know what to do.

> **Teacher strategies for Resourcefulness**
>
> ✭ Variety in questioning strategies
> ✭ Outcomes thinking
> ✭ Managing the moment of impulse

Reasoning

Reasoning is where you find the 'reasons' for something happening. A good 'reasoner' thinks problems through carefully. A good 'reasoner' collects all the important information, organizes it, compares it and then makes decisions. Reasoning is what you do when you make good choices and careful decisions.

21–25

If you scored 21–25, you see yourself as someone who thinks very carefully before making a decision. You like to work things through a bit at a time. If you get something wrong, you want to know why so that you can get better next time. As you try and solve a problem you think about how you are going about it. You will change the way you think about a problem to try to get the best answer. You will admit you are wrong if you see the proof of it. You can change your opinion if you are persuaded by evidence. You like to collect all the facts before you make a judgement. You think there are no problems that can't be worked out with the right method. You like explanations.

16–20

If you scored 16–20, you see yourself as someone who thinks carefully before making a decision. You prefer to work things through a bit at a time. If you get something wrong, you want to know why. As you try to solve a problem you can think about how you are going about it, though sometimes you just do it. You can change the way you think about something to try to get a correct answer. You will sometimes admit you are wrong if you see the proof of it. You can change your opinion if you are persuaded by evidence or by another person's point of view. You like to collect the facts before you make a judgement. You think there are no problems that can't be worked out with the right method with enough time. You like explanations.

11–15

If you scored 11–15 you see yourself as someone who thinks before making a decision. You mostly work things through a bit at a time. If you get something wrong, you sometimes want to know why. As you try to solve a problem you think about getting it finished and not about what you are doing. Sometimes you change your mind. You admit you are wrong if you are persuaded. Collecting facts is useful but less important to you than getting on with it. Some problems are too difficult to work out. Explanations are sometimes boring.

6–10

If you scored 6–10, you see yourself as someone who gets stuck with a problem. You can work things through a bit at a time with help. If you get something wrong, you don't want to know why, you want to do something else. As you try to solve a problem your mind can wander. Once you make up your mind it's hard for you to change it. Sometimes you admit you are wrong if you are persuaded to. You are not very interested in facts. You prefer just to do things. Some problems you can't work out. Explanations are often boring.

0–5

If you scored 0-5, you see yourself as someone who gets stuck with problems often. You can work things through a bit at a time but usually you need help. If you get something wrong, you get fed up and want to do something else. As you try to solve a problem your mind wanders. Problems that are hard are boring. Once you make up your mind you don't think about it again. You can admit you are wrong if you are persuaded to. Facts are dull. You prefer to do things. There are a lot of problems you can't work out. Explanations are boring.

Teacher strategies for Reasoning

* Open-ended problem solving
* Mapping techniques
* Templates
* Hierarchy of questions

Reflectivity–Reflexivity

R-R is being able to think about something afterwards and then learn from it. For example, when you have had an argument with a friend a good 'reflector-reflexor' would think about what happened and why and then think about different ways of getting a better outcome next time. R-R is important for learning because the first answer is not always the best. R-R helps you stop making silly mistakes. R-R is also about perfecting performance through practising. You cannot become a top performer – in sport, music or science, for example – without being good at R-R.

21–25

If you scored 21–25, you see yourself as someone who makes an effort to learn from mistakes. If you make a mistake, you do not feel that it is a disaster but an opportunity to get better. You plan your work beforehand. Before you start you have a clear sense of what you are going to do. You always go over work before you hand it in. You are the sort of person who enjoys practising. When you practise you change the routines around to get little performance improvements. Many things that used to seem really difficult you now find so easy they feel natural. You enjoy finding out how skilled performers improve. You often wonder why things occur the way they do.

16–20

If you scored 16–20, you see yourself as someone who tries to learn from mistakes. If you make a mistake, you will try to learn from it and 'not just avoid doing it next time'. You plan important work beforehand. Before you start you have a sense of what you are going to do. You usually go over work before you hand it in. You are the sort of person who practises to get better. When you practise, you notice your improvements. Some things that used to seem really difficult you now find much easier. You admire skilled performers and wonder how they improve.

11–15

If you scored 11–15, you see yourself as someone who can learn from mistakes. If you make a mistake, you will mostly try to learn from it, but sometimes avoid doing it next time. You think a little about work beforehand, but mostly you just get started. You rarely go over work before you hand it in. You are the sort of person who practises but would give up unless it was something you were really interested in. When you practise, you just get on with it. You think you are good at some things but not at others, and no matter how hard you tried you think you would never become good at them. You admire people who can do things really well.

6–10

If you scored 6–10, you see yourself as someone who avoids mistakes but often makes them. When you make a mistake you sometimes think about it to try to get better, but mostly you try to avoid doing it next time. When you complete work, you don't plan first. You never go over work before you hand it in. You don't re-read exam answers. You are the sort of person who practises until something more interesting comes along. When you practise, it's usually because you have to. You think you are good at some things but not at others, and no matter how hard you tried you know you would never become good at them. You admire people who do the things really well that interest you.

0–5

If you scored 0–5, you see yourself as someone who regularly makes mistakes. When you make a mistake you sometimes repeat the mistake. You get embarrassed about mistakes and try and avoid that work. If you complete work, you don't plan first. You don't go over work before you hand it in. You don't re-read exam answers. You are the sort of person who practises but only if made to, or if it's for something you are really interested in. You think some people are just naturally good at things.

Teacher strategies for Reflectivity–Reflexivity

★ Regular review
★ Post-analysis of student work
★ Emphasis on perfect practice

4

The self-esteem questionnaire

To do this questionnaire read each statement one at a time. Think about what it says. Then tick never, sometimes, always or don't know. Take your time. Do it on your own and think of your answers carefully.

Once you have filled in all your ticks your teacher will explain to you what they mean!

		Never	Sometimes	Always	Don't know
1	Do you ever want to answer a question but don't in case you look foolish?	☐	☐	☐	☐
2	Do you like to do well at school?	☐	☐	☐	☐
3	When you start something important do you finish it?	☐	☐	☐	☐
4	Do the others in the class listen to you when you have a suggestion?	☐	☐	☐	☐
5	Do you like reading?	☐	☐	☐	☐
6	Do your parent(s) like to hear about what you're doing at school?	☐	☐	☐	☐
7	Do you often feel lonely at school?	☐	☐	☐	☐
8	Do the others in the class ever pick on you?	☐	☐	☐	☐
9	If something is difficult, do you give up?	☐	☐	☐	☐
10	Does pleasing the teacher make you try harder?	☐	☐	☐	☐
11	When you close your eyes can you imagine yourself being really good at something?	☐	☐	☐	☐
12	Do you like watching television?	☐	☐	☐	☐
13	Do you think of things about yourself you would like to change?	☐	☐	☐	☐
14	Do you often feel sad because no one wants to play with you?	☐	☐	☐	☐
15	When you try hard at school do you get better?	☐	☐	☐	☐
16	Do you enjoy doing maths?	☐	☐	☐	☐
17	Do you ever dream about being someone better?	☐	☐	☐	☐
18	Are the others in the class pleased if you do well?	☐	☐	☐	☐
19	Do you try to better your last score?	☐	☐	☐	☐
20	Do other children often break friends with you?	☐	☐	☐	☐
21	Do you like to join in when there are group games in class?	☐	☐	☐	☐

The self-esteem questionnaire scoring table – for use by teachers with pupils

Scoring table

	Never	Sometimes	Always	Don't know
1	2	1	-1	0
2	-1	1	2	0
3	-1	1	2	
4	-1	1	2	0
5	ma.	ma	ma.	ma.
6	-1	1	2	0
7	2	1	-1	0
8	2	1	-1	0
9	2	1	-1	0
10	-1	1	2	0
11	-1	1	2	0
12	ma.	ma	ma.	ma.
13	-1	1	2	0
14	2	1	-1	0
15	-1	1	2	0
16	ma.	ma	ma.	ma.
17	2	1	-1	0
18	-1	1	2	0
19	-1	1	2	0
20	2	1	-1	0
21	-1	1	2	0

Questions 5, 12 and 16 are mask questions and should be disregarded.
For information:

Questions 7, 14 and 20 relate to belonging
Questions 6, 11 and 15 relate to aspirations
Questions 1, 8 and 21 relate to safety
Questions 4, 13 and 17 relate to identity
Questions 3, 9 and 19 relate to challenge
Questions 2, 10 and 18 relate to success

5 The emotional intelligence questionnaires

The five dispositions for lifelong learning – responsibility, resourcefulness, resilience, reasoning and reflectivity-reflexivity – correlate with what the American author Daniel Goleman calls 'Emotional Intelligence'. He argues that this emotional intelligence could be a more significant factor in a child's future than any other measure of intelligence. If a child has emotional intelligence, he will display responsibility, resourcefulness, resilience, reasoning and reflectivity-reflexivity.

The five sections of the following questionnaires correlate with what Daniel Goleman describes as the psychologist Salovey's five main domains of emotional or 'personal' intelligence. These five aspects of emotional intelligence, in short, are:

→ self-awareness

→ management of emotions

→ self-motivation

→ empathy

→ handling relationships.

In the ALPS teachers actively teach for emotional intelligence. But first teachers need to know the strengths and weaknesses of the individuals in the class. This can be done by careful assessment of children's reactions to different situations. The teacher's questionnaire opposite can also help you reflect on each child individually. The questionnaire can be used independently, or in conjunction with the child's questionnaire that follows. The child's questionnaire mirrors the questions in the teacher's version in a more simplified version. The third question in each section of the child's questionnaire is a mask question, which is included to minimize inaccurate responses. It can be used as a tool to gain the child's personal viewpoint about her level of emotional intelligence, which can then be used to compare the teacher's perspective with that of the child.

Teacher's notes for 'The child's emotional intelligence questionnaire': Questions 3, 6, 9, 12 and 15 are mask questions and should be discounted. For the other questions, score 1 point for a 'No' answer, 2 points for a 'Sort of' and 3 points for a 'Yes'. The sections A to E correspond to the categories in the teacher's questionnaire.

The teacher's emotional intelligence questionnaire

Many teachers find it is best not to try to complete this questionnaire for each child in their class in one session and take several short sessions to do this activity. Some work in pairs with another teacher who knows the class, such as the teacher who taught the class the previous year. Having a second perspective about a child can be a great help!

Take each child in your class in turn. Consider each question and mark the description that most closely describes that child. You may wish to use the space on the side of the page to make notes. Often the notes that you make will be of the greatest significance.

		Never	Rarely	Sometimes	Often	Always
Section A						
1	When provoked into feeling cross or upset, is able to calm down and rationalize the situation before reacting.	☐	☐	☐	☐	☐
2	After an upsetting or aggravating event, chooses to talk and express the emotions that he felt.	☐	☐	☐	☐	☐
3	Is able to shake off a bad mood.	☐	☐	☐	☐	☐
Section B						
4	Displays emotions that seem proportional to the event, whether excitement and happiness, or frustration and unhappiness.	☐	☐	☐	☐	☐
5	Takes an appropriate amount of time to shake off a bad mood.	☐	☐	☐	☐	☐
6	Shows a balance of different emotional states such as happiness, excitement, joy, sadness, frustration and anger.	☐	☐	☐	☐	☐
Section C						
7	Controls any tendency towards impulsive behaviour.	☐	☐	☐	☐	☐
8	Expects to succeed and is optimistic when faced with a new challenge.	☐	☐	☐	☐	☐
9	Has a hobby/interest/enthusiasm either in or outside school at which she seems to be determined to excel.	☐	☐	☐	☐	☐
Section D						
10	Mirrors the emotions of peers: if a friend is upset or angry, she displays similar emotions.	☐	☐	☐	☐	☐
11	Reports another child's emotional state to an adult and seeks help for others.	☐	☐	☐	☐	☐
12	Can describe in detail the emotions of characters in stories, films or books.	☐	☐	☐	☐	☐
Section E						
13	Is able to organize and lead groups of children and games on the playground.	☐	☐	☐	☐	☐
14	Effectively negotiates and settles arguments between peers.	☐	☐	☐	☐	☐
15	Is willing and able to work with any other child in the class.	☐	☐	☐	☐	☐

Your scores for each child should highlight individual areas of strength and weakness. On pages 211–14 we give some activities that can be done in class to develop each of these aspects of emotional intelligence.

The child's emotional intelligence questionnaire

For each of the questions below, tick one box. If you think that a description sounds exactly like you, tick 'Yes'. If it doesn't sound like you at all, tick 'No'. If it sounds a bit like you, tick 'Sort of'.

		No	Sort of	Yes
Section A				
1	When I feel cross or upset, I walk away from the person who has upset me.	☐	☐	☐
2	If I'm upset or angry, I find someone to talk to about what is bothering me.	☐	☐	☐
3	I always remember to watch my favourite TV programmes when they are on.	☐	☐	☐
Section B				
4	If I'm in a bad mood, it only lasts a few minutes.	☐	☐	☐
5	When I'm happy or excited, I like to show it so that everyone knows	☐	☐	☐
6	I am always allowed to go out to play when my friends call for me.	☐	☐	☐
Section C				
7	I never get in trouble for arguing or fighting at playtime.	☐	☐	☐
8	I have a hobby outside school that I work hard at to improve in.	☐	☐	☐
9	I never argue with my parents or brothers and sisters.	☐	☐	☐
Section D				
10	If my best friend gets upset, it makes me feel upset too, even if I can't do anything to help.	☐	☐	☐
11	I get upset and worry about characters in TV programmes or books, even though I know that they are make-believe.	☐	☐	☐
12	I like to spend time with my grandparents or cousins at weekends.	☐	☐	☐
Section E				
13	My friends often pick me to be captain of games at playtime.	☐	☐	☐
14	I like all the other children in my class and don't mind if I'm picked to work with any of them.	☐	☐	☐
15	If my teacher told my parents that I had been naughty in class, I'd be very worried.	☐	☐	☐

Five activities to develop emotional intelligence in the classroom

To develop self-awareness

Read aloud the script below, or make up one of your own. Extracts from books can be used effectively for this activity. Be as melodramatic as you like, stressing the emotional aspect of the text.

'Simon had always longed to have a dog. He had asked his mum over and over again. He had written the word 'puppy' on his Christmas list every year since he was old enough to write. He had also begged his grandfather to get him a dog.

'But Simon, you live in an apartment. How could you keep a dog there? A dog needs a garden, with space to run around,' they had said, over and over again.
'It could live with Grandpa,' said Simon, 'and I could just have it at weekends.'
'But Grandpa is too old to take on that sort of responsibility, and in any case, who would take it for walks?' his mum would say, and Simon knew that he was never likely to get a dog. One Christmas, his mum had tried to make him feel better by buying him a goldfish. Simon had tried to smile when she gave it to him, but he felt a bitter disappointment, like a large, sour pill stuck in his throat.

Then one evening, his mum told him some news. 'I've been offered a new job,' she said, 'it's a great opportunity, and comes with a big pay rise.'
'That's great, mum,' said Simon. He knew how tough it had been for his mum, since his dad had left them three years ago. His dad now lived down the road in a nice house with his new wife, Lorna, her ten-year-old son Jason, and their six-month-old baby, Samantha. Simon loved his dad, but sometimes he wanted to yell at him, 'Why? Why did you do this to mum? She was always kind to you, she cooked, she cleaned, she worked hard! Why did you have to go off with someone like Lorna?'

Lorna was everything that Simon's mum had been when she'd first married his dad, and wasn't now. Lorna was slim, pretty, well-dressed and always smelled of expensive perfume. She wore high-heeled shoes that Simon thought must be impossible to walk on. He had once tried them on for fun, and Jason had seen. Sneering, Jason had called Lorna, who had yelled at Simon and told him to leave her stuff alone. Later she had told his dad, who had said that he had to have more respect for his stepmother and stop causing trouble, or he'd not be allowed to visit when his dad wasn't there. Simon hadn't meant any harm by trying on her shoes, it was just a joke, he just wanted to see how she walked in them. He hadn't meant to cause trouble! Jason had smirked and pulled faces at Simon behind the grown-ups' backs. Simon had wanted to murder him. When they were out playing, sometimes Jason could be OK, even good fun. But the moment they were near Jason's mum and Simon's dad, there was trouble. Jason seemed so smug that he'd ended up living at the smart house, with his mum and Simon's dad, when Simon just lived in the pokey flat with his mum. Simon only got to visit his dad every other weekend, whereas Jason got to live in the house with the garden all the time. Sometimes Simon wanted to strangle him for being so smug!

In contrast to Lorna, who didn't go to work and only seemed to sit around the hairdresser's or having coffee with her friends, Simon's mum was often tired. She worked hard at the bank, and could rarely afford to have her hair done, let alone a manicure like Lorna had every Friday afternoon ready for the weekend.

Simon acted as if he liked Lorna when he went to his dad's house, but in fact he loathed her with a vengeance – he hated her neat house, her clean car and her manicured nails. Her nails were always painted a bright red. Simon far preferred his mum's natural look. His mum was a real mum, not a painted doll like Lorna. The only thing Simon liked about going to his dad and Lorna's house was seeing Samantha, although Lorna would spoil his visits by fussing over Samantha as if Simon was five years old, not ten-and-a-half and about to go to secondary school. 'Don't do that … put her down … no, don't touch her bottle, it'll get germs … Simon, please be careful, you'll hurt her' and so on and so on. Blah blah blah. Simon wished that Lorna would disappear in a puff of smoke and his mum could get back with his dad. Then she'd be able to get out of that pokey little flat and he'd be able to have a dog. Lorna wouldn't let Jason have a dog, but if Simon's mum lived in a house like that, she'd let him get one straight away.

Mum was still telling him about the job. 'It does mean that we'd have to move, though, Simon. You'd have to move schools.'
'Uh,' muttered Simon, still in a daydream about Lorna disappearing over a cliff in a puff of smoke, painted nails sticking out of the smoke trying to grasp at a ledge, rather like a wicked witch in a horror movie.
'I'll understand if you don't want to,' his mum went on, mistaking his 'uh's' to be a lack of enthusiasm for her new job. 'If you really don't want to go, I could turn it down.'
'Uh,' said Simon, not really listening, still deep in his vision of Lorna, high-heeled shoes disappearing into a cavern of green smoke.
'Of course, you could have a dog, if we do move,' went on his mum.

Lorna disappeared with a whoosh, and Simon stood up and yelled. 'Yipppeee! A dog, a real dog, I'll really be allowed a dog!'
He gave his mum a big smacking kiss on the cheek. 'Can I go to tell Grandpa?'
His mum nodded, taken aback at his sudden change of heart. Simon ran out of the room and out of the front door, yelling as he charged down the steps to the ground floor. 'Yippeeeeee! Yippeeeeee! Yippeeeeee!' echoed up the stairs.
'Life,' thought Simon, 'is good!'

When you have finished, ask the children to reflect on their feelings. Follow up with a discussion of how they felt, either in pairs, groups or as a class. With older children you may wish to ask them to write down keywords to express their feelings. Alternatively, you may wish to brainstorm keywords for the emotions that children express, writing them up on the board or on cards, or a memory map. Saying the words with passion in a tone that enhances the feelings will add impact to the activity.

Once you have a list or memory map of the children's reaction to the text, you may wish to open up discussion about whether it is necessary to control those emotions and if so, how this could be done. For example, one would not wish to rationalize and control any joy felt about an unexpected gift or treat, nor is it healthy to subdue grief at the death of a pet. However, the anger felt when a Lego® model is accidentally dropped is best rationalized and managed, rather than leading to a fist-fight or outburst of tears and screams. Children often need to be taught the difference between appropriate and inappropriate displays of emotions. This can be done in discussion, through written responses to the texts, or through roleplay.

Other issues that you may wish to explore with children by finding appropriate published texts or by devising your own could include:

❖ bereavement

❖ loss of a pet

❖ jealousy of a sibling or new baby

❖ fear of bullies

❖ having an operation or medical treatment

❖ the theft of a bike or a favourite toy

❖ the break up of a friendship

❖ an argument with the family or friends

❖ starting a new school or class.

To develop the management of emotions

After an activity such as the one above, ask the children to roleplay a part of the scenario from the script. For example, in pairs the children could explore how Simon felt when Jason and Lorna told his dad that he had tried on her shoes. Encourage the children to display the emotions that they would feel in that situation: the embarrassment at having been caught, the resentment about the situation of Simon's mother as opposed to that of his stepmother, the anger against Jason for telling on him, his fondness for his half-sister, and the expectation that he must act as if he liked Lorna when his feelings were quite different.

First, encourage the children to really express their feelings aloud. Allow them to start impassioned arguments, imagining that they can say whatever they feel. Encourage them to act out their roleplays to other groups. Then start to explore the possible outcomes of Simon actually saying aloud what he feels about Jason and his stepmother. Consider the effect on Simon – such as an instant sense of satisfaction and relief, followed by guilt and discomfort. End the activity with a discussion about the emotions felt and the appropriateness or inappropriateness of verbalizing these emotions rashly. Discuss where it might be best for Simon to explore these feelings, maybe with his mother at home, or his dad, or with a grandparent or a teacher. Finally, make a note of the key points on the board to help the visual learners in the class.

To develop self-motivation

Create situations where children can set personal targets and challenge themselves. Do so in non-academic ways in addition to setting academic targets and encourage an optimistic approach. For example, in PE lessons set challenges, such as shooting basketball goals. Give children notebooks to record personal achievements. Ask them to predict their next score. Allow time for practise. Analyse technique, such as, 'When Joanne put her weight on her back leg her throw seemed more controlled.' Create an 'I bet I could' display board in the classroom and encourage every child to display their personal targets and challenges.

Change the challenge regularly, so that all children have a chance to excel. Draw attention to the power of positive thinking. For example, 'I bet I could run three laps in two minutes next time' is more likely to lead to success than, 'I'll try but I'm no good at running fast'. Allow children to decide on activities and targets, and discourage competitive behaviour – the competition is against oneself, trying to set a personal best. Include out-of-school activities and ask children to report targets and successes from both inside and outside school. Display the key criteria for successful completion of targets in the classroom:

- ☺ Think positive
- ☺ Aim to improve a little at a time
- ☺ Record your progress
- ☺ Analyse your performance
- ☺ Celebrate your success!

To develop empathy

In roleplays such as the ones above, ask children to consider the feelings of the other characters in each scenario. For example, after allowing Simon to express his feelings of anger and hurt, ask the child playing Jason to start to put his point of view across. Explore Jason's feelings about Simon and his father. Perhaps Jason feels that Simon is his father's favourite, and that he and Samantha will always come second. Perhaps he knows that Simon doesn't like him and also that Simon wishes his mother would disappear so that Simon's dad could remarry Simon's mum.

As you gradually build in the second person's perspective on the situation, ask the children to consider the impact of Simon's original outburst on the other character. Swap characters and get each child to experience the feelings of the other character. Ask the child playing Jason to express his feelings, just as Simon expressed his. Stress the fact that both characters have a perspective and encourage an empathetic response to both.

To develop social competence

Create group times where children take it in turns to be allocated the role of leader. Decide before the activity what qualities the group leader will need. Set up systems for the group leader to develop these skills. For example, give a soft toy to the group leader, which he hands to each individual to give him permission to speak. Everyone should get a turn to hold the toy and speak, but only the person with the toy can speak at any one time. Or play a piece of music, during which everyone can speak. At the end of the music, the group leader must reflect back what was said and draw conclusions. Give a structure in which the group leader can use his social skills. Help him by creating rules and enforcing them.

The homework questionnaire

This is not a competition. Everyone will get different scores for different sections of the quiz. A higher mark does not mean that you are better or worse, it just shows how you are different. Your teacher is going to use the information from your scores to decide what sort of learner you are and help you to improve even more! Everyone will end up with a set of targets when they have finished this exercise.

Read each statement and decide how well it describes you. If you think this is exactly like you, give it a score of 5. If it is not at all like you, give it 0. If it is somewhere in between, give it a score between 0 and 5. The higher the score, the more closely the sentence describes you.

For example, read the following statement:

'I always choose to do my homework the minute I get home.'

If this is true, you always choose to do your homework the minute you get home, and never leave it until later, give yourself a score of 5. If this is not at all true because you like to do your homework after you have eaten, give yourself a score of 0. If you nearly always do your homework the minute you get home, give yourself 4, or if you rarely do your homework immediately, give yourself 1, and so on. Try to answer quickly and do not spend too long thinking about each one. Just think how well the sentence describes you and give it a mark.

Section one   Score
1 When I do my homework, I always have to look for a different sort of pencil or something.   ____
2 I always lend my pencils and pens to my friends.   ____
3 I keep lots of stuff in my schoolbag and I have to rummage around to find things.   ____
4 I get fed up because when I go to use my pens many of the lids are missing.   ____
5 I often forget where I have put my school things at home.   ____
Total:

Section two   Score
1 Adults in my family often have to remind me to do my homework.   ____
2 I prefer to go to play or watch TV before I do my homework.   ____
3 I often ask an adult in my family to write a note to say I didn't have time to do my homework.   ____
4 I am often late handing in my homework.   ____
5 I am often late to school because I have been doing my homework in the morning.   ____
Total:

Section three   Score
1 I often do not understand what I am supposed to do when I sit down to do my homework.   ____
2 I often ask an adult in my family to write me a note to say that I didn't understand the homework.   ____
3 I can only do my homework if someone helps me.   ____
4 I often forget what the homework is and have to phone someone.   ____
5 I often ask my teacher to explain the homework the next day and do it the next evening.   ____
Total:

Section four   Score
1 I like to do my homework with the TV or the radio on.   ____
2 I often chat to my family while I do my homework.   ____
3 I hate to do my homework in a room on my own.   ____
4 If the phone rings, I always rush to answer it.   ____
5 I like to leave my homework part of the way through and come back to it later.   ____
Total:

Now add up your scores for each section and write each in the box. In which section did you score highest? This is the area that you need most help with, so your teacher will give you a set of targets to help you with those. When you have succeeded with all those targets, your teacher will give you a set for the section that you scored your second highest mark in, then the third, then the fourth. This means that the targets are tailor-made for you!

Homework Target Card: Section one

The targets on this card are aimed to help you to become tidier and more organized. It is no good if you are ready to do your homework, but do not have all the pens and pencils you need. Work your way through the targets and suggestions below, and you will find that you will never have to go searching for your belongings again!

1 Put all the lids on your pens. Throw away any that do not work.
2 Put all your pens and pencils into one pencil case.
3 Never put a blunt pencil or a pen without a lid back into your pencil case.
4 Sort your school bag and put things into plastic zip-up wallets.
5 Agree with your teacher or parents a weekly time to tidy your school bag and pencil case.
6 Keep one plastic wallet especially for finished homework.
7 Agree with your parents one place at home where you will always keep your schoolbag.
8 Agree with your parents where in your bedroom you will keep your school things.
9 Organize this place with plastic wallets, containers and holders. Label them.
10 Ask your teacher to help you to establish some rules about borrowing and lending equipment.

Homework Target Card: Section two

The targets on this card should help you to manage your time more effectively. Often you aim to do your work but the time slips past and you end up in a rush. You need to decide on a plan for how to manage your time and then ask your family and friends to help you to stick to it.

1 Write a list of the times that you do things each evening, such as supper, bath and bedtime.
2 Make a timetable, putting in the activities that you do regularly, such as clubs or sports.
3 Think about the times that you work best, such as before you have eaten, or in the morning.
4 Sit down with an adult in your family and work out the best times each day to do homework.
5 If necessary, tape your favourite TV programme to watch after you have done homework.
6 If you agree to do homework in the mornings, set your alarm at an earlier time.
7 Draw up your timetable clearly. Display it at home where the whole family can see it.
8 Tell your friends when you plan to work. Ask them not to call for you during this time.
9 Put a copy of this timetable on your desk at school for the first few weeks to remind you.
10 Ask a member of your family to work at the same time as you for the first few weeks.

Homework Target Card: Section three

These targets should help you to understand what homework you need to do so that you do not feel confused or muddled about what to do. You need to become more aware of what is being explained and make sure that you are really listening to instructions.

1 If you do not have a diary for writing down homework tasks, you need to get one.
2 When your teacher explains homework, make sure that you look at her.
3 When your teacher explains homework, think about what she says and make brief notes.
4 Do not look at worksheets unless your teacher tells you to – look at her and listen instead.
5 Never try to do the work as your teacher is explaining – you will miss an instruction.
6 When you have written your notes, check them with another child.
7 Explain the work in your own words to a friend before you leave for home.
8 Ask your friend to explain the work to you in his own words.
9 If you are still unsure, wait until after school, then check your notes with your teacher.
10 As soon as you get home, get out your notes and explain the work to an adult.

Homework Target Card: Section four

This set of targets is aimed to help you deal with distractions when you are working. You cannot concentrate fully if you are watching TV, playing with pets or talking while you work.

1 Talk to the adults in your family about the various places that you could do your homework.
2 Agree on a place where you can sit at a table with space to work.
3 Agree that while you work, the television and radio will be turned off.
4 Look up television programmes in a TV guide and tape favourites to watch later.
5 If you like music, agree on suitable classical music, not anything that will tempt you to sing!
6 Agree with the adults in your family that while you do homework, you will not answer the phone or door.
7 Ask your family to tell anyone who calls for you during homework time to call back later.
8 While you work, make a rule that brothers and sisters either work, or leave the room.
9 Make a rule that you always finish your work in one go, and never leave half way through.
10 Ask to co-ordinate the family's homework plan, so that you all do your work at the same time.

Contact list

Accelerated Learning in Training and Education, (ALiTE), 45 Wycombe End, Beaconsfield, Bucks HP9 1LZ   tel: 01494 671444   fax: 01494 671776
office@alite.co.uk
www.alite.co.uk
Training in school and classroom approaches described in this book.

Anglo-American Books	Bookstore tel: 01267 211880; www.anglo-american.co.uk
ASCD	The best US organization for principals and headteachers www.ascd.org
Association for Neuro-Linguistic Programming	Promotes NLP in UK www.anlp.org
Binoh Centre	Training in Feuerstein's Instrumental Enrichment approaches
Campaign for Learning	Advocates for lifelong learning (www.campaign-for-learning.org.uk)
CASE/CAME	Application of thinking skills in subject areas – CASE Administrator Kings College, London tel: 0207 872 3134
Critical Thinking Books & Software	Excellent thinking materials from a California-based publisher www.criticalthinking.com
DEMOS	Independent think-tank publishing good material on learning to learn www.demos.co.uk
IAL	International Alliance for Learning – dedicated to improving performance through accelerated learning (www.ialearn.org)
London Leadership Centre	Leading thinking on the management of schools http://ioewebserver.ioe.as.uk
Model Learning	Specialists in mapping techniques for schools tel: 01277 202812; www.modellearning.com
National College for School Leadership (NCSL)	Learning and development for existing and aspiring school leaders; active in research and development, and online learning www.ncsl.org.uk
Questions Publishing Company	Publishes thinking skills materials for schools tel: 0121 212 0919; www.education-quest.com
SAPERE	Society for Advancement of Philosophical Enquiry & Reflection in Education tel: 01278 68347; www.sapere.net
SEAL	Society for Effective Affective Learning (www.seal.org.uk)
University of the First Age	Promotion of alternative learning opportunities for pupils tel: 0121 202 2347; www.ufa.org.uk

Key vocabulary and definitions for pupils

Attention	when you concentrate on one thing and nothing else
Big Picture	what is about to happen
Brain breaks	exercise for the brain
Brain food, strain food	food that's good for you and food that isn't
Connecting the Learning	connecting what you are doing now to previous lessons
Feedback	learning how to improve
Five dispositions for learning	resilience, responsibility, resourcefulness, reasoning and reflectivity–reflexivity
Keywords	the important words you have to know
Magic spelling	practising spelling by seeing the word, saying it and pretending to write it up above your eyes and to the left
Memory mapping	maps that help you think
Mental rehearsal	when you go over how you will do something by thinking about it first
Metacognition	being aware of your own thinking
Multiple intelligences	different ways of being clever
Pole-bridging	talk yourself through it
Primacy and recency	beginnings and endings
Review	going over things so you don't forget
Self-test	testing that you have got it right
Self-esteem	see, hear and do
SPECS	memory secrets: see, personalize, exaggerate, connect, share
Targets	when you say how you will improve something and write down what you will improve
VAK	Visual, Auditory, Kinesthetic

The ten best of everything (almost)

Brilliant books for teachers by topic

Carter, Rita, *Mapping the Mind* (Weidenfield and Nicholson, 1998)
Comprehensive and beautifully illustrated tour of mind and brain for a lay audience

Claxton, Guy, *Wise Up: The Challenge of Lifelong Learning* (Bloomsbury, 1999)
Idiosyncratic and well written argument for learning to learn

Goleman, Daniel, *Emotional Intelligence – Why it Matters More than IQ* (Bloomsbury, 1996)
The book that launched the fad. Very readable

Gopnik, Alison et al., *How Babies Think* (Weidenfield and Nicholson, 1999)
Why Piaget got it wrong! Leading-edge research on babies' mental processing

Hannaford, C., *Smart Moves: Why Learning Is Not All In Your Head* (Great Ocean Publishers, 1995)
Quirky rationale for brain breaks, hydration, impact of dominance on learning

Howard, Pierce J., *The Owners Manual for the Brain*, 2nd edn (Bard Press, 2000)
Marvellous and very full summary of research relating to psychology of learning and
performance. Very readable

Jensen, Eric, *Teaching with the Brain in Mind* (ASCD, 1998)
One of many books Jensen wrote to provide a link between neuroscience and the classroom

Kagan, Spencer, *Multiple Intelligences: The Complete MI Book* (Kagan Co-operative Learning, 1998)
Everything you need to know for classroom practice in MI in one – very large – volume

Springer, Sally, P. and Deutsch, George, *Left Brain, Right Brain: Perspectives from Cognitive
Neuroscience* (Freeman, New York, 1998)
Succinct summaries of research in topics such as gender and the brain, laterality, handedness

Sapolsky, Robert, *Why Zebras Don't Get Ulcers* (1999)
Compelling insights into stress and what it does to you

... and some more

Bowkett, Stevphen, *ALPS StoryMaker: Using fiction as a resource for accelerated learning* (NEP, 2001)
Caviglioli, Oliver and Harris, Ian, *MapWise: Accelerated Learning through Visible Thinking* (NEP, 2000)
Smith, Alistair, *Accelerated Learning in Practice* (NEP, 1998)
Smith, Alistair, *Bright Sparks: Motivational Posters for Pupils* (NEP, 2001)
Smith, Alistair, *Leading Learning: Staff Development Posters for Schools* (NEP, 2001)
Smith, Alistair, *The Brain's Behind It: New knowledge about the brain and learning* (NEP, 2002)
Smith, Alistair and Call, Nicola, *The ALPS Approach: Accelerated Learning in Primary Schools* (NEP, 1999)
Rockett, Mel and Percival, Simon, *Thinking for Learning* (NEP, 2002)
Wise, Derek and Lovatt, Mark, *Creating An Accelerated Learning School* (NEP, 2001)
Call, Nicola and Featherstone, Sally, *The Thinking Child* (NEP, 2003)

Websites by topic

http://www.acceleratedlearning.co.uk   contact Nicola via her website
http://www.alite.co.uk   contact Alistair via his website
http://www.newhorizons.org   a publisher specializing in brain-based learning
http://www.cainelearning.com/   brain-based learning site with good links
http://www.21learn.org   the 21st Century Learning Initiative
http://pzweb.harvard.edu/Research/Research   the official Harvard Project Zero site
http://www.musica.uci.edu/index.html   music and learning
http://www.brainstore.com   Eric Jensen's site
http://www.nauticom.net/www/cokids/teacher   early years and brain-based learning
http://www.cdi.page.com   the Child Development Institute

Index of resources

Bold type indicates pages that can be photocopied.

A

Accelerated Learning Cycle (poster), **28**
action research projects, 194
action rhymes for gaining attention, 75
affirmation phrases, 91
ALPS method, how schools begin with, 193
attainment, way to recognize, 89
attention, ways to obtain, 73
audit forms for display, **80**

B

base camp
    creating (poster), **76**
    useful items for, 78
BASIC activities for classrooms, 85
Big Picture, 153
books for teachers, 220–1
brain break
    apparatus, 137
    activities, 133
    indicators, 138

C

contact list, 218
curriculum, sharing with children and
    parents, 122

D

desk labels
    activity, 92
    games, 94
    list of one hundred, 93
    list of twenty cool, 93
diffusion activities, 168
display
    ALPS, 79
    places, 79
    policy, 79

F

feedback
    positive, 118
    without giving grades, 121
    without marking, 119
five dispositions (poster), **47**

G

good looking, asking, answering (poster), 72
good sitting, good listening (poster), 70
grades
    as tools, 120
    to motivate, 121
    principles of, 120
groups
    choosing, 157
    organizing, 156
group-working, protocols, 158

H

homework
    list of fifty good, 125
    monitoring assignments, 130
    motivators, 129
    parental feedback form, 130
    questionnaire **215**
    target cards, **216–7**
Horsenden Code of Conduct at KS1, 13
Horsenden Primary Reception Literacy through
    VAK, 17–18
Horsenden's Magic Spelling strategy, 16

J

jokes, 141

K

key vocabulary, **219**

L

language of progression in class, 112
life map, creating a, 61

M

managing impulsivity, 169
mapping
    for older children, 54
    for young children, 54
marking
    codes, 116
    focused, 115
    stamp, 117

memory and recall improvement, **176**
memory maps
   for assessment, 55
   for revision, 59
memory techniques, PRECIPITOUS, 178
motivational posters, **10, 20, 22, 32, 36, 38, 52,**
   66, 80, 86, 88, 90, 98, 110, 114, 124, 126, 132,
   134, 142, 152, 178, 180, 182, 192
multiple intelligences, 174–5
music in the classroom, using, 144

P

Plan, Do, Review, 158
pole-bridging, 169
primacy and recency, maximizing, 153

Q

questioning strategies, improving, 113
questionnaires
   'About me'
      for older children, **102**
      for younger children, **104**
   brain-builder, **34**
   emotional intelligence
      for children, **210**
      for teachers, **209**
   five dispositions for teachers, 50
   homework, **215**
   'how good am I at learning?', **197**
      total sheet, **198**
   self-esteem, **206**
      scoring table, 207
   VAK learning preference
      for children, **163**
      for parents, **165**
      for teachers, **166**
      score meaning, 164
questions to ask if stuck, 109

R

reasoning, promoting, 51
reflectivity–reflexivity, promoting, 51
remember, helping children to, 177
resilience, promoting, 49
resourcefulness, promoting, 49
responsibility, promoting, 49

S

SATs
   sample preparation policy, 183
   steps to prepare children for, 181
   ways to prepare children for, 184
scripts
   mental rehearsal for success, 187
   relaxation, 186
   visualization, 188
self-talk
   changing low to high can-do, 111
   helping children be positive, 109
   negative into positive, 91
starting lessons positively, 154

T

target
   cards **216–7**
   helping class to set good, 108
   prompt sheet, 108
   with parents, 107
target setting, National Curriculum, 103
Target Terminator, recognizing a, 107
targets and rules, display, 117

V

VAK
   jokes, **160**
   jokes voting form, **162**
   learning preference questionnaire
      for children, **163**
      for parents, **165**
      for teachers, **166**
      score meaning, 164
   proforma, **14**

W

websites, 221
what the teachers said, 26

Y

your engagement chart, **196**

A selection of titles from Network Educational Press

THE SCHOOL EFFECTIVENESS SERIES

Book 1:   *Accelerated Learning in the Classroom* by Alistair Smith
Book 2:   *Effective Learning Activities* by Chris Dickinson
Book 3:   *Effective Heads of Department* by Phil Jones & Nick Sparks
Book 4:   *Lessons are for Learning* by Mike Hughes
Book 5:   *Effective Learning in Science* by Paul Denley and Keith Bishop
Book 6:   *Raising Boys' Achievement* by Jon Pickering
Book 7:   *Effective Provision for Able & Talented Children* by Barry Teare
Book 8:   *Effective Careers Education & Guidance* by Andrew Edwards and Anthony Barnes
Book 9:   *Best behaviour and Best behaviour FIRST AID* by
            Peter Relf, Rod Hirst, Jan Richardson and Georgina Youdell
            Best behaviour FIRST AID (pack of five booklets)
Book 10:   *The Effective School Governor* by David Marriott *(including free audio tape)*
Book 11:   *Improving Personal Effectiveness for Managers in Schools* by James Johnson
Book 12:   *Making Pupil Data Powerful* by Maggie Pringle and Tony Cobb
Book 13:   *Closing the Learning Gap* by Mike Hughes
Book 14:   *Getting Started* by Henry Leibling
Book 15:   *Leading the Learning School* by Colin Weatherley
Book 16:   *Adventures in Learning* by Mike Tilling
Book 17:   *Strategies for Closing the Learning Gap* by Mike Hughes and Andy Vass
Book 18:   *Classroom Management* by Philip Waterhouse and Chris Dickinson
Book 19:   *Effective Teachers* by Tony Swainston
Book 20:   *Transforming Teaching and Learning* by Colin Weatherley, Bruce Bonney, John Kerr and Jo Morrison
Book 21:   *Effective Teachers in Primary Schools* by Tony Swainston

ACCELERATED LEARNING SERIES   General Editor: **Alistair Smith**

Accelerated Learning in Practice by Alistair Smith
The ALPS Approach: Accelerated Learning in Primary Schools by Alistair Smith and Nicola Call
MapWise by Oliver Caviglioli and Ian Harris
The ALPS Approach Resource Book by Alistair Smith and Nicola Call
Creating an Accelerated Learning School by Mark Lovatt and Derek Wise
ALPS StoryMaker by Stephen Bowkett
Thinking for Learning by Mel Rockett and Simon Percival
Reaching out to all learners by Cheshire LEA
Leading Learning by Alistair Smith
Bright Sparks by Alistair Smith
Move It by Alistair Smith

ABLE AND TALENTED CHILDREN COLLECTION

Effective Resources for Able and Talented Children by Barry Teare
More Effective Resources for Able and Talented Children by Barry Teare
Challenging Resources for Able and Talented Children by Barry Teare

MODEL LEARNING

Thinking Skills & Eye Q by Oliver Caviglioli, Ian Harris and Bill Tindall
Think it–Map it! by Oliver Caviglioli and Ian Harris

OTHER TITLES

The Thinking Child by Nicola Call with Sally Featherstone
StoryMaker Catch Pack by Stephen Bowkett
Becoming Emotionally Intelligent by Catherine Corrie
That's Science! by Tim Harding
The Brain's Behind It by Alistair Smith
Help Your Child To Succeed by Bill Lucas and Alistair Smith
Tweak to Transform by Mike Hughes
Imagine That... by Stephen Bowkett
Self-Intelligence by Stephen Bowkett
Class Talk by Rosemary Sage

For more information and ordering details, please consult our website www.networkpress.co.uk